POLITICS AND PEOPLE

The Ordeal of Self-Government in America

POLITICS AND PEOPLE

The Ordeal of Self-Government in America

ADVISORY EDITOR

Leon Stein

EDITORIAL BOARD

James MacGregor Burns

William E. Leuchtenburg

The Washington Correspondents

by Leo C. Rosten

ARNO PRESS
A New York Times Company
New York — 1974

Reprint Edition 1974 by Arno Press Inc.

Reprinted from a copy in The Newark
  Public Library

POLITICS AND PEOPLE: The Ordeal
of Self-Government in America
ISBN for complete set: 0-405-05850-0
See last pages of this volume for titles.

Manufactured in the United States of America

➡️

Library of Congress Cataloging in Publication Data

Rosten, Leo Calvin, 1908-
    The Washington correspondents.

    (Politics and people: the ordeal of self-government
in America)
    Reprint of the ed. published by Harcourt, Brace,
New York.
    Bibliography: p.
    1. Journalists--Washington, D. C. 2. Press--
Washington, D. C. 3. Government and the press--United
States. I. Title. II. Series.
PN4899.W3R6 1974   301.44'46   73-19175
ISBN 0-405-05896-9

THE WASHINGTON
CORRESPONDENTS

THE WASHINGTON
CORRESPONDENTS

The Washington
Correspondents

by Leo C. Rosten

HARCOURT, BRACE AND COMPANY

NEW YORK

Typography by Robert Josephy

PRINTED IN THE UNITED STATES OF AMERICA
BY QUINN & BODEN COMPANY, INC., RAHWAY, N. J.

To Pam

Contents

Contents

Acknowledgments

I WISH to express my gratitude and thanks to the one hundred and twenty-seven Washington correspondents who were generous enough to submit to interviews, questioning, questionnaires, and the near-impertinences of research during the sixteen months in which the materials for this study were being collected. Without the co-operation of these men and women this book could never have been written. I am particularly indebted to the following, who may be singled out for their special interest and help: Clifford A. Prevost of the Detroit *Free Press*, Paul W. Ward of the Baltimore *Sun*, Arthur Krock and Delbert Clark of the New York *Times*, Robert S. Allen of the New York *Post*, the Philadelphia *Record* and the "Daily Washington Merry-Go-Round," Richard L. Wilson of the Des Moines *Register and Tribune*, Paul R. Leach of the Chicago *Daily News*, Erwin D. Canham of the *Christian Science Monitor*, and Marquis W. Childs of the St. Louis *Post-Dispatch*.

The entire study was made possible by a grant from the Social Science Research Council, a pre-doctoral field fellowship for 1935-36.

I wish to acknowledge the aid of Stephen T. Early, Assistant Secretary to the President, James Allen of the Securities and Exchange Commission, Leona B. Graham, executive assistant to the Secretary of the Interior Arthur

Hays Sulzberger, publisher of the New York *Times,* Morris L. Ernst, attorney for the American Newspaper Guild, and E. S. Gardephe of the Press Intelligence Service of the government.

It gives me genuine pleasure to acknowledge the encouragement and guidance of Professor Charles E. Merriam, chairman of the department of political science at the University of Chicago. Many discussions with and suggestions from Professor Harold D. Lasswell of the same institution can be acknowledged only in these inadequate words. Valuable comments on the manuscript were made by Professor Leonard D. White and Dr. Charles Ascher.

Brief extracts from the book appeared as articles in the *Public Opinion Quarterly* for January, 1937, and the *Journalism Quarterly* for June, 1937, and September, 1937.

My wife deserves a tribute for the patience and skill with which she organized the reference notes, managed the bibliography, read proof, and helped prepare the book for publication. The index was constructed with a happy disregard of the difficulties by Emily Fogg Mead.

Any or all of the above are cheerfully absolved of responsibility for the pages which follow.

LEO C. ROSTEN

Author's Note

THE AIM of this book is to give a picture, an analysis, and an interpretation of the Washington newspaper correspondents. In a democracy, we depend upon the press for a presentation of the facts upon which our political opinions are based and the issues around which our political controversies revolve, but we know nothing of the men, the women, the problems, the devices behind the dispatches and columns which begin with the portentous date-line "WASHINGTON, D. C.—" This book describes the personalities and techniques of the reporters who are at the heart of the opinion-making process. It is a study of a group of highly significant journalists in a society in which journalism has been accorded the dignity and the prerogatives of constitutional status.

The book is intended to be neither an "exposé," an apology, nor a polemical tract. It is an analysis—the result of sixteen months of investigation in Washington, under a fellowship from the Social Science Research Council of New York. Most of the information was gathered from discussions with 154 members of the press corps, ranging in age from twenty-three to seventy, in salary from $1,500 to $22,000 a year, in conviction from the most "radical" to the most "reactionary." I tried to get the newspaper-man's point of view to his work, his news-sources, his publishers, and his function. I was permitted to attend press

conferences and participate in the vicissitudes of the correspondent's day. I talked to special correspondents, columnists, reporters for the press associations, government press
agents, lobbyists, newspaper publishers, and editors. Facts
were checked by referring to the literature on journalism,
public opinion, and propaganda.

After several months of contact with the press corps, I
drew up a questionnaire (see p 151) which was submitted
to the men whom I had interviewed. This questionnaire
was designed to discover who the correspondents *are*, in
terms of social origin, education, professional training,
experience, the economic stratum from which they come,
the newspapers and magazines they read, and so on. It
was filled out in patient detail by 127 Washington correspondents. A second questionnaire (see p. 152) was then
constructed to find out what the correspondents *believe:*
their personal philosophy of politics, which papers they
consider reliable and which they consider dishonest, their
attitude to their jobs and their publishers, their consciousness of newspaper "policy," their conception of the freedom with which they are permitted to exercise their function. This questionnaire was anonymous in form and was
submitted to those who had filled out the first. One hundred and seven returns were received.

I arrived in Washington on September 3, 1935, and
carried on the investigation until the end of December,
1936, making five trips to New York in between. The
first months in the capital were devoted to meeting as
many correspondents as possible and explaining the nature
of the study to them. I found that it was necessary to
emphasize the fact that the work was being pursued under

a grant from an academic body with no political interests, that the study sought to prove no preconceived thesis, that it was the press corps as a group which was the subject of inquiry, and that all information would be published in a form which would not name individual informants. The initial problem, obviously, was to win the interest and, if possible, the confidence of the persons upon whose co-operation the success of the study depended.

The newspapermen were, on the whole, gratifyingly responsive to the purposes of the investigation. Some of them were flattered; others were interested, but skeptical of the number of men who could be induced to "talk" or fill out questionnaires; most were curious. There was less amused superiority to the idea of an "academic" analysis than I had been warned to expect. There were sporadic expressions of distaste at the idea of "serving as guinea pigs"—but those who resisted were amenable to persuasion. In many cases personal friendships grew up and helped the progress of the work greatly. I was free to drop into certain offices at any time to discuss problems as they arose.

Interviews were carried on as often and as informally as possible: in the offices of special correspondents, before and after press conferences, over lunches in the Press Club, the Cosmos Club, or the Willard Hotel, in the dining rooms of the Senate or the House of Representatives, in the White House press room, in the press galleries of the Senate and the House of Representatives, in the bar, lounge, and library of the Press Club, sometimes in a correspondent's home. The discussions lasted anywhere from half an hour to four and five hours. Many correspondents

were interviewed at regular intervals; several were seen
two and three times a week for eight months. Membership
in the National Press Club opened up a field for more
continuous and informal contact with the correspondents
and facilitated the creation of a working rapport.

Where no objection was shown to the taking of notes
during an interview, this was done. In other cases the content of the discussion was recorded immediately after-
wards. The degree of error involved in recalling verbal
information was reduced to a minimum. The only factual
information used with reference to correspondents' biographies, attitudes, and preferences (the subject matter of
Part Two of the book) was obtained from the answers
which the correspondents made to the two questionnaires.

Half a dozen letters sent to me by members of the press
corps are interesting commentaries on the newspaperman's
attitude to a study of this type:

"Every time I look your questionnaire over, I feel like a
guinea pig. However, I have no objection to anyone knowing
the following facts about myself."

"All this delay in answering has been intentional. Here is
the damn thing anyway. Good luck."

"My heart goes out to you. . . . It is a fruitless quest. But
here is my record."

"You are doing a swell job. I hope you raise plenty of hell."

"As I have promised to do, I have answered your questionnaire completely and frankly, although in filling it out I have
disclosed facts regarding my education which I have withheld
from even my closest business and personal associates. . . . I
am asking this request: that the material I give you be handled

so that my identification will not show up through any 'case record' or anything like that."

"I have dutifully filled out your questionnaire, in spite of a strong objection to questionnaires in general and a feeling that the information I have given you in this one in particular can be of no earthly interest to anyone. . . . I must beg you to use my name under no circumstances and to make sure that no general picture is created as would point to me."

I was interested in making this study for several reasons. University training in political science and international relations, with public opinion and propaganda as the area of special interest, suggested the value of enriching marginal theories with realistic research on the actual persons and relationships involved in the subtle mechanisms of opinion-making. This book is a study in public opinion and falls somewhere in that field of the social sciences which is bounded by psychology at the one end and sociology at the other.

The statement by Robert S. Lynd in the preface to *Middletown in Transition* suggests the methodological axis around which I tried to build a work which was fascinating from the outset:

". . . Knowledge cannot advance without both insight and data, and the need is obviously for the maximum admixture of both, the one constantly checking the other in the endless game of leapfrog between hypothesis and evidence as understanding grows."

L. C. R.

THE ONE HUNDRED AND TWENTY-SEVEN

Adams, Phelps H.	*New York Sun*
Allen, Robert S.	*New York Evening Post, United Features Syndicate, Philadelphia Record*
Alsop, Joseph W., Jr.	*New York Herald Tribune*
Anderson, Paul Y.	*St. Louis Post-Dispatch*
Bargeron, Carlisle	*Free-lance columnist*
Barkley, Frederick R.	*Baltimore Evening Sun*
Beal, John R.	*United Press Associations*
Belair, Felix, Jr.	*New York Times*
Benson, George A.	*Minneapolis Journal*
Black, Ruby A.	*Portland (Me.) Evening News, Jamestown (N. Y.) Evening Journal, Madison (Wis.) State Journal, Green Bay Press-Gazette, Eau Claire (Wis.) Telegram, Daily Northwestern, Oshkosh (Wis.), Worcester (Mass.) Gazette*
Brackett, J. R.	*Associated Press*
Brandt, Raymond P.	*St. Louis Post-Dispatch*
Brayman, Harold	*Philadelphia Evening Public Ledger*
Brooks, Ned	*Cleveland Press, Cincinnati Post, Toledo News-Bee, Columbus Citizen, Akron Times-Press, Youngstown Telegram, Kentucky Post*
Brown, Ashmun N.	*Providence Journal, Providence Bulletin*
Brown, Robert S.	*Cleveland Press, Toledo News-Bee, Columbus Citizen, Akron Times-Press, Youngstown Telegram, Cincinnati Post, Kentucky Post*
Browne, Merwin H.	*Buffalo Evening News*
Bruner, Felix F.	*Washington Post*
Butler, James J.	*New Britain Herald, Utica Observer-Dispatch, Schenectady Gazette, Niagara Falls (N. Y.) Gazette, General Press Association*
Canham, Erwin D.	*Christian Science Monitor*
Catledge, W. Turner	*New York Times*
Childs, Marquis W.	*St. Louis Post-Dispatch*
Chipman, Stanley	*Providence Journal, Providence Bulletin*
Clapper, Raymond	*Scripps-Howard Newspaper Alliance*
Clark, Delbert	*New York Times*
Cornell, Douglas B.	*Associated Press*
Cotten, Felix T.	*Central News of America*
Cottrell, Jesse S.	*Charlotte Observer, Arizona Daily Star, Anderson (S. C.) Mail, Anderson (S. C.) Index*

Kilgore, Bernard	*Wall Street Journal*
Kluckhohn, Frank L.	*New York Times*
Krock, Arthur	*New York Times*
Lambert, John T.	*Washington Herald, Universal Service*
Lawrence, David	*Columnist, United States News*
Leach, Paul R.	*Chicago Daily News*
Lehrbas, Lloyd	*Associated Press*
Lewis, Edward W.	*United Press Associations*
Lincoln, G. Gould	*Washington Star*
Lindley, Ernest K.	*New York Herald Tribune*
Little, Herbert	*Buffalo Times*
Malcolmson, Charles	*Philadelphia Record, New York Post*
Mallon, Paul	*North American Newspaper Alliance*
Manning, George H., Jr.	*Harrisburg News-Patriot, Troy Record, Camden Courier and Post, Scranton Republican, Toronto Star, Elmira Star-Gazette, General Press Association*
McGahan, Paul J.	*Philadelphia Inquirer*
McKee, Oliver, Jr.	*Boston Evening Transcript*
Michael, Charles R.	*New York Times*
Miller, Joseph L.	*Associated Press*
Mobley, Radford E., Jr.	*Akron Beacon Journal, Reno Gazette, Rock Island Argus, Omaha World-Herald, Richmond Times Dispatch, Mobile Press Register*
Morhart, Frederick H., Jr.	*Indianapolis News*
Mosher, Clinton L.	*Brooklyn Daily Eagle*
Mulligan, Ralph C.	*Worcester (Mass.) Telegram, Columbia (S. C.) Record*
Murray, K. Foster	*Norfolk Virginian-Pilot, Savannah Morning News, Charleston News and Courier*
Neal, William S.	*International News Service*
O'Donnell, John P.	*New York Daily News*
Oliver, D. Harold	*Associated Press*
Pearson, Drew	*United Features Syndicate*
Perkins, Frederick W.	*Pittsburgh Press*
Prevost, Clifford A.	*Detroit Free Press*
Price, Byron	*Associated Press*
Reed, Fred A.	*Chicago Daily News*
Robertson, Nathan W.	*Associated Press*
Simpson, Kirke L.	*Associated Press*
Skinner, Carlton	*Wall Street Journal*
Smith, Kingsbury	*International News Service*
Stafford, Lawrence E.	*Grand Rapids Press, Saginaw News, Jackson Citizen Patriot, Flint Journal*
Stark, Louis	*New York Times*
Stern, Max	*New Mexico State Tribune (Albuquerque), San Diego Sun, San Francisco News, El Paso (Tex.) Post*
Stimpson, George W.	*Houston Post*
Stokes, Thomas L.	*New York World-Telegram*

Strout, Richard L.	*Christian Science Monitor*
Thistlethwaite, Mark	*Indianapolis News, Fort Wayne Journal Gazette, Evansville Courier Journal, Terre Haute Tribune*
Thompson, Harold O.	*United Press Associations*
Timmons, Bascom N.	*Houston Chronicle, Cleveland News, San Antonio Express, Dallas Times-Herald, Tulsa World, Shreveport (La.) Times, New Orleans States, Arkansas Democrat*
Trohan, Walter	*Chicago Tribune News Service*
Trussell, Charles P.	*Baltimore Sun*
Waltman, Franklyn, Jr.	*Washington Post*
Ward, Paul W.	*Baltimore Sun*
Warner, Albert L.	*New York Herald Tribune*
Watkins, Everett C.	*Indianapolis Star, Terre Haute Star*
Weil, Arthur T.	*Buffalo Evening News*
Weir, Frank H.	*Philadelphia Evening Public Ledger*
Wiggins, J. R.	*St. Paul Pioneer Press, St. Paul Dispatch*
Wile, Frederic William	*Joliet Herald-News, Washington Evening Star*
Williams, Gladstone	*Miami Herald, Fresno (Calif.) Bee, Modesto (Calif.) Bee, Atlanta Constitution, Sacramento Bee*
Wilson, Lyle C.	*United Press Associations*
Wilson, Richard L.	*Des Moines Register and Tribune*
Wimer, Arthur C.	*Hartford Courant, New Castle News*
Wooton, Paul	*New Orleans Times-Picayune*
Wright, James L.	*Buffalo Evening News*
Young, Marguerite	*New York Daily Worker*
Zon, Henry	*Federated Press*

PART ONE

PART ONE

The Washington Correspondents

Introduction

WASHINGTON, D. C., is the center of diffusion of political news in the United States. It is one of the richest and most significant news locales in the world. Politics is news. Politicians are news. Personalities are news. Washington is a mélange of politics, politicians, and personalities. In the capital, politics is vivified and made dramatic: it is politics-in-action, with personalities to symbolize it, and with strategy, pressure, and negotiation to lend it plot.

There are 504 accredited newspaper and magazine correspondents in the capital, a body larger than the House of Representatives and almost as large as the Senate and the House combined. These 504 men and women have been described as a third house of Congress and a fourth branch of the federal government. They are the representatives of newspapers, press associations, syndicates, trade journals, editorial services, and magazines. They are charged with the responsibility of reporting events at the hub of political action.

The Washington correspondents, more familiarly known as "the capital press corps," enjoy a semi-official status. They are listed in the *Congressional Directory*. They have access to conferences with the officers of the government from the President of the United States down. They have special quarters set aside for their exclusive use in all

3

government buildings, including the White House. Official documents, statements, reports, statistics, are made available to them. They receive advance copies of speeches and announcements. They have special sections reserved for them in the galleries of the House of Representatives and the Senate, and at Congressional Committee hearings. A committee of their own choice governs them in the press galleries, formulating rules for admission and enforcing discipline.

The Washington correspondents consort with statesmen. They dine with Ambassadors and Cabinet members. They are fêted at the White House in a special reception and ball. They are not strangers to full dress or the perquisites of social status. Their help is sought by persons and organizations trying to publicize an issue; their displeasure is avoided. They are aware, by virtue of the deference paid to them and the importance attached to their dispatches, that they are factors of political consequence. They have launched Congressional investigations and wrecked political machinations. They are the antennae of newspapers all over the nation. They are private citizens working for private employers; yet their status is such that they are granted quasi-official prerogatives. The agencies of the federal government co-operate with them, with varying degrees of efficiency and ingenuousness, in the process of informing the United States about what is going on in its capital.

The press corps is a professional skill-group with a high morale, a strong tradition, a vigorous if unarticulated code of ethics, and a body of specialized techniques. Now a profession may attract personalities of a generic type by its very nature, and a community of interest, experience, and skills tends to stamp professional perspectives with an identity of form. Despite the anonymity which journalism usually imposes upon its practitioners, newspapermen do not live in either a social or an intellectual vacuum. The journalist is sensitized to the observation of aspects of the real world, with a talent for translating segments of reality into the grammar of "news stories." In the inflections which creep into his recording of events there is imbedded, however obscurely, a personality—and an autobiography. "Objectivity" in journalism is no more possible than objectivity in dreams. Even under the mobilization of arid facts in a dispatch on the Budget there is a structure of professional reflexes and individual temperament.

It may be said that the driving impulse of the scientist is to know, of the soldier—to act, of the journalist—to tell. What the newspaperman tells, what he considers worth telling, and how he tells it are the end products of a social heritage, a functional relationship to his superiors, and a psychological construct of desire, calculation, and inhibition. These are the problems with which this book is concerned.

One hundred and twenty-seven Washington correspondents have supplied most of the information upon which this book is based: ninety special correspondents for individual newspapers or newspaper chains, twenty-five press association reporters, columnists, and bureau heads, twelve columnists who are syndicated nationally. These 127 members of the press corps are *political* correspondents and columnists for the six major press associations, the news and feature syndicates, and for 186 daily American newspapers of a general (rather than trade or technical) circulation of over 75,000. This detailed description is important. It was impossible and unnecessary to include all the newspapermen and women in the capital in this study. For of the more than five hundred listed in the *Congressional Directory* a large number are representatives of trade journals, magazines, foreign papers, and the foreign-language press in the United States; many are feature writers who do not devote themselves to news political in content (some of the press association reporters cover "the women's angle" in Washington; some cover scientific developments; some are special writers on technical government research in agriculture). The local Washington newspapers each have from ten to fifteen representatives listed in the *Congressional Directory*, but some of these are publishers, city editors, telegraph editors, society columnists, local reporters interested only in the civic news of the District of Columbia. If we exclude all those who do not cover national political events for a press association or an American newspaper of large circulation, about 208 correspondents are left.* The 127 who have contributed to this study are the most prominent of these.

This book is not a dissertation on The Press, American Journalism, or Publishers. It is a study of the newspapermen who translate our political environment in the service of journalism. It is concerned with the function, the techniques, and the composition of the press corps, and the relationship of the Washington correspondents to the news,

* The method by which the 127 were chosen is described at length in Appendix A.

to their news-sources, to their employers, and to their
society. The aims of the study may be encompassed by
several questions: Who are the Washington correspondents, in terms of social origins, personality type, and intellectual orientation? How do they get news, how do they
treat it after they have gotten it, and why? What are the
factors (human, technical, implicit, or overt) which enter
into the process of informing the public of political events
in the capital? Given the nature of the American newspaper system and the premises of a democratic order, does
the public get an accurate and intelligible picture of the
problems which our government faces and the methods
by which it meets them?

The public has had to regard the Washington correspondent as a romantic but anonymous figure. It seems
ironic that in a society which moves according to the man-
date of public opinion, we have been more concerned with
the talents of men who incarcerate animals in public
pounds than with those of the men who have the license
to disseminate information about the political order under
which we live. A dentist is not permitted to polish the
molars of the citizenry until he has demonstrated his
ability before examining bodies which guard "the public
welfare"; but we accept the information which is the
source of our knowledge about our government and the
men who constitute it, without concern about either the
qualifications of those who write the news or the motivations of those who publish it. Considerations of this type
are fundamental to any understanding of the nature of
democracy.

Washington has become the matrix of political news. News from Capitol Hill, the White House, and the administrative Triangle has ascended to increasing importance as the federal government widened its scope and power. This was no sudden phenomenon. It is not the fruit of the New Deal or of President Roosevelt's personal design. From one point of view the movement of political power to a central point, the most striking characteristic of contemporary political life, is a manifestation of an historical trend which began on the plane of economics and invaded the sphere of politics. In the United States this movement has subordinated the theory of federalism to the reality of administrative centralization. The acts of the present administration and the tactics of the President are, in this context, points on a political line reaching from the past to the future.

In the late nineteenth century the economic centers of gravity began to shift: the particularistic competition of individuals gave way to the concentration of power in monopolies and trusts. Organization took large-scale form. The outlines of the economy began to approximate the shape of a gigantic pyramid. "Bigness" and monopoly bestrode society.

The growth of modern economic life effected a reconstruction of the political framework within which the economy operated. To the land-holder, the employer, and the entrepreneur was added a new economic "type"—the industrial worker. Mass education, universal suffrage, unionization movements, the experience of collective bargaining—these were expressions of a new political energy and inculcated in the masses of democratic society a consciousness of the potential power which was theirs. As men of property and finance exerted pressure on government, seeking to manipulate political power for the sake of defending and expanding their vested interests, men without property were driven to demand protection from the state and improvement in the conditions of their life. In the face of industrial crises, financial catastrophes, agricultural disasters, and wide social dislocations, the democratic state, reduced by theorists to a policing power, found positive responsibilities thrust upon it. It was forced to intervene in fields which were once extra-political. In government and administration, as in the economic order upon which they rested, the maturing of capitalist-democratic society shifted power, thrusting it from the various points on the periphery to the point at the center. The traditional legalistic compartments of the American political structure were undermined by federal laws which dealt with problems as varied as interstate commerce, loans for highway construction, crop culture, or the consumption of alcohol. The political order was being re-created on functional rather than philosophic lines. The federal government was driven into even wider fields of authority after the cataclysm of 1929. That may not have been desirable but it was imperative. The influence of the capital in relief services, public works, soil conservation, social services, permeated the smallest localities of the nation. The political scientist observes that we are passing from a *Staatenbund* to a *Bundesstaat*. Washington, D. C., once called "a talking club on the Potomac," has become the seat of real national power.

This book is not concerned with the equities involved

in this political transformation, nor with either the problem of bureaucracy or the threat of federal despotism. What is relevant for our purposes is that the intensification of federal power has heightened the meaning of what takes place in Washington. The capital has entered into the consciousness of the American people to a degree unparalleled in times of peace. This assigns an unprecedented importance to news from Washington. It increases the significance of the role which the Washington correspondents play in the drama of public opinion.

I. The Capital

REPORTERS are human beings. As human beings they are subject to the influence of the environment in which they live and work. This truism applies with more particular force to newspapermen than to the average citizen. For the reporter is thrown into contact with his environment with a directness and immediacy which is not possible to men who work in shops or sit in offices. In the final analysis, indeed, the journalistic function is to describe the environment-in-change. The reporter's daily routine is a kind of ethnological field trip: he meets the environment at various points, seeking to discover in it and extract from it that which is "new," different, startling. The environment sets the tempo at which life moves—the reporter with it—and in which events materialize. Reporters must be sensitive to the "feel" and the color of their milieu, and must be skilled in describing it.

It is fundamental to this study of the Washington newspaper correspondents that we examine, first, the city in which their activity is laid.

Washington is an unreal city. It has no industries, no large employer class, no "proletarian" base, no financial nerve-centers, no agricultural extremities. It is a prosperous city; its temper is one of affluence. Its history has been marked by steady growth and economic well-being,

11

because its fortune is joined to the one major industry in American which knows no depressions—politics. It is free from the economic catastrophes which convulse metropolises. It is inbred and secure. It is isolated from the vitals of the body politic. It cannot grasp with any degree of immediacy, because it does not experience them at firsthand, the living significance of industrial warfare, agricultural disaster, or financial chaos. Such phenomena occur at distant points and Washington becomes aware of them only by report and repercussion. It reacts to crises by legislative action and debate. And these formal devices, used to cope with dynamic problems, tend to dull its perception. It is significant that government officials find it necessary to make regular trips "into the field" so that they may experience once again the living aspects of the nation with whose government they are concerned. In the same manner editors often order their Washington correspondent back to the home office, to freshen a perspective which has become adjusted to the insular psychology of the capital.

Unlike other major capitals of the world, Washington makes no organic cultural contribution to the nation which it governs. London, Paris, Moscow, Tokyo—these have a civilization quite apart from their political activity. They are incubators of art, letters, and music. They create a rich urban culture. In such matters Washington is sterile: were its political arteries to be severed, the city would sink into the dreary anonymity of a small town in the South.

The social structure of Washington resembles that of a feudal estate. On June 1, 1936, almost one-fourth of its 594,000 residents (117,103) were in the service of the government. Twenty-five percent are Negroes.[1] These figures do not fully indicate the stratification which cuts the population into mutually exclusive circles. Washington is a combination of Mayfair and Middletown. The government clerks form a vast army, dull, tired, commonplace, without contact with their official superiors or their social inferiors. Lost in the depressing minutiae of administration, most of them have the turgid security of the civil service employee and his lack of imagination as well. On a different level is the upper administrative personnel of the government: departmental executives, sub-executives, aides, policy makers. This is the most important governmental group, because of its function rather than its size. Its members are active, immersed in the excitement of participating in the actual process of governing, full of political intrigue, buzzing with gossip, rife with factionalism. The thousands of experts in the capital are isolated into little groups with specialized preoccupations: scientists, economists, technicians, statisticians, consultants. In a segregated world lives the Army and Navy set: officers (either retired or "stopping off" pending re-assignment), their wives and families, a clique which is arrogant, conservative, and, in social matters, uninformed. The more than five hundred Congressmen form a stratum almost in themselves, with Senators enjoying a social prestige not ordinarily given to politicians. At the top of this strange organism of a city are two groups in one: the diplomatic set, and Society. This is the aristocracy of Washington: elegant, cosmopolitan, and sophisticated to the point of decadence. Drawn from the social élite of the United States on one hand, and the political élites of the world on the other, they live a life which is described in the apt platitude, "the social whirl."

During the height of the Season, Washington is an endless sequence of cocktail parties, formal dinners, and official receptions, charged with pomp and gossip, heavy-laden with ambassadors and dowagers, Senators and debutantes, cabinet members and political celebrities.

In Washington, social life and official life are not divorced from each other. The mechanisms of practical politics, the making of "contacts," the spinning of alliances, the formulation of political tactics—these germinate in the innumerable "parties" which characterize life in the capital. The administrative machinery of the government is housed in ponderous Greek buildings, but the inter-personal nerve-centers run through living rooms, lounges, and private bars. In Washington, party politics is buttressed by cocktail-party politics.

Lord Northcliffe once remarked with exasperation that Washington is nothing but a large whispering gallery. This is not surprising. In Washington all conversational roads lead to political gossip; the theme is omnipresent and inescapable. In Washington, indeed, conversation becomes coterminous with gossip. And because of the political influence of those who indulge in it, gossip in Washington is more significant than its name suggests. It is gossip about exalted persons and high deeds. It forms a channel for communicating information about that sublimated warfare which characterizes politics-in-action. In Washington, gossip represents the "pre-official" aspects of politics. It is a guide to the whole drama of personal relationships which is, at bottom, the administrative and bureaucratic machine of government. Gossip in Washington is invaluable as a source of information and a framework for political analysis. The Washington correspondents have learned to use it for both purposes. For nearly a year before the appointment of Joseph E. Davies as Ambassador to Moscow, the teas of the capital were busy with talk of the moves which Mr. Davies, abetted by his wealthy and ambitious wife, was making to secure a diplomatic post—preferably at a capital like Paris. The newspapermen could get little information concerning these maneuvers from either the State department or the White House; but the society columns, relying on gossip and inference, charted the entire affair with accuracy. In such matters, said Paul W. Ward of the Baltimore *Sun*, "gossip has a strange veracity." [2] To it there is communicated much of the texture and the profile of official affairs.

Washington newspapers devote considerable space to society news. In no other city, probably, are the society columns followed with such care.[3] This is easy to understand, since society has a semi-official character in the capital. It may be of subtle import that Ambassador X was a guest of honor at the home of Secretary Y, with Senator Z and the chairman of an important government board "among those present."

Gossip in the capital has become institutionalized. It is encouraged by implicit social sanction. Washington is a small city, with the small city's love of personal information. There are not the many separate élites which, in a city like New York, create a special financial set, an "old family" set, or a theatrical set. The social pyramid of the capital is crowned by the political-social. Washington's society is fairly small, thrown together of necessity, and closely integrated. In such a setting, gossip has rich soil.

Gossip flourishes for another reason. In any bureaucratic

structure (the word is used without invidious intent), gossip thrives. Employment in a huge impersonal machine precipitates a sense of insignificance in many individuals, a melancholia of inconspicuousness. Antagonisms are generated against superiors when personal ambitions are frustrated by political exigency, or when private expectations are thwarted by the tyranny of red-tape. The government clerk has a fixed status and a routinized existence. In gossip many of them find a safe outlet for their grievances and a sense of compensation for their unimportance. They can talk with condescension about the great and about great deeds. They can "talk out" their grievances, wreaking symbolic vengeance on the villains of their personal dramas. Disappointed clerks and ambitious officials indulge in verbal criticisms of the "higher-ups," deriving a sense of power from petty disclosures of "what goes on."

Washington is a city of people who do not think of it in terms of permanent residence. Its important inhabitants identify themselves as "coming from" some place or expecting to "return to" another. There is little civic tradition. There are no communal bonds to cement a common identification with the place of residence. Washingtonians have no franchise, for example: they do not vote on either municipal or national affairs; when they vote it must be in the state of their "voting residence" or as absentee voters.*

The debilitating influence of Washington's summers should not go unobserved. They are long, hot, and ener-

---

* The District of Columbia is under the governing authority of Congress and Executive Commissioners, named by the President and confirmed by the Senate. Congressional Committees set taxes.[4]

vating. And since they coincide with the period when Congress is not in session, when the White House is practically closed, and when all of the higher officials have left for their vacations, the newspapermen spend at least ten weeks of the year in a dull, uneventful doldrum. Summer, which begins in spring and invades fall, sets a tempo of living which, unlike the tempo of thinking, is leisurely. One Washington correspondent, in taking leave of the capital, remarked that he was leaving because he was "afraid to get old . . . [In Washington] ruts rise everywhere to fit the feet. Washington is life set to slow motion, a dreamy place with an exotic climate and habit-forming influences." [5]

The influx of visitors, the constant re-shifting of personnel, the periodic turnover of Congressmen—these give the city something of the character of a hotel lobby. Governors, mayors, convention delegates, lobbyists, business leaders, publicity seekers, job hunters—visitors, day in and day out, inject the life and the color of the nation outside the capital into the local scene. Washington is a whirlpool of news, and tidbits of information are carried with incredible speed across the dinner tables, the teacups, and the highball glasses of the city.

Participation in the social life of the capital is a necessary part of the life of the Washington correspondent. The premium on "inside information" makes some newspapermen a social asset to a party. Moreover, the wives of most correspondents, like the wives of most Congressmen, are eager to share in the brilliant life of capital society, and encourage their husbands to seek a foothold on the social ladder. The Washington correspondents "learn their way around"; they develop a talent for obtaining news from the widest variety of sources and on the most informal occasions.

Occasionally a correspondent will come upon a big story through the most innocent clue. He may sense an explanation for some forthcoming political move in a remark which a Senator passes to his dinner companion. He may gain insight into some impending shake-up by the animus with which a personality or official is discussed. He may find a last link in a chain of evidence in the fact that some guest of prominence leaves early to attend a special meeting. At the times when politics is moving at a "hot" pace the social atmosphere is charged with meaning.

The intellectual climate of Washington is hectic. There is an emphasis upon "inside stories," rumors, tips. There is an avid interest in personal feuds and party intrigues. It is an atmosphere which is not conducive to a sober analytic perspective. It fosters a dominantly impressionistic political orientation. In Washington, news becomes a disjointed combination of event, conjecture, and inference.

The composite impression is one of extravagance. To listen to the talk of the capital is, even to the initiated, "like sitting through a series of newsreels. . . . In the gossip of its salons and saloons, in the discussion of the newspaper offices, in the government departments, on the floor and in the cloak rooms of the Senate and the House of Representatives, the confused din of a continent echoes and re-echoes." [6]

II. Press Conferences

EACH important official in the government, from the President down, holds conferences with the representatives of the press.* Any accredited correspondent, regardless of the paper for which he works or the political complexion of his dispatches, is entitled to admission. At these conferences the newspapermen are free to ask direct questions. The official, in turn, answers as he chooses: he may give a frank and detailed reply; he may refuse to answer; he may meet the question with a witticism or evade it with an ambiguity; he may offer information which can be printed as a direct quotation, on his authority; he may offer information which may be printed but not as a quotation, and without naming him; he may submit facts for the enlightenment of the press corps alone, with the stipulation that the facts are "off the record."

* President Roosevelt, Secretary Morgenthau, and Secretary Ickes meet the press twice a week; Secretary Hull, daily. In the early days of the New Deal, press conferences were held often and regularly; but in the last year, partly because of a decline in dramatic "spot" news, both the frequency and the regularity of press conferences suffered. Madame Secretary Perkins and WPA Administrator Harry Hopkins have one press conference a week scheduled, but cancellations are not uncommon. The Secretary of War holds a press conference only on special occasions. Attorney-General Cummings and Secretary Roper receive the newspapermen once a week. Secretary Swanson's weekly conferences are called off frequently. In recent months RFC Chairman Jesse Jones has met the press only over long intervals.

Anywhere from ten to two hundred correspondents attend a press conference, depending upon the importance of the official and the occasion. This type of mass-interview has become imperative, since the extraordinary growth in the size of the press corps has made it impossible for any official to meet newspapermen individually or in small groups.

The most important press conferences are those of the President of the United States. The President is, of course, bigger news than any other single person in the capital. He is the symbol of the state, the leader of his party, the directing will of the government, and the personification of authority. He is one of the few men so well known to every reader in the land than anything he says, does, or thinks is big news. From a wider point of view Presidential press conferences are important because they represent the most concrete contact which correspondents have with the guiding will and intelligence of government. It is the President who sets the tone for the entire administration's relations with the press. His attitude seeps through to the conferences of each administrative officer; his technique is generally copied. For these reasons it will prove valuable to discuss Presidential press conferences in some detail.

THEODORE ROOSEVELT

Mass press conferences at the White House, as a formal institution, are comparatively modern. Most Presidents, from Thomas Jefferson to Ulysses S. Grant, kept the press informed of public affairs by giving stories and announcements to one or more newspapermen whom they trusted. (Lincoln, among others, was suspicious of newspapers and reporters alike.) In general, the President's secretary was the link between the Chief Executive and the press, with cabinet members and Senators close to the White House serving as informal sources of information. Presidential announcements were made either in the form of a public statement or a letter to a political official or a prominent person, which the recipient then made public. Grover Cleveland was called "dignified" in his relations with the press. President McKinley was colorless and hesitated to communicate news directly to the newspapermen, even though he had known many of them when he was in the House of Representatives. Mark Hanna, McKinley's political godfather, served as the President's spokesman.[1]

It was Theodore Roosevelt, cognizant of the value of publicity and not reticent about projecting his ego into the front pages of the land, who first began to treat the newspapermen with a consideration calculated to have its rewards. In 1895 a reporter for the Washington *Star*, William W. Price, had begun the practice of standing outside the gates of the White House, interviewing visitors as they came out. Other correspondents followed suit and soon this type of catch-as-catch-can interviewing became a common practice. President Roosevelt saw Price and several others at their post one rainy day and, either touched or inspired, ordered an anteroom set aside for them. This became the White House Press Room.[2]

After the comparative isolation of Cleveland and the tepid piety of McKinley, the strident personality of Theodore Roosevelt was seized upon by the press. Roosevelt had vitality, color, and a flair for the dramatic. He was conscious of the use to which newspapermen might be put, and he enjoyed and encouraged the propagation of news calculated to emphasize his virility and glorify his person. He made friends with a few correspondents, with whom he would gossip freely at breakfast or while being shaved, and favored them with exclusive news stories. He did not see the press corps *en masse*, preferring to play favorites. On launching the First Conservation Congress he did call forty to fifty correspondents together in order to announce and publicize the event.[3]

The glamor of Theodore Roosevelt's personality and the animal magnetism which he exuded robbed many of the correspondents of their detachment and anaesthetized their powers of discrimination. He was probably the first President to use newspapermen deliberately for the publication of "trial-balloon" statements for which he accepted no responsibility. Roosevelt was strong-willed and imperious. He barred one correspondent from the White House and all executive departments by a formal executive order, because of an innocent story the man had published. When he did not like a correspondent, or when he resented the tenor of a newspaperman's dispatches, the President would demand that the man be replaced. He often accused reporters of falsification—generally newspapermen who had resisted emotional affiliation with what was tantamount to a Roosevelt cult. He damned many an honest correspondent by consigning him to the famous "Ananias Club." He repudiated well-founded dispatches blithely. He often warned the newspapermen who were close to him that he would deny the very information he was giving them.[4]

Oswald Garrison Villard said that Theodore Roosevelt "did more to corrupt the Washington newspapermen than anyone":

> However opposed politically one might be, it was impossible not to yield to his personal charm and the extraordinary stimulus which came from association with him. He flattered [the press corps] not a little by confiding freely in them and consulting them on matters of state. . . . Most of them . . . worshipped [him]. They created what remains a legendary Roosevelt. . . . They helped mightily in the making of his vast reputation.[5]

TAFT

William Howard Taft was not so fortunate in his dealings with the press, nor so skillful. He made an effort to hold weekly conferences with all the members of the corps, although this was not a regular practice. He was good-humored, healthy, competent; the newspapermen liked him. The corps was not permitted to quote President Taft directly or indirectly; they could merely say, "The President is considering . . ." or "The President is concerned about . . ." Taft openly favored Gus J. Karger, correspondent for the Cincinnati *Times-Star*, which was owned by Charles O. Taft, the President's half-brother. Karger had access to the White House at all times, and often advised the President. He was given much inside information and many exclusive stories, and the newspapermen received a good deal of their information about executive affairs from him.[6]

During the famous Ballinger-Pinchot feud, which

threatened to become a major scandal in the Taft administration, Theodore Roosevelt, presumably retired from political life, plunged into the controversy by supporting Pinchot and breaking with Taft. The intrusion of Roosevelt's belligerent personality presented a difficult problem to the Washington correspondents. They were torn between two allegiances. Many of them, still fascinated by the bravura figure of Roosevelt, rallied to their first love. President Taft felt that the corps was being neither fair nor impartial. He felt that the newspapermen were on the side of Roosevelt and he became more hostile in his attitude to them. After the Ballinger-Pinchot crisis, Taft's relations with the Washington corps were less congenial.[7]

WILSON

Woodrow Wilson assumed office with a statement to the press corps which suggested that he would be co-operative, frank, and accessible. He welcomed the newspapermen and asked them to serve as antennae between him and the public, reporting the currents of public opinion to him as well as from him. He promised to take the Washington correspondents into his confidence. He inaugurated the mass press conference, open to all correspondents on equal terms, to be held at specified times.[8] For two years Wilson met the press regularly, twice a week. Despite his original intentions it was difficult for him to create an intimate atmosphere with the correspondents. He rarely volunteered information; he was cautious in his statements; he was withdrawn in his attitude. He was the father of the "official spokesman" device, or the camouflage of "a high authority." Misquoted on several unfortunate occasions, he was obliged to establish the rule that the President may be quoted directly only by express permission.

There was in Wilson's manner something of the professor facing a classroom. He regarded newspapermen as intellectual inferiors and, at bottom, probably feared them. He was angered by the stories which revolved around the apocryphal engagements of his three daughters. Wilson displayed little ease in the presence of the corps; he felt that he could not place much trust in their discretion. He was excessively thin-skinned. He resented criticism of Secretaries Bryan and Daniels. Nothing describes his attitude to the correspondents better than his own words:

I came to Washington with the idea that close and cordial relations with the press would prove of the greatest aid. I prepared for the conferences as carefully as for any lecture, and talked freely and fully on all large questions of the moment. Some men of brilliant ability were in the group, but I soon discovered that the interest of the majority was in the personal and trivial rather than in principles and policies.[9]

After the *Lusitania* was torpedoed President Wilson put an end to press conferences, either because of his hypersensitivity or because he felt that the foreign correspondents were reporting confidential information to the embassies. He did not wish to segregate them and hold separate conferences for foreign and American correspondents.[10] The entry of the United States into the World War concentrated all information services in George Creel's Committee on Public Information. The press saw very little of Woodrow Wilson during the last years of his administration. Secretary Joseph Tumulty kept the policies and acts of the White House before the public.

HARDING

In Warren Gamaliel Harding, the newspapermen found a publisher, an ex-newspaperman, and a brother under the skin. President Harding resuscitated the practice of regular press conferences. He was affable and communicative, the epitome of good-fellowship. He met the corps twice a week and enjoyed a high degree of popularity. He was the first President to divulge, quite carelessly, what went on at Cabinet meetings.[11] Harding talked to the press freely—freely enough, at any rate, to display an astonishing incompetence in dealing with the post-War problems with which, unfortunately, he was compelled to be concerned. Even in the easy atmosphere of press conferences his thinking was confused, uncertain, and misleading. "His original proposition for a substitute for the League of Nations in an 'association of nations' was in its inception a careless, offhand remark to the newspaper group, and he was, doubtless, greatly surprised by the furor it created." [12]

It was President Harding's unfortunate fate to be compelled to institute the rule that all questions from the newspaper corps be written out and submitted in advance. This extreme measure was taken after he had, in a press conference, made a disastrous *faux pas* which had international reverberations. During the Washington Conference for the Limitation of Armaments in 1921, Secretary of State Hughes and several leading statesmen had informed the press that the Four-Power Pacific Pact involved the protection of the main Japanese Islands in the Pacific, even though that fact was cleverly concealed in the text of the treaty itself. At one of the bi-weekly conferences with Mr. Harding one correspondent asked, in the midst of a barrage of questions, whether protection of the Japanese Islands was to be drawn from the implications of the Four-Power Pact. The President replied quickly that it was not. When this story was printed in the American newspapers it created a sensation. Japan and other powers protested that the interpretation given by the President of the United States was directly opposite to that which had been agreed upon by the diplomatic representatives. Secretary Hughes, chairman of the conference, rushed frantically to the White House and got an official correction. He prevailed upon the hapless Harding to agree that in the future only written questions, submitted in advance of Presidential press conferences, would be considered. At his next meeting with "the boys" President Harding, with some humiliation, announced this new policy.[13]

There was probably another reason for this self-protective device. Mr. Harding, a not subtle intelligence, feared that if in the give-and-take of a press conference he refused to answer certain questions, his refusal might be misinterpreted or might form the subject of unfavorable comment. Later he liberalized the "written questions" rule slightly by permitting oral questions, if *he* opened discussion on any subject.[14]

Most Washington correspondents labored under no illusions concerning Mr. Harding's intellectual gifts or the political skullduggery of those with whom he surrounded himself. Yet he fared well with the press. "No President will ever be more carefully and more generously protected than he was." [15]

During the Harding administration newspapermen began to protest against the practices of government officials who offered information but refused either to be quoted on it directly or held responsible for it indirectly. A vigorous criticism of this evil was made in 1920 by Paul Hanna, a correspondent covering the State Department:

The Cabinet officer can fill the press with his own propaganda without being responsible for a line that is printed, and never has to deny or acknowledge anything so far as the public is concerned. . . . Reporters, fortunately, get cynical. . . . But the constant dropping of propaganda wears a hole in their indifference, and State Department reporters must produce copy. What the Secretary of State knows has not been revealed. What he has said may not be repeated, paraphrased, or in any manner indicated as coming from him. The inevitable alternative is the "dope" story, and the safest of all "dope" is an echo of the Cabinet member's generalizations, for which the reporter and his paper become exclusively responsible. [16]

CALVIN COOLIDGE

In Harding's successor, the press conference was brought to a point of subtle perfection. Calvin Coolidge avoided every semblance of the publicity seeker. There was in his press technique and his public manner either an extraordinary design or a monumental ingenuousness. He did not court the newspapermen, as Theodore Roosevelt had done. He did not indulge in the congenialities of Warren G. Harding. On the surface he appeared colorless, withdrawn, and, on many occasions, irritable. And yet few Presidents received so flattering a press. There was high art in Mr. Coolidge's artlessness. Its full success may be measured by the singular tenacity with which the legend of "the strong, silent man," "the sage from Vermont," is rooted in the public mind. There is historical irony in the fact that in the 1936 Presidential campaign one of the first slogans devised for candidate Alf M. Landon was "The Kansas Coolidge."

The circumstances under which Coolidge came to the White House were, of course, pregnant with drama. Here was a taciturn, tight-lipped politician, practically unknown to a nation which had not yet been endowed with the identifying symbol of "Throttlebottom." He was sworn in by the light of an oil lamp in a rustic setting which excited the political romanticism of the public. There was a feverish demand for news about "this man Coolidge."

At his first press conference Mr. Coolidge faced an eager, news-hungry group of correspondents. An account of that first meeting, written in 1927 by J. Fred Essary of the Baltimore *Sun,* is illuminating:

Although bearing a reputation for taciturnity . . . President Coolidge gave his newspaper visitors a surprise the very first time they foregathered with him. He talked at length. He answered every question propounded and elaborately elucidated his answers. He was communicative almost to the point of garrulousness. And he has been ever since.[17]

To the correspondents who were anxious to outline the nature of Mr. Coolidge's policy and program to an expectant public there was, unfortunately, little "news" about which to write. The new President's contributions to political philosophy consisted chiefly of statements to the effect that he would follow "the policies of President Harding." The press corps found itself with little of positive content to offer its public. As editors grew more insistent, and as the public displayed an ever-increasing appetite for news about the man whom they did not seem to know very well, the newspapermen in Washington were driven to heights of resourcefulness.

Interest in Mr. Coolidge was shifted from what he *did* —which was not particularly spectacular in the first days after he took office—to what he *was*. What peculiar or unique quality did this man possess which might stamp him into the public mind? The Washington correspondents hit upon an "angle." Every popular hero has a particular "angle" around which his personality is built in terms of newspaper treatment. Colonel Lindbergh's angle is modesty; Greta Garbo's, tantalizing seclusion; General Johnson's, robust invective. What was President Coolidge's "angle"? The most striking characteristic about the new President was his lack of a striking characteristic. And the correspondents in Washington were compelled to exploit just that. News about Mr. Coolidge centered around the comparative absence of news. The President's policy was to offer no obstacles to the rising tide of prosperity and the rising prices of stocks; to keep government expenses down, preach economy, and let the financial and business momentum of the country proceed undisturbed by political interference. This, needless to say, was scarcely big news-matter. The press was driven, both by public interest and the laws of competitive journalism, to confer positive values upon utter negativism.

Newspapermen versed in the magic of inflating personalities into "good copy" hit upon the angle of Mr. Coolidge's silence. Not just silence—journalism deals in superlatives—but extravagant silence. A silence that was unexpected, anomalous, unparalleled. The press began to feature stories about the silent nature of Calvin Coolidge. But silence is inextricably allied to strength in the lexicon of political caricature, and silence is regarded as a mighty virtue in a society which bears the stamp of its Puritan heritage. Mr. Coolidge's "silent strength" became the core around which the ballyhoo rotated. And since a reputation for "silent strength" leads inexorably to the imputation of wisdom, Mr. Coolidge was endowed with heroic sagacity and labeled with another slogan, "the Sage from Vermont." "Silent Cal, the Sage from Vermont." It was simple to buttress these flights of fancy with argument and homely details: the President's dry New England humor, his pleasure in fishing (a solitary joy), his homely aphorisms.

The technical conditions which Calvin Coolidge laid down for his press conferences will suggest the shrewdness behind his cultivated inarticulateness. Mr. Coolidge enforced the rules laid down by President Harding, that questions from the press be written out and submitted in advance. He was never to be quoted directly, except by express permission (a standard White House rule). But Mr. Coolidge objected even when quoted indirectly. Further, he ordered that his failure or refusal to comment upon a question could not be mentioned in the dispatches.[18]

On several occasions he protested, with marked annoyance, because the whole press did not approve of his decisions. (The landing of Marines in Nicaragua, for example; or his policies concerning the War Debts, Mexico, and the Chinese situation.) At times Calvin Coolidge seemed to proceed upon the theory that the function of newspapers was to support the administration, *sans* exception.

The dictum which did not allow newspapermen to quote Mr. Coolidge even indirectly imposed a serious handicap on the correspondents, who had perfected the technique of "writing around" Presidential remarks, reporting them obliquely, offering a reliable account of the substance, if not the language, of the President's words. Under Mr. Coolidge's ruling the press corps was forced to perfect the elaborate fictions of "a White House Spokesman," "an official spokesman for the President," "a source close to the White House." [19] The remarks attributed to these mysterious personages were, of course, those of the President. The device served Mr. Coolidge admirably, since it publicized information for which he disclaimed responsibility. It was a fool-proof version of the "trial-balloon."

A specific illustration will suggest the invulnerability of this tactic. On December 24, 1924, Ambassador Jusserand of France delivered an eloquent speech in which he pleaded for a change in the American attitude to the French war debt. At a press conference Mr. Coolidge was asked to comment on this plea. The President, with unconcealed irritation, dismissed Jusserand's words with the tart comment that no attention be paid to them; by clear implication, and to the understanding of most of the newspapermen present, he criticized the Ambassador for having made such a speech. When this was published, attributed to "the White House spokesman" of course, Ambassador Jusserand was placed in an embarrassing light, and the French Embassy registered the proper degree of diplomatic injury. Secretary of State Hughes hastened to the White House. An official statement appeared, on the President's authority, saying that Ambassador Jusserand had in no way been criticized.[20] The Washington correspondents were held responsible for a gross misrepresentation. Mr. Coolidge's reputation for statesmanship remained unimpaired.

The practice of never speaking "for publication" had more serious consequences. The New York *World* pointed out that on a single day in April, 1925, the President had expressed his opinion on ten important public questions without once speaking "for publication." The subjects ranged from tariff plans and foreign affairs to the Soviet-Japanese Treaty. Because of Mr. Coolidge's ambiguity, and because of the absence of a definite statement which the reporters could be free to examine and quote from, newspaper dispatches showed a surprising disagreement on the "facts." Two dispatches said Mr. Coolidge was "not looking with favor on private loans which might be used for military purposes;" one account found him "unalterably opposed;" one found him "not disturbed" by the matter, believing that "the government has nothing to do with such negotiations." [21]

On another occasion, when a question arose about the recognition of the Soviet Government, surely a problem of public interest, one newspaper stated that Mr. Coolidge was, once again, "unalterably opposed;" another, that he was "moving toward recognition;" another, that recent developments would cause "a reconsideration" of American policy; another, that "the Hughes policy was unchanged;" another, that the government's attitude had been stated "three years ago;" another, that the government's position "was greatly misunderstood." [22] The last alone had an unintentional verisimilitude.

These examples should suggest the difficulties under which the Washington corps worked. The newspapermen were driven to equivocation and camouflage in the interpretation of Presidential remarks. They could not press Coolidge orally for more definite or intelligible commitments than he cared to make. One reporter tried to interrogate him after a particularly vague statement and Mr. Coolidge mobilized his powers of refrigeration and "froze the poor fellow with an icy stare." [23] Strange talents were called into play in the process of trying to inform the public what was in the Presidential mind; miracles took place under the journalistic necessity of dramatizing dull routine events. If Mr. Coolidge would remark, "I am not in favor of this bill," the dispatches the next day would read: "In a fighting mood, President Coolidge today served notice on Congress that he would combat, with all the resources at his command, the pending bill. . . ." [24] The Washington correspondents developed imagination and versatility under the Coolidge regime.

According to Henry Suydam, then correspondent for the Brooklyn *Eagle*, "Mr. Coolidge, with an art that almost defied deception, used the press conferences for the dissemination of trivia which, under the deft, inflating touch of the correspondents, became important and significant." [25]

Mr. Coolidge permitted "the dissemination of trivia" to pass without protest. He enjoyed it. There is evidence that he encouraged it. White House correspondents believe that he told homely little stories of White House life to the Secret Service men, who passed them on to the press corps. In some cases, believing that the stories were being conveyed *sub rosa,* the correspondents assigned an importance to them which they scarcely deserved. (News is often valued in indirect ratio to the ease with which it is acquired or the explicitness with which it is proffered.) The country was flooded with tales about the President's habit of reading the Sunday paper in his galluses, his table-talk, his household economies. These entrenched "the man Coolidge" in the public heart.

On the pictorial plane Mr. Coolidge's talent for publicity reached full bloom. He demonstrated a curious inability to resist photographers. It was a standing joke among the cameramen at the White House, according to Jay Hayden of the Detroit *News,* that the President was willing to pose for almost any picture, at almost any time, in almost any costume.[26] The nation was regaled with strange pictures of its Chief Executive, in cowboy suit, in Indian headdress, in overalls; foot on spade, fishing rod in hand, pitching hay. (In all of these, Mr. Coolidge preserved an austerity of expression which was a triumph of restraint and a tribute to his sense of humor.) These infantile representations—especially incongruous in a man of Mr. Coolidge's conspicuous unathleticism—may have irritated the intelligentsia, but they left a sweet and lasting impress on the voters. The burgher, the grocer, and the suburbanite felt at one with such a man.

The public, reveling in the euphoria of rising profits and wages, devoured idle and amusing tales of political vaudeville on the Potomac. Dispatches from the capital sank to a low level of quality. One Republican newspaper, after several years of this type of political correspondence, withdrew its representative from Coolidge's summer camp in the Black Hills, and declared that the President's vacation was "the most over-reported event in secular history."

It is doubtful whether the newspapermen who ground out the Coolidge legend in daily episodes ever believed in their own creation. They regarded it as a part of their job. Raymond Clapper, then head of the United Press bureau in Washington, said that "the Washington correspondents worked with their tongues in cheek." [27] And Calvin Coolidge expressed admiration for the ingenuity of the newspapermen and, with irony, urged the publishers to raise their salaries. [28]

There is a deeper reason for the popularity of Mr. Coolidge and for the persistence of the Coolidge legend. For, unwittingly, Calvin Coolidge was admirably suited to the needs of the day. After the exhausting idealism of Woodrow Wilson and the shocking corruptions of the Harding administration, the American public was content to pursue the dream of competitive materialism without being disturbed; to earn much, spend freely, and enjoy the fruits of speculative investment. It welcomed a President who did not warn them of disaster, who did not harass them with the bogey of monopolies, who did not disturb their consciences with the contrast between their Christianity and their social barbarism. The public needed a leader who would lend moral sanction to the frenzied quest for wealth and luxury. That is what Mr. Coolidge did. His economic philosophy reflected the temper of the day and the myth which it pursued. He was an exponent of moral capitalism. He preached an astringent ethic. His political addresses today read like quasi-religious sermons:

If society lacks virtue it will perish. . . . The classic of classics is the Bible. . . . The nation with the greatest moral power will win.[29]

His conception of industrial society was pious and eminently reassuring:

The man who builds a factory builds a temple, and the man who works there worships there, and to each is due not scorn and blame, but reverence and praise.[30]

In an economy which was still expanding, Mr. Coolidge's practices met the deepest impulses of the land. He simply refused to interfere, on any grounds, with the "automatic" mechanism of economic competition. He refused government aid in the tragic struggle between the anthracite miners and operators in 1925. He refused the aid of price-controlling methods to the farmers. He pocket-vetoed Senator Norris's bill for the government operation of Muscle Shoals. He refused to recognize the basic contradiction which we injected into the problem of the War Debts by our high tariff policy. The sum of Mr. Coolidge's statesmanship was to sit tight and utter moral homilies on the goodness of it all. And he basked in the glowing hymns of a press which, like the public mood it reflected and to which it catered, sang the glories of an arid philosophy.

Practically every important newspaper in the country printed encomia about Mr. Coolidge for another reason. The Mellon tax-reduction plan played a significant role in eliciting choruses of praise from the publishers. Since the federal debt was being diminished and since federal revenues were creating great surpluses in the public treasury, there was no reason to exact great sums from the taxpayers in excess of administrative expenses. Tax reductions were inevitable. The Coolidge-Mellon group made big headlines by changing tax schedules before the 1924 election, with a certain ballyhoo of their own to emphasize the wonder of it. This was greeted as a heavenly benediction by the press, to whom tax reductions meant higher profits. Mr. Mellon was acclaimed "the greatest Secretary of the Treasury since Alexander Hamilton." * Mr. Coolidge was delineated simply as a Yankee Messiah. The Democratic candidate's chances were strikingly negligible in 1924 and the ecstatic "Coolidge press" swept Messrs. Coolidge and Mellon into four more years of innocuous statesmanship.[31]

The Washington correspondents had been presented with the considerable task of popularizing a man of no historic talents, no engaging graces, no compelling personality. They had to transform a New England politician into a statesman. In pursuit of circulation, and grateful for tax refunds, the press hammered the Coolidge legend into the public mind. Mr. Coolidge was astute enough to let newspapermen pressed for copy endow him with ex-

*See exhibit 2 in Appendix H.

travagant talents which he did not possess, and magnify him to a stature which he could not have achieved by deliberate exertion.

In Calvin Coolidge the dream of the twenties came true: high profits and, occasionally, homage unto God.

HERBERT HOOVER

The story of Herbert Hoover and the press corps forms an episode which is unique, unpleasant, and informative. Mr. Hoover came into office enjoying the respect and confidence of the newspapermen. This was due to the excellence of his relations with the press when he had served as Secretary of Commerce in the Harding Cabinet. At that period Herbert Hoover welcomed newspapermen to his office and discussed national affairs with them frankly and informally. The press corps felt that he was the best "grape-vine" in Washington.

The first warning of a change came during his 1928 Presidential campaign, when Mr. Hoover showed annoyance with the correspondents who asked him to elaborate with greater specificity on those issues which, in his speeches, he treated with the ambiguity of conventional oratory. A more surprising attitude was manifested on his good-will tour to South America, as President-elect, when he imposed a censorship on the twenty-odd reporters who accompanied him. All news copy had to pass through the hands of George Barr Baker, a former War-time censor. Writing displeasing to Mr. Hoover was deleted. It was remarkable that the correspondents submitted to this censorship without a murmur.[32]

In the White House Mr. Hoover established three categories of news: news for which he could be quoted directly; background information which might be used to improve the content of dispatches, but on which he was not to be quoted; strictly confidential information, to be used in no way whatsoever. He abolished the irritating fiction of "the White House Spokesman" but he followed the Coolidge-Harding policy of requiring written questions. He exploited the possibilities of this scheme (1) by demanding that questions be submitted at least twenty-four hours in advance of press conferences; (2) by ignoring any questions he did not wish to discuss. When the gentlemen of the press asked for comments on questions which they had submitted and which had not been discussed Mr. Hoover used the simple tactic of denying that he had received the questions at all.[33]

As his administration ran into the difficulties of the emerging economic crisis, Mr. Hoover became suspicious and irritable. He chastised correspondents openly for interpretations, however legitimate, with which he disagreed. He reacted with anger to news accounts which criticized him. He denounced an article in the Baltimore *Sun* (concerning air-mail contracts which had been so phrased that only one company could have bid on them) with a passion that shocked the corps. He began to invite newspaper publishers to the White House, using the occasion to complain about correspondents whom he did not like and suggesting that he would prefer to have them transferred. Several newspapermen accused the President of taking personal reprisal against them.[34] Relations with the press were hardly improved when Mr. Hoover openly curried favor with certain correspondents. Mark Sullivan, William Hard (his biographer), Leroy Vernon, and Richard V. Oulahan were placed in positions of special privilege; the newspapermen called them "trained seals." *

Mr. Hoover began to make unannounced automobile trips to his Rapidan Camp, leaving the correspondents behind. A Washington correspondent and his wife wrecked their car and suffered serious injury trying to keep up with the 55-mile per hour pace of the President's "flying cavalcade." When a story appeared in which the speed of the Hoover party was mentioned, the President ordered the secret service to make an official investigation of the "leak." [35] At the Rapidan Camp, which became a kind of week-end White House, the correspondents were kept at a distance. Trying to report the President of the United States became a matter of long-range guesses which had little factual substance and less official support.[36]

In another sphere Mr. Hoover's press policy brought ill-feeling to a high point. He excoriated the correspondents for writing innocent human-interest stories: that the President asked carpenters to stop work on White House repairs so that he might take a nap; that Mrs. Hoover was taking sound tests to study and improve her speaking voice; that a dog from the President's kennels had bitten a marine; that there was a patch on one of the White House curtains.

Mr. Hoover ordered his secretary, Theodore G. Joslin (who had succeeded George Akerson), to tell the Washington correspondents that "as a result of a series of leaks,

* Mr. Hard later renounced his favored position by bold critical reporting.

only such news as is given out through stated channels of the executive offices should be presented by the newspapers." [37] A committee of newspapermen protested against the attempt to funnel all news through Mr. Hoover's secretary. The President repeated the ultimatum coldly. He refused to supply the correspondents with facts which they had been accustomed to receiving: the names of White House visitors and guests, for instance, or the movements of the Hoover family.

In several instances the newspapermen caught Mr. Hoover in what was alleged to be direct prevarication. He issued a statement during the London Naval Conference to the effect that the United States would hold up the building of three cruisers; this was proved to be false by Harold Brayman of the New York *Evening Post* and Phelps Adams of the New York *Sun,* who showed that construction was going on as per schedule.[38] In August, 1931, he denied having received a letter from Franklin D. Roosevelt, then Governor of New York, concerning negotiations between the United States and Canada regarding the St. Lawrence River waterway project. When Governor Roosevelt announced that he would make public his copy of the letter, the White House admitted that the letter had been received. Then the White House denied having denied knowledge of the letter and, at the same time, denied that there had ever been any negotiations. This fantastic confusion, thrice confounded, brought down a storm of anger and resentment from the press corps.[39]

Mr. Hoover's figures on unemployment, the federal deficit, and business conditions were proved to be wrong by the newspapermen on several occasions.[40] His spurious optimism ("Prosperity is just around the corner") became the subject of irony. The Wickersham Committee Report on Prohibition was the occasion for more disaster. Mr. Hoover insisted on interpreting the report as if it were favorable to Prohibition despite the fact that seven of the eleven commissioners had taken a distinctly "wet" stand.

Newspaper editorials rang with criticism of Hoover's press policy. The correspondent for *Editor and Publisher* reported:

Utterly disregarding editorial warnings in scores of newspapers from coast to coast that the public business of the national government must be openly conducted . . . President Hoover and a determined group of bureaucrats have literally thrown down the gauntlet to the Washington correspondents on the question of censorship. . . . True, verbal denials persist, from the White House down, that there is any thought of censorship . . . but these declarations are accompanied by "suggestions" that it might be more discreet and consonant with public interest to write only what is handed out officially.[41]

On the night of September 4, 1931, the bankers composing the Advisory Council of the Federal Reserve Board met at the White House. President Hoover refused to comment on the matters discussed. The Washington correspondents interviewed the bankers as they left the conference and "broke" the story. The discussions had involved the possibility of extending the moratorium on foreign debts, the legalization of three per cent beer, and plans for liquefying the frozen assets in real-estate projects and closed banks. On none of these critically important problems did Mr. Hoover feel it necessary to enlighten the public.[42]

When the corps continued to issue dispatches on the severity of the crisis the President's secretary summoned the Washington correspondents to his office for one of his periodic lectures, and urged them to "consult with this office" before sending out stories. There were cries of censorship once more. Mr. Joslin held another conference, denied the charges and, with an exquisite disregard of consistency, asked the correspondents to refrain from publishing both his request that they consult his office and his denial that it was censorship.[43]

The tension between the press corps and the President came to a head on October 6, 1931. A bi-partisan conference on unemployment and other problems of the depression was scheduled to meet at the White House. At his morning press conference Mr. Hoover asked the correspondents *not* to report the meeting. He said there would be no announcement, not even a statement of the persons attending or of the general program discussed. He told the newspapermen not to "waylay" participants as they left the conference. The head of the New York *Times* bureau, Richard V. Oulahan, and Jay Hayden, veteran reporter for the Detroit *News*, promptly told the President that it would be out of the question to expect the newspapermen not to supply the public with information about one of the most important events of the year. They suggested that it would be wiser for Mr. Hoover to make the facts available. The President refused. The press corps ignored the President's objections and dispatched their stories, getting information by interviewing those who participated in the conference. Mr. Hoover and his office maintained a sullen silence.[44]

The President's unfortunate press methods were reflected in other departments. The correspondents held Mr. Hoover responsible, indirectly at least, for the obfuscation which characterized the behavior of cabinet officers and departmental heads. Officials refused to answer either oral or written questions, and refused to elaborate on handouts which were either equivocal to the point of uselessness or misleading to the point of prevarication. The Department of Justice denied any knowledge of an investigation of the New York building rackets which had been begun, the newspapermen discovered, several months earlier. The same department withheld information from a correspondent who had printed a story which they did not like. The Federal Farm Board refused to give the public the names of organizations applying for loans, or the amount of the loans applied for. The Shipping Board instituted a policy of silence and chastised newspapermen for "butting in" when they tried to get information.[45]

Secretary Stimson's conferences were curtailed. Secretary of War Hurley criticized the correspondents for their accounts of the famous "Battle of Anacostia," in which an army of veterans was forcibly ousted from the capital. Mr. Hurley implied that there had been no violence and accused the reporters of falsification. The correspondents proved that their news accounts had been correct and unexaggerated.[46] The Farm Board abandoned its weekly conferences with the press altogether. Newspapermen could get no answers from any officials to the questions pouring in from the farm areas.[47]

In September, 1931, over 100 correspondents signed a petition calling on the Board of Governors of the National

Press Club to select a committee which would study the government's refusal to provide information on public activities.[48] It was a striking expression of the bitterness into which Mr. Hoover had driven the press corps.

From June 1 to November 25, 1932, President Hoover met the press only eight times. From September 13 on, Secretary Joslin merely handed out formal statements to the correspondents, without further comment or elaboration. Presidential conferences were canceled without warning. At those conferences which were held the correspondents filed in, listened to Mr. Hoover read an announcement, filed out, and then waited for the antiquated mimeograph office of the White House to distribute copies of the same announcement. Attendance at the press conferences fell off sharply. Mr. Hoover complained that the press corps was boycotting him.

Latent hostility turned to open war. Hoover's friends maintained that the day-by-day dispatches of the Washington correspondents did as much to defeat him in 1932 as all the efforts of Charles Michelson and the Democratic party. The photographers joined the conflict and many of the unflattering pictures of Mr. Hoover which appeared in the newspapers can be traced more directly to bitter feelings than to bad light.[49]

From September 13 to November 25, 1932, the President of the United States did not hold a single press conference with the Washington correspondents, representatives of the newspapers of the nation.[50] The press policy of Herbert Hoover had reached its logical conclusion.

FRANKLIN D. ROOSEVELT

The circumstances under which President Roosevelt took office were peculiarly auspicious. After the negativism of Calvin Coolidge and the intransigence of Herbert Hoover, an executive with an engaging manner, a modicum of wit, and an appreciation of newspaper problems was destined to receive an enthusiastic welcome from the Washington press corps. Mr. Roosevelt's insight into publicity techniques effected a revolution in White House press relations. The social setting in 1933 was, of course, made to order for a man who knew how to dramatize himself and his program in terms understandable to the common man. From 1933 through 1934, news dispatches from the capital publicized his talents and extolled his political astuteness. The newspapermen who swarmed to press conferences at the White House were convinced that "here was a politician to make Machiavelli, Mark Hanna, Talleyrand, and Boies Penrose hang their heads in utter shame." [51] Publishers began to complain that Mr. Roosevelt had hypnotized their reporters with his charm and misled them with his "propaganda."

Mr. Roosevelt's earlier experiences with the press had not presaged such success. As Assistant Secretary of the Navy in the Wilson cabinet he had offended newspapermen, partly because of an "arrogant Harvard manner," in the words of one correspondent, partly because of several news hoaxes he played upon reporters covering the Navy Department. In his Vice-Presidential campaign of 1920, Mr. Roosevelt had irritated the press by denying remarks which the newspapermen recalled his having made. When he was Governor of New York, friction between him and the press had broken out. At one point he "threatened" reporters for speculating on his disposition of charges against Mayor James J. Walker. In Albany, some reporters avoided his conferences altogether.[52]

If these memories persisted in the minds of the newspapermen, they were swiftly dispelled when Mr. Roosevelt entered the White House. His policy was simple enough: press conferences were to be held regularly twice a week, more often when necessary. Contact between the administration and the reporters was to be informal and systematic. Press-relations officers in each department would facilitate rather than retard the dissemination of news. The "White House spokesman" was to be forgotten. The use of any form of written questions was abolished. There were to be four categories of news:

1. The President could be quoted directly only by permission, a standard procedure.

2. The substance of the President's remarks, however, might be incorporated into dispatches and attributed to him in indirect quotation. This represented a considerable liberalization of White House practice.

3. Background information would be offered by the President for the sake of enriching the correspondents' understanding of official acts and policies: such material could be used in dispatches but was not to be attributed to the President.

4. The President would give a good deal of strictly confidential information "off the record." Such material was meant only for the guidance and understanding of

the correspondents: it was not to be publicized in any form
—not even, in the strictest sense, to the correspondents'
own editors.[53]

At his first meeting with the newspapermen, on March
8, 1933, Mr. Roosevelt announced that the correspondents
would be free to ask direct oral questions. The President's
advisers had warned him against oral questioning as an
unnecessary and hazardous procedure; they awaited it with
anxiety, the correspondents with skepticism. The President's technique and the spirit which pervaded that first
press conference are worth describing in detail; they have
become something of a legend in newspaper circles. Mr.
Roosevelt was introduced to each correspondent. Many of
them he already knew and greeted by name—first name.
For each he had a handshake and the Roosevelt smile.
When the questioning began, the full virtuosity of the
new Chief Executive was demonstrated. Cigarette-holder
in mouth at a jaunty angle, he met the reporters on their
own grounds. His answers were swift, positive, illuminating. He had exact information at his fingertips. He showed
an impressive understanding of public problems and administrative methods. He was lavish in his confidences and
"background information." He was informal, communicative, gay. When he evaded a question it was done frankly.
He was thoroughly at ease. He made no effort to conceal
his pleasure in the give and take of the situation.[54]

The correspondents were exhilarated. Mr. Roosevelt's
first interview with the reporters of the capital ended in a
spontaneous outburst of applause, a phenomenon unprecedented in White House annals. One of the oldest and
most respected correspondents in Washington, Henry M.

Hyde of the Baltimore *Evening Sun,* called it "the most amazing performance the White House has ever seen." [55]

> The press barely restrained its whoopees. . . . Here was news—action—drama! Here was a new attitude to the press! . . . The reportorial affection and admiration for the President is unprecedented. He has definitely captivated an unusually cynical battalion of correspondents.[56]

Even the editor of *Editor and Publisher* was ebullient.

> Mr. Roosevelt is a great hit among newspapermen at Washington. I rubbed my ears (*sic!*) and opened my eyes when I heard hard-boiled veterans, men who had lived through so many administrations and been so disillusioned that there are callouses in their brain, talk glibly about the merits of the White House incumbent. If Mr. Roosevelt fails the craft, by any false word or deed, he will break a hundred hearts that have not actually palpitated for any political figure in many a year.[57]

The reasons for this hero-worship by presumably "hard-boiled" newspapermen are not difficult to isolate. Mr. Roosevelt's colloquial manner soothed journalistic egos still smarting under the rebuffs of his predecessor. The laughter at press conferences was in the nature of a catharsis: in it was vented some of the hostility which Mr. Hoover had aroused. Newspapermen admired President Roosevelt's adroit handling of questions. He won professional approbation for his news sense, his ability to "time" a story so that it broke with maximum force, his skill in investing even routine affairs with news value. "He never sent the reporters away empty-handed . . . and reporters are all for a man who can give them several laughs and a couple of top-head dispatches in a twenty-minute visit." [58] Above all, the positivism and range of Mr. Roosevelt's action, pouring climax upon climax in a remarkable sequence of political moves, won newspapermen, no less than lay citizens, after the obstinate inertia of the last White House occupant.

A man who is able, without batting an eye, to launch NRA, AAA, a $3,000,000,000 public-works program, the Civilian Conservation Corps program, slam the banks shut, go off the gold standard, revalue the dollar, take on every sort of discretionary power instead of trying to shoulder off on Congress a share of the responsibility, was bound to register with a corps of newspapermen who were weary of trimmers, pussyfooters, and people who had not given them a new idea to write about since the World War. [59]

The Washington correspondents were pleased by Mr. Roosevelt's obvious efforts to win their good-will. They were flattered by "off the record" comments. Their professional ethic was gratified by the fact that Mr. Roosevelt cultivated them as a group, playing no favorites and breeding no "trained seals." * Many of them were won by the hospitality shown at picnics, receptions, and Sunday afternoon teas at which the President and Mrs. Roosevelt played host to the press.

Mrs. Roosevelt broke the tradition of Presidential wives and became a personality of consequence in her own right.

---

* In February, 1937, the President gave his first "exclusive" story to a Washington correspondent, in an interview with Arthur Krock of the New York *Times*. (It was printed in the *Times* on February 28.) At his next press conference Mr. Roosevelt said that his "head was on the block," apologized for the exclusive story, and promised that it would not happen again.

She held press conferences with women correspondents; in her way she was often more effective than her husband.[60] She won widespread respect and affection.

The President's influence permeated every department and bureau of the government. During the critical days of the bank crisis, Secretary of the Treasury Woodin supplied information in an informal, non-technical fashion. Postmaster General James A. Farley indulged in a winning frankness and good humor. Secretary of Agriculture Wallace was sincere, co-operative, appealing. Secretary of the Interior Ickes became a first-rate news source because of his aggressive personality and his gift for picturesque language. Such figures as General Hugh S. Johnson added brilliant colors to the news scene.[61]

The President's influence was more directly perceptible. When one executive in NRA refused to co-operate with the press he was discharged on orders from the White House. When Major Dalyrymple of the liquor division of the Internal Revenue Office (the Alcohol Tax Unit) rebuked newspapermen and told them "not to hang around my office," he was chastised in a manner certain to win the correspondents' hearts. When Henry Morgenthau, Jr., on becoming Acting Secretary of the Treasury, issued his General Order Number 1, on November 20, 1933, ruling that all departmental news must come directly from him or his press agent, the Treasury Correspondents Association wired their protest to Hyde Park and got a modification of the rule.* There was general agreement among the Washington correspondents that the New Deal was trying to pro-

---

* Some correspondents complain that certain news-restrictions persisted in the department.

vide accurate news, and that the press agents of the various governmental agencies were doing a commendable job. Even handouts, later the subject of considerable criticism, were praised for their veracity and the service which they afforded hard-pressed newspapermen.[62]

It was "a newspaperman's administration." Arthur Sears Henning, head of the Washington bureau of the Chicago *Tribune*, stated that never had relations between the press and the White House been so happy. George R. Holmes, bureau chief of International News Service, praised the President for his policy, called him "his own best press relations man," and said that in the twenty years he had been in Washington he had "never known a time when the administration seemed more honest in giving out news." Arthur Krock, of the New York *Times*, said that Mr. Roosevelt was the greatest reader and critic of newspapers he had ever seen in the Presidential office; and, the final accolade, "He could qualify as the chief of a great copy desk." [63]

The honeymoon could not last. The Washington correspondents had propagated the impression that Franklin D. Roosevelt was a paragon of talents and a repository of supreme political skills. Events which shattered this idea released that iconoclasm which is the successor to faith.

In 1935 dispatches began to reveal a more aggressive and critical journalistic temper. In Washington newspaper circles one encountered less hero-worship, more skepticism of both the President's personal graces and his political acumen. Ashmun Brown of the Providence *Journal*, honorably mentioned in the 1936 Pulitzer Prize awards, wrote an astringent article in the *American Mercury* for April, 1936, and insisted that "the Roosevelt Myth" was no more. Other newspapermen in the capital began to write caustically of Mr. Roosevelt's "dictatorial" aspirations, the menace of his "propaganda" or the various follies of the New Deal.[64]

The correspondents began to falter in their emotional allegiance as the structure of the New Deal began to totter. In some dismay they were driven to the conclusion that Mr. Roosevelt's More Abundant Life was overdue. Unemployment figures began to worry them—particularly since they could not get exact ones from government sources. Some began to murmur that, for all the ballyhoo, the New Deal was less an integrated program than a series of adventures in the realm of political economy. Many newspapermen found it difficult to reconcile the politics of Mr. Farley, for whom they had a genuine personal affection, with Rooseveltian moral purpose.

At a press conference in February, 1935, the President was asked whether he would support state NRA legislation. He answered in the negative. The correspondents hastened to send off their dispatches and in some places special editions appeared. That afternoon Governor McNutt of Indiana, campaigning to stimulate NRA legislation in his state, called the White House by telephone; Mr. Roosevelt assured him that he (the President) had been misquoted. He sent a telegram to the Governor which was made available to the press. It read, in part:

I have no hesitation in making perfectly plain to you the extraordinary misinterpretation put upon my reply at press conference.

At his next press conference Mr. Roosevelt chided the correspondents for their "misinterpretations." He warned the corps not to draw unwarranted inferences from his failure to comment on "pending legislation," since "80 per cent" of such conjectures were incorrect.[65] The newspapermen were surprised. They felt that the President had wriggled out of a difficult situation, leaving them to hold the bag.

After the "Dred Schechter decision," to use one of H. L. Mencken's more palatable phrases, Mr. Roosevelt delivered his famous "horse and buggy" stricture against the Supreme Court, in the press conference of May 31, 1935. Some correspondents thought the comments petulant and impolitic. Those who regarded the Constitution as a parchment of divine origin called the President's comments heresy. To others it was simply the most unforgivable of political sins: bad strategy.

On June 24, 1935, the President held an emergency conference with congressional leaders. When it was over, Senators Harrison and Robinson, spokesmen for the administration, declared that a decision had been made to push through the President's recommendations for so-called "Soak the Rich" legislation, by attaching them as a rider to a bill pending on excise taxes. A howl of protest went through the editorials of the land. At his next press conference, June 26, 1935, Mr. Roosevelt announced that he had *not* recommended such legislation. "The correspondents . . . gasped in amazement. The questions which followed reflected their anger and incredulity." [66]

Several blunders of another caliber saddened correspondents who had come to believe in their own reports

of Mr. Roosevelt's infallible political acumen: his letter
of July 7, 1935, to Representative Sam Hill, apropos the
Guffey Coal Bill ("I hope your committee will not permit
doubts as to constitutionality, however reasonable, to block
this legislation."); his public reversal of attitude on the
propriety of corporation gifts to charity; the flagrant error
involved in the cancellation of the air-mail contracts, permitting the Army, with inadequate resources, to fly the
mails—with tragic consequences; the affair of the "preacher
letters," in which it was discovered that by some colossal
carelessness the White House secretariat had sent out an
inquiry to several thousand clergymen which was in part
a verbatim copy of a letter sent six months earlier by Governor La Follette of Wisconsin.[67]

Liberal correspondents were offended by the President's
high-handed disposition of the case of Dean S. Jennings, a
reporter discharged from the San Francisco *Call-Bulletin;*
the affront was particularly sharp because it hit the American Newspaper Guild, which has an energetic chapter
among the Washington correspondents. In the Ickes-
Moses controversy, many newspapermen felt that the
President was settling an old political grudge against a
capable public servant in New York. The castigation of
General Hagood, creating a public scandal over a negligible issue, did not increase Mr. Roosevelt's stature as a
political Machiavelli.[68]

Other sources of irritation were less explicit, but no less
corrosive. The correspondents were disillusioned when the
President, in answering one newspaperman who had persisted in asking an embarrassing question, said tartly:
"This isn't a cross-examination." [69] To newspapermen who

had come to feel that they had a right to cross-examine
the President on matters of policy, if not on affairs of state,
this was a distressing blow.

Newspapermen began to feel that the exercise of Presidential wit to evade a question was less of a novelty than
an irritant. The use of correspondents' first names was resented by some as a form of psychological bribery. Mr.
Roosevelt's debonair manner offended those newspapermen who thought the dignity of the office called for
lugubrious intonations, or those who could not forgive a
personality exuberant in the face of adversity. Liberal correspondents mourned the President's compromises with
the Right; conservatives, his flirtations with the Left. The
Roosevelt smile was maliciously likened to a faucet, turned
on and off with calculated purpose. One heard repeated
displeasure with Mr. Roosevelt's facial gestures ("mug-
ging").

There was growing antagonism to the "off the record"
remarks. They were called "silly" or "unnecessary"; it
was said that they no longer divulged really confidential
information, but more often acted "to sew up a story"
which some correspondents were ready to write.[70] Arthur
Krock, after praising the President and his aides for their
newspaper policy, and after granting the great service of
the press releases, suggested that the administration was
guilty of "more ruthlessness, intelligence, and subtlety in
trying to suppress legitimate unfavorable comment than
any other I have known." [71]

With the spread of critical sentiment, Mr. Roosevelt
was charged with faults for which his responsibility was
questionable. For instance, at each press conference the

same group of correspondents (generally from the press associations) stand in the front row, directly before the President's desk. These men, it was darkly hinted, "play the stooge": they laughed too heartily at Mr. Roosevelt's puns. The "front row" ordinarily supplies the "Thank you, Mr. President" which is the informal signal for the end of the conference; some newspapermen suggested to this writer that the technique was being used to rescue Mr. Roosevelt from embarrassing situations. It was said, too, that reporters in "the front row claque" permitted themselves to be used for "planted questions" (i.e., questions suggested to them by one of the President's secretaries) for which Mr. Roosevelt was primed with a ready and devastating answer.

Now some of these charges were legitimate, some absurd. The whole array, including many which must seem picayune, is given here because it is undeniable that there are newspapermen in Washington who harbor a resentment against Mr. Roosevelt, for one or another of these reasons, which is reflected in the tenor of their news dispatches. In the very fervor with which he was delineated in the first days of his administration lay part of the animus for that reversion of sentiment which took place once it became clear that not even Mr. Roosevelt could fulfill the extravagant expectations of the newspapermen. They had accepted as real not merely their glorification of a man, but their fabrication of a superman. No agnostic is so bitter as one disenchanted of a desperate and adolescent faith.

In the myth about Mr. Roosevelt which the Washington correspondents propagated, and in the energies de-

voted to the later deflation of it, there is an illuminating
lesson for analysts of public opinion. Neither the myth-
making nor the myth-destroying was an inexplicable or
unique phenomenon. The same journalistic process has
operated before; and it will be repeated with future Presidents and by future correspondents. The dynamics of that
process form a study in the psychology of journalists, and
are discussed at length later.*

It will serve to round out this section by pointing out
that when the concerted attack on Roosevelt began in 1936,
by the American Liberty League, "Jeffersonian Democrats," the Southern Committee to Preserve the Constitution, the Hearst chain, the Chicago *Tribune,* the Los Angeles *Times,* the Detroit *Free Press,* and most of the newspapers in the country, this writer took an anonymous poll
on the question: "Of the current candidates for President,
who is your choice?" The returns came in from February
to May of 1936, before the Republican candidate had been
chosen, when Governor Alf M. Landon, Senators Vandenberg and Borah, and Colonel Frank Knox were competing for Republican favor. Eighty-four members of the
press corps specified their choice.

Roosevelt	54
Landon	8
Vandenberg	8
Borah	4
Norman Thomas	4
Hoover	2
Knox	1

* See Chapter XI.

Thus, of the eighty-four returns, fifty-four (65.2 per cent) of the Washington correspondents expressed a preference for Franklin D. Roosevelt. The combined vote for all Republican candidates was twenty-six (30.8 per cent). The press corps still favored Mr. Roosevelt against any Republican candidate by more than two to one.

THE PRESS CONFERENCE: COMMENT

The press conference makes news available on equal terms to all correspondents at regular intervals. This insures many newspapermen, especially those from smaller papers or those overloaded with duties, against much of the fear of being "scooped" on news of major importance. Like the handout, the press conference saves time and energy; it obviates the necessity of several hundred men running around for information which may just as well be given them collectively. It removes a great deal of the tension of covering Washington.

The press conference has other advantages. It offers newspapermen an opportunity to obtain concrete impressions of the men who run the government. It provides them with a chance to interrogate important officials and, often, to extract information which has not been revealed in handouts. The correspondents were responsible for exposing the basic contradictions of NRA when, through shrewd questioning, they involved General Hugh S. Johnson, Administrator Ickes, and Attorney General Cummings in a revealing public fight. The newspapermen precipitated the housing controversy of 1934, between James A. Moffet and Secretary Ickes.*

The press conference also opens the possible strategy of "pegging" a story. Suppose a correspondent has collected facts, through his own research and private sources, for which no "spot" occasion exists (i.e., the facts have no salient news value in terms of some immediate event). In a press conference this reporter can ask a question designed to elicit an answer around which he can orient the information which he has been holding in reserve; thus he creates a "peg" upon which to hang his story.†

Some correspondents complain that the press conference *en masse* makes personal contact impossible between officials and individual reporters. Newspapermen criticize the "channel publicity system" by which the press agent becomes the central point of contact between the press and the departments.[73] Some press agents decide which persons shall or shall not be interviewed and pass on the newspapermen's request for information on given subjects. In some cases, this system has definitely improved the quality

---

* The conflict reached such proportions that a White House conference between the two belligerents was called. After the conference the following handout was issued:

"It seems a pity that either misrepresentation or a desire to stir up trouble where no trouble exists should have given rise to stories which created the impression that there is a divergence of views between the Housing Administration and the Public Works Administration. No conflict or overlapping exists."

This was greeted with irony by the press.[72]

† It does not matter whether an official denies or confirms the substance of a question. In either case his answer can be made to serve as a point of departure for a story.

of the information which the public receives (in the departments of Justice, Commerce, and the Treasury, for example). But, say some reporters, the system itself is bureaucratic and has elements of news suppression in it. It is obvious that handouts and press agents protect government officials. As for press conferences *en masse*—in the days when the corps in the capital was smaller it was easy to have interviews between an official and a few newspapermen at which an intimate atmosphere prevailed. But the press corps has grown to such unmanageable size that such a practice is impossible without gross favoritism. At its worst, the present method has become a necessary evil.

Correspondents often criticize press conferences when they mean to criticize the officials who conduct them. The success of the conference depends to an overwhelming degree on the personality of the official and the competence with which he can meet oral questions. Officials who are intimidated by the sight of a hundred or more correspondents, as was Secretary of State Stimson, for example, retreat into an uncommunicative shell. They offer little news which might not better be incorporated into a handout. They offend the correspondents by their timidity, and are offended by the newspapermen's cross-examination. In the present cabinet the unfortunate experience of Madame Secretary Perkins is a case in point. Few correspondents bother attending the press conferences of Secretary of Commerce Roper because of their uninspired tone.

The significance of the press conference as a democratizing influence should not go unnoticed. Erwin D. Canham, head of the *Christian Science Monitor* staff in Washington, says that press conferences have become "the fifth wheel of democracy" and introduce the benefits of the interpellative devices of English and French parliamentary government into the less flexible pattern of American politics.[74]

Professor Whittlesey of Princeton, criticizing the press conferences of the Hoover regime, has suggested that cabinet members be questioned regularly in the houses of Congress instead.[75] But Percy S. Bullen, formerly Washington correspondent for the London *Daily Telegraph*, said that even during the days when the inept "White House spokesman" formula was in force, the American press conference was a better device for communicating with the public than anything which Europe could offer: for exactitude, the interrogations in the House of Commons did not yield better results.[76]

Much of the objection to the press conference lies in the inescapable nature of the situation. A horde of from fifty to two hundred newspapermen, primed with questions, crowd into an official's office. As soon as the conference opens the barrage begins. Questions come in a swift, confusing, and diverse stream. They range from generalized matters of policy to queries on technical facts. Time is limited, extended discussion difficult. Answers must be given by the official with little time for reflection. He is forced to be cautious. He recognizes some questions as being "loaded" (i.e., framed so that any answer may be interpreted unfavorably). He has learned that a mistake or a careless comment may have serious results. The official sees the reporters as a pack of persistent news-vultures. The correspondents see the official as evasive and over-sensitive. To the official, the newspapermen are "trying to get something on me." To the correspondents, the official is "trying to hold something out on us." Both are right.

The character of political information militates against an uninterrupted harmony of relations between official and reporter. There are many occasions, in the course of practical politics, when officials feel it is not wise to publicize certain facts or where premature publication may have undesirable consequences. The element of surprise is important. Success often depends upon secretly conducted tactics. At such times the official is not too eager to cooperate with the press.

It is just to point out, too, that the person who has been misrepresented or singled out for journalistic attack develops a defensible suspicion of reporters. The officer who saw a sober and scholarly analysis of consumers' problems in women's dresses burlesqued into a subject of national derision learned to place future information in the hands of a press agent who had an understanding of the journalistic mind.*

On March 10, 1936, Secretary of Commerce Roper ordered all employees of the department to get written permission before giving out news, after he had discharged two officials of the Steamboat Inspection Service for a "news-leak." [77] From the point of view of Mr. Roper this was a necessary and realistic protective measure. To the correspondents it represented the elimination of a fruitful channel of news.

When the NRA decreed that no interviews with mem-

---

* Walton H. Hamilton, formerly of the Consumers' Advisory Board of NRA.

bers of its staff were to be granted until arrangements had been made with press-relations officers, many correspondents vented their indignation and raised the cry of censorship. Arthur Krock was rather more realistic and declared that the policy was justified; that co-ordination of information services led to greater efficiency. The burden for getting news, he stated, rests upon the correspondents and not the officials.[78]

The essential point is that officials and newspapermen meet for essentially conflicting purposes. The official wants to present information which will reflect most favor upon him. The newspaperman, motivated by the ancient values of journalism, is interested in precisely that type of news which the official is least eager to reveal. In the final analysis the press conference reduces itself to a contest between reporters skilled in ferreting and officials adept in straddling.

Two quotations, from gentlemen of experience, will illustrate the point. The first is from William Jennings Bryan. In his farewell to the press corps upon resigning as Secretary of State, he used a homely simile:

I have been like an old hen. My secrets have been my chickens which I was seeking to protect with my wings, while you were trying to get them out from under me.[79]

The other is from Premier Bennett of Canada, who expressed the basic antagonism of purposes with laudable and unfamiliar frankness to the 150 newspapermen who covered the Imperial Economic Conference at Ottawa in 1932.

Your business is to get news, I know, but mine is to see that you do not get any that will hamper the negotiations in progress. Your business is to find something to write about. Ours is to work for the benefit of the Empire as a whole.[80]

III. The Handout

IF you sit in the office of a Washington correspondent you will hear, several times within the course of an hour, the swish of an envelope being dropped through the slot in the door. If you examine the contents of his wastebasket at the end of a day you will find from fifty to 150 printed, mimeographed, or multigraphed press releases: pamphlets, booklets, announcements, speeches. Anywhere and everywhere in Washington there is evidence of the ubiquitous publicity device known as the "handout." There has been so much written about the handout which is either uninformed or misleading that it will be wise to discuss it at length.[1]

The handout is simply a press release issued by any person or group (public or private), and distributed gratuitously to newspapers. These press releases present facts, figures, or statements of policy upon which publicity is desired. Handouts are issued upon the initiative of the organization desiring to publicize an event or a point of view. They are not offered apologetically. They are not circulated nefariously. They are not illegal. They are not accompanied by threats or compulsion. They may be used in part or in whole, or they may be discarded, at the pleasure of the recipient. Many of them are of value since they provide material of news interest. Handouts are issued not only by governmental agencies but, with equal

67

freedom and fecundity, by each of the innumerable pressure groups which make Washington the most productive propaganda center in the nation.

The handout was adopted by the government as a publicity device during the World War, when it became necessary to control and co-ordinate the dissemination of official news. A "voluntary censorship" was recommended by the government and agreed to by the Washington correspondents.[2] Press agents, skilled in the arts of publicity, were installed in the departments of the federal government. Every effort was made to focus attention upon the glory, the moral purpose, and the assured victory of our side; and on the diabolism, demoralization, and certain defeat of the enemy. Facts of pessimistic significance were suppressed; facts strengthening optimistic impressions were energetically circulated. Since it was important that there should be no leak of secret information, and that certain facts should not be published prematurely, the authorized channel for communicating information which could be quoted became the handout. Handouts were prepared with infinite care and were checked by experts sensitive to the vagaries of the public mind and the power of the public press.

After the War there was a heightened consciousness, in industry as well as in government, of the value of "getting a good press," of creating and maintaining favorable public response. Publicity techniques were refined and a specialized group of experts, versed in the subtle craft of eliciting public sympathy, emerged in the robes of a new profession. Press agents became permanent adjuncts to large corporations and public personalities. Shortly after the War the newspapers of New York took a census of the number of press agents regularly employed in New York City, and discovered no less than 1,200 of them.[3] The movement spread to the government bureaus. In Washington, press agents were attached to the information services of the several departments, being listed as "public relations officers," "special advisors to the Secretary," "research assistants," or officers of "information services."

Since the handout is a simple, inexpensive, and direct method of bringing a given body of information to the attention of newspapermen it was adopted by all groups desirous of stimulating publicity for a cause. A press agent, a mimeograph machine, and a messenger boy became basic equipment for pressure groups in the capital. It has been suggested that because of its availability to organizations with limited funds, the mimeograph machine has become the last buttress of democracy.

Objections to the handout began to appear at an early date. In 1923, Washington correspondents were already complaining about the evil of government press agents and the menace of government handouts.[4] During the administration of President Hoover, pervaded by the ideal of efficiency and the ethic of "good business," *American Press*, a trade journal, estimated that the federal government was spending $3,000,000 a year on handouts alone.[5] One Washington correspondent received ninety-six separate pieces of material from government bureaus in a single day in July, 1931, ranging from a brief statement to an eighty-three page decision of the Board of Tax Appeals.[6] Another writer testified that in one day he received no less than 178 handouts from public and private organizations in the capital—enough to fill a week of newspapers.[7]

It should be clear that, contrary to the opinion held in some quarters, the Roosevelt administration did not invent the handout.[8] It did exploit its possibilities. The great flood of New Deal press releases may be attributed to several obvious reasons. In the dramatic action of the first Hundred Days of Mr. Roosevelt's regime, news charged with spectacular public interest was being created at an unprecedented pace. The persons with whom the President surrounded himself were sensitive to the necessity of supplying a steady stream of officially approved information to the public. Washington was crammed with news, news-events, and news-personalities. Emergency boards, councils, and commissions sprang up like mushrooms, manned by persons fervent in their conviction of the significance and the originality of their achievements. The key officers of the government realized, as did the President, that it was imperative to enlist public favor and create public sympathy for the New Deal. Those who attacked the Administration on the ground of publicity-seeking ignored the obvious fact that everything in Washington became "hot news," from Treasury announcements to Department of Labor statistics. The public's demand for news in the dramatic days of 1933 was literally insatiable.

The contagion of publicity-consciousness swept through the organs of the government. Sedate departments like the Treasury and the Department of Justice installed public relations experts and issued attractive handouts. Newspapermen were drawn into the government service by high salaries and, in some cases, by the prospect of work in which they could believe.* The NRA and the Agricultural Adjustment Administration had staffs in their press sections so large that they were organized like the city room of a metropolitan newspaper; publicity agents directed policy and supervised a personnel which included reporters, rewrite men, copy readers, statisticians, research workers, and special writers. In less than a year, NRA alone issued 5,200 handouts and AAA almost 5,000.

From March 4, 1933, to March 21, 1937, the publicity section of the Department of the Interior, under Michael W. Straus, turned out 6,295 press releases.† Up to the same date the Federal Emergency Relief Administration publicity section, under Morton M. Milford, had produced 2,926 releases.‡

It was not long before critics opened fire on government "propaganda" and "the colossal waste of the taxpayer's money." Washington correspondents began writing stories

* It is significant that many New Deal press agents are former correspondents for newspapers which were in violent opposition to the policies of the administration. The Hearst organization contributed Michael W. Straus (Public Works Administration), Marion L. Ramsey (Rural Electrification Administration), Kenneth Clark (Resettlement Administration), Edward Roddan (Democratic National Committee). The Chicago *Tribune* contributed John Herrick (Office of Indian Affairs) and Guy McKinney (Emergency Conservation Work). One Hearst correspondent is known to have left his post to take a New Deal job which paid him $1,000 a year less than he was getting from the New Deal's most vehement antagonist.

† Of these 2,825 were for the Department of the Interior, 2,220 for the Public Works Administration, 1,175 for the old Petroleum Authority and the new Petroleum Administration, and 75 for the National Resources Board and the Mississippi River Authority.

‡ The CWA and the FERA were responsible for 1,271 of these, the WPA for 1,455, and the National Youth Administration for 200.[9]

about "the Ballyhoo Men of the government," and on dull days filled their dispatches with stories about the menace of government publicity. One free-lance writer, writing under the pseudonym "George Michael," and believed to be affiliated with a private pressure group not distinguished for reputability, rushed into print with a hysterical volume entitled *Handout* which was a triumph of delusion over fact.[10] The "handout menace" became a favorite theme of attack. It was said that the press was being propagandized and prostituted by a ruthless bureaucracy.

The press corps agrees that no correspondent can possibly handle the full quantity of news-matter being created day by day in the capital. The handout and the press conference have systematized the flow of information; they have offered newspapermen, regularly and efficiently, responsible accounts of official acts. The handout has made the life of the Washington correspondent immeasurably easier, removing the confusion and the uncertainty which would exist without some institutional link between complex events and overworked reporters. Some news is so technical (e.g., news from the Treasury and the Federal Reserve Board) that it has to be interpreted to the reporters and simplified for their purposes.[11] Handouts have grown as specialized administrative agencies have grown.

A distinction should be drawn between the handouts of government agencies and those of private pressure groups. The former, except for statements from officials, are largely statements of fact; the latter are, more generally, expressions of opinion. Handouts from private organizations are clearly designed to represent a special point of view and, according to Arthur Krock, in a speech to the National Republican Club, "nothing in any of them could fool anyone who could resist a bargain offer of the Brooklyn Bridge from a perfect stranger." Mr. Krock said of thirty-seven NRA handouts which he received one day, that "all were accurate and useful reports of acts and proceedings interesting to industry, entirely colorless." Of government press releases in general Mr. Krock said, "Rarely has any statement been disproved in fact." [12]

Handouts save the correspondent's time, they spare his legs, and they provide him with information for which an official agency assumes responsibility. In the absence of the handout each correspondent would be thrown upon his own resources; he would find it necessary to get the same facts by the time-consuming process of telephone calls, interviews, visits to innumerable offices, and hasty research. One correspondent told this writer: "It would take me three days of bench-warming and nagging to get the facts which are in a handout—and then I'd not be certain of their accuracy or be able to quote a responsible authority for them." In the words of another, "The men who moan about the handouts are the ones who would yelp most loudly if they were abolished."

The chief objection to the handout is that it offers those facts which the press agent *wants* publicized. There are no handouts on the failures, scandals, dissensions, and inconsistencies of an administration. There was no handout on the famous AAA purge by which Jerome Frank was maneuvered out of an important position. There was no handout on the fact that the Import-Export Bank, headed by George Peek, had made only one loan in its entire year of existence—$4,000,000 to Cuba: a miserable record considering the purposes of the organization and the fanfare with which it was set up.[13] There are no handouts on the political deals, the intramural squabbles, the clashes of personality, the sterilizations of policy, which are woven into the fabric of the governing process. "The rules of the game prescribe that an administration shall not even be candid about such terrible blunders as the cancellation of the Air Mail contracts." [14]

This is not surprising. It is true of any administration and any organization, private or public. It is to be expected that the human beings engaged in publicity work, whether in government or in private industry, will try to mobilize their facts and turn their phrases so that a picture of success will be created. It is fair to say that efforts have been made by government departments to avoid *crude* propaganda in their official publicity. Stephen Early, special secretary to the President and overseer of the New Deal's press relations sections, instructed the press agents in the different parts of the government to handle their jobs "just as though you were working for a newspaper" and "without propaganda." [15]

Nevertheless, from time to time it has appeared that censorship was being exercised by certain bureaus to prevent unfavorable facts from coming to light. An article in the *New Republic* alleged that the Department of Agriculture suppressed a devastating report on the conditions of Southern share-croppers, long a touchy subject with the administration.[16] A dispatch in the *Wall Street Journal* for February 13, 1936 (page 2), showed that there had been a manipulation of figures in a cotton report issued by a government department.

But to generalize with the flat charge that handouts are "dangerous propaganda" seems to miss the point. Any statement made with the intention of influencing people or of eliciting publicity is, analytically, propaganda. The positive value of the handout cannot be swept aside lightly. As long as it can be charged and demonstrated publicly that certain government handouts present inaccurate facts or suppress significant ones, then the dangers of the device may be held in check. It is more proper to criticize the *use* which correspondents make of handouts. Those newspapermen who accept handouts at their face value, without critical analysis or the suspicion which is presumably part of a competent reporter's psychology, are responsible for passing "propaganda" on to the public and disseminating, without investigation, only that version of the facts which has been purged of features displeasing to the official point of view. The resourceful correspondent has little to fear from the handout. He can interpret for himself the facts and information contained in press releases. Many a handout, launched with the purpose of reflecting glory on a government agency, has turned into a boomerang because some correspondent has had the energy and intelligence to go beyond the facts proffered.

It is important to remember that since handouts cannot parade in disguise they are approached with suspicion by competent newspapermen. It is part of the newspaperman's job to examine information and expose its limitations. The statistics on re-employment issued by the Department of Labor at regular intervals are not given much "play" by Washington correspondents because a general feeling has grown up that their authenticity is not to be trusted.[17] The experienced newspaperman treats handouts from the Department of Commerce as critically as those from the Chamber of Commerce.

There is a self-correcting aspect to handouts, because the device is open to all comers. Thus, it was possible to find side by side on the same table of press releases at the National Press Club, a handout from the American Federation of Labor stating that unemployment had decreased slightly, one from the Department of Labor proving that unemployment had declined sharply, one from the Republican National Committee demonstrating that it was increasing, and one from the American Liberty League proving conclusively that never in our history had it been so bad. Each handout was supported by impressive statistics. The Washington correspondent can take his choice of these equally suspect claims, or he can indicate their true nature by placing them in juxtaposition to one another. If the handout is obviously colored it is a simple enough matter to reveal its purpose, using the language of the handout itself as evidence.

It should be noticed that the handout competes for attention with the other news available on any given day. A reporter with several good stories will ignore the handout; another, pressed for news, will "play one up" into a front-page dispatch. During the dull summer months handouts receive microscopic and grateful attention.

Handouts are dangerous insofar as: (1) they so simplify the task of covering Washington that they become, for many correspondents, the sole source of information;

(2) they succeed in creating the impression, by sheer cumulative effect, that there are no other facts, or no other versions of the facts, than those contained in the press releases. It cannot be denied that the incessant flow of "easy information" and ready-made stories has a debilitating influence on those newspapermen who are susceptible to the temptation to use the easiest way of covering the capital.

Publishers with correspondents in the capital who lack the resourcefulness and the critical insight which are the first requirements of a good journalist should not be surprised to receive dispatches which are little more than regurgitations of officially written news stories. In these cases the fault lies with the reporters rather than with the handouts. Publishers who load their correspondents with so many routine duties that they are left with little time to explore the contents of handouts should not expect political correspondence of a high level. In any event it is reasonable to point out that handouts are but one device in the total process of getting news and that, *within the limited sphere* in which they should be put to use, no effective substitute for them has been suggested.

IV. News-Sources and Restraints

NEWS-SOURCES

I. CONGRESSMEN

HANDOUTS and press conferences offer correspondents a steady supply of routine news. But the correspondent who wishes information of a more revealing nature is obliged to cultivate private news-sources. In this field the value of friendships with Senators and Representatives is very high. For many years, particularly before the inauguration of White House press conferences, Senators were the chief sources of news in the capital.[1] They are still invaluable. Senators are well-informed on the confidential aspects of political life because: (1) they have power over appointments and recommendations; (2) their committees are important incubators of news and news-events; (3) Senators often initiate action for legislation of interest to their home state or locality; (4) they have their own information machines among political dependents and those whom they have recommended for appointive offices. It is of the highest importance for a special correspondent to cultivate the Senators from his state and maintain a friendly liaison with them. Since no correspondent has the time to make a daily canvass of all the agencies, departments, bureaus, and commissions in the capital, Congressional figures of importance serve as excellent short-cuts to the founts of information.

The special correspondent makes the rounds of his home delegation regularly. "A Tennesseean sitting on the Ways and Means Committee . . . or an Oregonian serving as chairman of a major committee often passes to a newspaper friend from his own state a story of national or international bearing." [2]

Most newspapermen in the capital develop fairly responsive contacts with from five to fifteen Congressional leaders: generally, the legislators from their states and several members of key Congressional committees. It is not necessary to court more than a few Congressmen; the majority are poor news-sources because they are neither men of public interest nor occupants of important committee posts. But the competent correspondent has an "in" with at least one member of the House Ways and Means Committee, one member of the Senate Finance Committee, one Representative on the House Appropriations Committee, one on the Senate Committee on Foreign Relations.

It is not difficult for a correspondent to get news from Congressmen, however solemnly they may be sworn to secrecy. Newspaper publicity is the legislator's life-line, his most potent method of keeping "the folks back home" alert to his achievements and his stature. The Congressman who has aspirations for re-election cannot afford to adopt a cavalier air to the newspaperman who controls the news which his constituents read. Magnus Johnson, former Senator from Minnesota, once invaded the Senate press gallery and harangued the correspondents for some of the stories they had been writing. The press corps boycotted him. Stories about Senator Johnson suddenly ceased to appear.* The political damage he suffered was inestimable.[3] The corps' boycott of ex-Senator Thomas Heflin was carried on with equal success after that statesman had indulged in some of his more offensive oratory.†

There are professional, social, and personal bonds between legislators and newspapermen. Eleven Congressmen are members of the National Press Club, and no less than forty-five have been, or still are, newspapermen. Senators Arthur Capper, Carter Glass, and Arthur Vandenberg are newspaper publishers today. Senators Harry Byrd and Joseph C. O'Mahoney (Wyoming) were once editors. Senator Royal S. Copeland is an active columnist for the Hearst papers, and Henry Cabot Lodge, Jr., was formerly a member of the New York *Herald Tribune's* Washington bureau. Thirteen Representatives still edit or publish a newspaper. Louis Ludlow of Indiana was a Washington correspondent for thirty years and was President of the National Press Club. It is natural to expect a common body of interest and experience between such men and the active journalists in the capital, and to find that the former have an understanding of newspaper practices and problems which is gratifying to the latter.

Many Congressmen are friendly with certain news-

---

* The correspondents for some papers, e.g., the New York *Times,* did not join the boycott.

† The Baltimore *Sun* and *Evening Sun,* apparently following the strategy of "publicizing their enemies in order to make them ridiculous," frequently devoted much space to Heflin's speeches, with extensive direct quotations which created an unforgettable impression in cold print.

papermen, play poker with them, meet them socially, and do not hesitate to offer them friendly tips. Many Congressmen realize that correspondents are an incalculable aid in publicizing a program and bringing facts into prominence. The prominence of Fiorello LaGuardia when he was a Representative from New York owed a great deal to the consistent publicity given to him and his work by Ray Tucker. The prestige of such figures as Senators Norris, Wagner, La Follette, and the late Bronson Cutting, or of Representatives like Maury Maverick of Texas, owes much to the sympathetic treatment given their activities by correspondents who admire them and find them honest, intelligent, and conscientious public servants.

It is not unknown for Washington correspondents to put ideas into the heads of their political favorites and, sometimes, to put felicitous words into their mouths. A Washington correspondent may type out a statement and ask a statesman if he "would not like to say that for publication." In 1930 a correspondent for the Washington *Post* ran around the Senate getting endorsements for a vigorous personal campaign against the London Naval Conference.[4]

The late Huey Long was first greeted in the capital with ridicule, but several correspondents were attracted to him and told Long that John J. Raskob and the late Senator Robinson were "selling out" the Democratic party to Wall Street. After several weeks of suggestion, during which Senator Long was impressed by the fact that he had the power to stampede the next Democratic convention, he began to ponder on his political position. Suddenly, to the surprise of everyone, Huey Long made political overtures to Senator Norris and launched into a vigorous attack on Senator Robinson's leadership of the party.[5]

Some Congressmen feel under a psychological obligation to newspapers which have supported them in election campaigns, and are eager to curry favor with those whose support in future campaigns is uncertain. A Congressman knows that papers which helped elect him can also help to defeat him. It is clear that the loquacity of legislators springs from a rational motivation.

After a secret committee meeting in which seventeen Senators participated, two correspondents attempted, on a bet, to discover how many men they could coax into telling what had gone on in the conference. With no particular effort they succeeded in getting the salient facts from thirteen Senators within one afternoon.

Congressional "leaks" are common. When President Hoover called in Congressional leaders of both parties in June, 1931, and received their advance approval for the moratorium he was planning to announce a week later, the story was being telegraphed to newspapers all over the country within a few hours.[6] Mr. Hoover polled many members of Congress by telegram; the news broke more easily because of this.

The alertness of Congressmen to favorable publicity for themselves and the programs in which they are interested may be seen in the manner in which Congressional committee hearings are conducted. Paul Mallon has pointed out that the modern inquiry is arranged with an eye to providing a "hot story" regularly at noon each day, to give the afternoon papers a striking "lead," and another one late in the afternoon, to give the morning papers a

fresh lead. He suggests that investigators are careful not
to develop too many important points at once, but gauge
their pace so as to hold the public's attention as long as
possible.[7]

Some Senators, cognizant of the power of the press,
hold press conferences of their own. The Honorable William Edgar Borah holds forth on regular occasions in his
chambers in the Senate Office Building. His technique is
well-known: he pretends he does not want to give out a
story, but inculcates the impression that an important story
does exist. Just before the interview ends, he drops the
facts into the conversation. The correspondents regard Mr.
Borah as an excellent fellow despite his penchant for elo-
cution. So sensitive is the Senator to the efficacy of Washington as a sounding-board that he remains in the capital
after Congress is over and comes back before it convenes,
in order to make maximum use of the opportunities.[8]

Congressmen and correspondents help each other, and
exploit each other. They are united in purpose insofar as
both are eager to have news printed; the nature of the
news to be printed, however, often precipitates conflict.

II. OFFICIALS

Government officials, of both major and minor rank, are
also serviceable news-sources. Why, it may be asked,
should an appointed official offer news to the correspondents, apart from that made available in press conferences?
Unlike the Congressman his political life does not depend
upon continuous favorable publicity. But officials, like
Congressmen, are eager to have their work presented in

the most favorable light. The public's reaction to their work does have a bearing on their careers. Some of them, like Congressmen, suffer from the diseases of publicity-seeking. In the Fabian warfare of politics, the adroit utilization of the press as a weapon of attack and a method of defense is of paramount importance. Suppose, for example, that Senator Resplendent P. Smith has attacked a cabinet Secretary on a political issue. Now the Secretary may not be too well-equipped in the arts of controversy and invective, or may not consider the Senator worth answering. But an official in the department may be indignant over this insult to the work with which he has identified himself. He may be enraged because the Senator has misstated the facts or concealed important evidence. If this official is contacted he may be induced to give the other side of the story, under a guarantee that his name is not to be used. He may point out that the Senator has a standing grudge against the Secretary of the department because the XYZ Corporation, which is the largest contributor to the Senator's campaign funds, has declared war on the Department for its intervention in certain labor troubles.

Intra-administration feuds, personal strife, factionalism, a competition for public support or the favor of the President—all these encourage the communication of confidential information. Malcontents in government bureaus who came into the service with high hopes of achievement and who have seen worthy programs sabotaged and hamstrung for personal, party, or political reasons, are excellent pipelines of "inside stories." Those souls upon whom the incompetence, friction, or obstructionism of governmental routine imposes a psychological burden are not reluctant to voice their discontent, as long as their identity will be concealed. The operation of an impersonal bureaucratic structure places a psychic premium on the externalization of discontents. The Washington atmosphere of gossip, and the lack of inhibitions upon gossip, facilitates revelations of "inside" information. One correspondent in Washington, with a string of important "exclusive" stories to his credit, cultivates the "young radicals" in government offices, the men whose frustrated idealism or ambition is conducive to the communication of information embarrassing to those higher up. In this connection it is interesting to point out that Jerome Frank, upon being ousted from the AAA, told his story to a friendly columnist who gave the facts behind the news and attacked Secretary Wallace and Administrator Chester C. Davis for their conduct in the famous AAA "purge." [9]

III. THE PRESS GALLERIES

In the galleries of the Senate and the House of Representatives there is a special section, immediately behind and above the Speaker, which is reserved for the representatives of the press. The corridors behind these galleries have been converted into press rooms, in which newspapermen type their stories, telephone their offices, lounge, talk, sleep, or play cards. The press associations and the larger newspapers have direct telephone lines from their offices to the gallery. Admission to the press galleries is strictly limited to "bona fide correspondents of reputable standing" for daily newspapers or press associations, who dispatch news *by telegraph*. This keeps out reporters for trade journals, private news-letter services, pressure group representatives, and others.* The correspondents, through their Standing Committee, authenticate applications for admission and enforce their own discipline. The committee co-operates with the Speaker of the House of Representatives and the Committee on Rules of the Senate, to whom violations of the privileges of the galleries are reported.

The major burden for covering the House and the Senate falls upon the reporters for the press associations, to whom the Senate or the House is a permanent "beat" and an exhausting ordeal. These men are faced with the task of sending "running accounts" of debates, keeping newspapers in almost minute-by-minute touch with legislation, oratory, and filibusters. A correspondent assigned to the galleries must be able to condense long-winded remarks into brief paragraphs, and give the gist of technical bills in succinct language. He must interview Congressmen. He must cover committee hearings. Since he is stationed at a fixed beat there is great routine, exacting detail, and much tension attached to his job.

Consider a typical day in the life of one of the correspondents covering the Senate for a press association. If a committee hearing is being held he must cover it, from about 10 A.M. to noon. This requires the sending of frequent leads to his office as the news breaks. He will file several bulletins, write a running account, change the lead at different points in the investigation, and write a final

* The rule also serves to bar Negro correspondents from the galleries.

story summarizing the day's events, which afternoon papers can use. Then he may write a special story which morning newspapers can use the next day, with still another lead. When the Senate convenes he returns to the galleries. Relieved every fifteen minutes or half hour by one of his colleagues (press association men covering the Houses of Congress must work in shifts), he keeps in close touch with his office by telephone. If there is some important news-break he may run down to the corridor on the floor of the Senate and ask to interview a Senator, who will give him added information on what is going on. He is obliged to stay in the gallery after the Senate adjourns, writing a story for late afternoon and evening editions, and another for the next morning's press. All through the day he is being queried by his office, which feeds him questions coming in from different parts of the country, gives him instructions or leads on possible angles to cover, or supplies him with information on events which have broken in other parts of the capital but which are relevant to the news breaking on his beat.

Covering the House or the Senate lacks the variety and color of the job which is the special correspondent's. One press association reporter wrote no less than eleven stories in one day, plus half a dozen bulletins and new leads, and was on constant call in between. It is not uncommon for the men to eat a quick sandwich lunch at their typewriters or while calling to their offices. The nervous strain on them is great; the routine is tiring; the tension of covering an incessant flow of news is acute.

The special correspondent visits the press galleries regularly, especially when some bill in which he is interested is under discussion. He does not, of course, worry about being "scooped" because his newspaper gets an uninterrupted flow of dispatches from the press associations. Since covering Congressional action is largely a routine job, and since the press association reporters stationed in the galleries concentrate on it, the special correspondent finds it useful to devote his time to other spots and specializes on an entirely different type of story.*

IV. CO-OPERATION AND "BLACKSHEETING"

No one correspondent covers Washington. The Washington newspaper corps covers Washington. This is a point which deserves emphasis. Contact between correspondents is continuous, professional morale is high, co-operation is widespread. Information is shared, advice given freely, the fruits of individual labor pooled. The National Press Club serves primarily as a clearing house for the exchange of facts, tips, leads, and gossip. After any press conference, for instance, correspondents compare notes, consult colleagues on the "angle" to be followed in interpretation, and seek the opinion of reporters more expert in certain fields of news.

The advantages of co-operation are obvious. (1) Through a division of labor with friends, one correspondent is "covered" on events which he could not possibly report in person. (On some days there are four or five press conferences scheduled.) (2) Co-operation entails a sharing of expert knowledge. During the labor difficulties in the automobile industry, correspondents called upon

* See Chapter V.

their confreres from Detroit to supply them with detailed information about the background of the dispute, the technical set-up of the automobile industry, and its labor policies and record. A correspondent who is at home with news emanating from the Department of the Interior may need help with information stemming from the Treasury. (3) In the same way, familiarity with regional situations is put to co-operative uses. Representatives of California papers find it profitable to consult newspapermen serving Pennsylvania, for example, when a full understanding of certain news depends upon a knowledge of local conditions in Pennsylvania.

Co-operation reaches its most explicit form in the "Blacksheet." The Blacksheet is a carbon copy of a news-dispatch, which one newspaperman gives to another. The correspondent receiving a Blacksheet from a colleague is free to treat it as he sees fit. Generally he uses it as a guide and a source, incorporating only its substance into his own news-story. He may reorient the facts with an eye to regional emphases, angles most attractive to his readers, or a point of view more consonant with his paper's policy.* Rarely does a newspaperman transmit another man's Blacksheet *verbatim*, although this has been done—with amusing results. The stories on Herbert Hoover's acceptance of the Republican Presidential nomination, which appeared in the Baltimore *Evening Sun* and the New York *Herald Tribune* in August of 1932, were practically identical and betrayed the undiscriminating use of the Blacksheet.

* See Chapter X.

The use of the Blacksheet has been both underestimated and misunderstood. It was inevitable that newspapermen confronted with the complex task of covering Washington would resort to every device which would prove helpful. There is, after all, no reason why correspondents from, say, Philadelphia, Chicago, Los Angeles, and New Orleans should not co-operate. They are not competitors; their news-markets are removed from each other. Their publishers do not know, and probably do not care, if the news-dispatches coming to any one paper represent the combined efforts of several men. On the contrary, if an editor receives dispatches which are the fruit of several correspondents' work he is getting an extra service for which he does not have to pay. There is neither deception nor disloyalty in co-operation, nor in the use of the Blacksheet. In newspaper circles there is no effort to conceal or deny the practice. Correspondents who cover the same events, eat together, think alike, meet socially, discuss news, share leads, and consult one another can hardly be blamed for extending their reciprocity to its logical conclusion: the exchange of news-dispatches. Through Blacksheets and co-operation special correspondents often beat the press associations, either in terms of time or content.

Blacksheeting is carried on informally. Co-operative groups tend to form on the basis of personal compatibility, a community of interest, and the fact that the papers of the men in the group do not compete with each other. (Sometimes reporters from the same city co-operate on routine stories.) Younger correspondents are more likely to exchange Blacksheets with correspondents not much older. Correspondents working for arch-Republican or arch-

Democratic papers, or themselves allied emotionally with either party, will tend to find in each other's Blacksheets a gratifying coincidence of attitude. Members of the Gridiron Club tend to exchange Blacksheets with others who sport the insignia of the order. The location of offices plays a role of some consequence in the formation of these groups. The newspaper offices of special correspondents are concentrated in three buildings, and these form a rough foundation for co-operative enterprises. The twelfth floor of the National Press Building, the ninth floor of the Colorado Building, and the sixth and seventh floors of the Albee Building are centers where there is easy access to and from newspaper offices.*

What with formalized press conferences, handouts, the excellent services of the press associations, the news-ticker, the flow of gossip and tips, and the co-operation of the home office, some correspondents find their life pleasant, secure, and not unduly tense. The following comment by a veteran Washington newspaperman is in point:

Probably "Washington Correspondent" is the easiest and most sumptuous berth any reporter can get in this country. There is small work connected with it. Groups work together, swapping news and writing each other's stories. Friendships grow up all around and the tranquil family life of Washington appeals. Into this pleasant and placid existence why should enmities and acrimony and consequently more work intrude.[10]

An interesting example of the importance which press-corps co-operation may achieve as an opinion-molding

* Obviously, all of the newspapermen in the capital do not use Blacksheets, but the practice is indulged in, with varying degrees of frequency, by a majority of the press corps.

force is to be found in the following episode When Premier Laval of France came to the United States to discuss international economic problems with President Hoover in October, 1931, Senator Borah was used as a decoy by which the American attitude to the French position on the Versailles Treaty might be publicized without involving either the President or the official position of the government. Senator Borah is a first-rate news-personality in Europe; he is regarded as the spokesman of the Senate on international affairs and his opinions get wide notices in the European press. Mr. Borah made a forceful statement to a group of foreign correspondents which left no doubts concerning American antagonism to the intransigent attitude of the French to Germany. That afternoon a French correspondent who had come over to cover Laval's visit, eager to minimize the implications of Borah's statement, met one of the Washington correspondents for the St. Louis *Post-Dispatch* at a cocktail party and pretended that Senator Borah had been sympathetic to the French in his point of view, aye! almost Francophile. The American was skeptical; he promptly called Senator Borah, whom he had long known, and got the real story. Then this correspondent:

... who was all for having some red-blooded American give the French a bit of his mind, proceeded to telephone to other newspaper friends to tell them what a very sensational story there was in the Borah interview. Within an hour ... the excitement had been raised to a pitch where the interview, of which stenographic copies were by this time available, had become the big story of the evening, and even those who wanted to soft-pedal it had to treat it as such. The following morning all newspapers gave it great prominence and several printed it verbatim.[11]

The danger which Blacksheeting involves is simply that a correspondent may not exercise sufficient discrimination in using someone else's Blacksheet. During the negotiations in Washington in 1933 between industrialists and workers of the automobile industry, under Section 7A of the now defunct NRA codes, several correspondents, plagued with work, relied upon the dispatches of Detroit correspondents familiar with the automobile industry and the Detroit scene. Now several Detroit correspondents were sending their papers dispatches which, for "policy" reasons, strained desperately to suggest that the negotiations were going smoothly, that the interests of both labor and industry were being considered equitably, and that a compromise fair to all would be reached. When the conferences ended, the Detroit correspondents acclaimed the results as fair and just. The correspondents using their Blacksheets took the same tack and suggested the same halcyon finale. But one Detroit correspondent knew that the negotiations had not been fairly concluded; although his dispatches hailed the final agreement as a fair compromise, privately he said: "Compromise, hell! It was jammed down labor's throat! I had to play up the brotherly-love angle for my newspaper." And it was this angle which those who used this man's dispatches with too much credence broadcast through their own news columns.

In the same way, one correspondent may "go out on a limb" on a story (i.e., make a prediction or analysis which he is unable to support with proof or which is based on incomplete evidence) and other newspapermen, without checking upon the authenticity of the account, will use his Blacksheet as the basis of their dispatches. This practice is condemned by experienced reporters. It is probably confined to overworked and none too resourceful correspondents.

The Washington corps is split into competing groups of non-competing reporters. An interesting study might be made of the preponderance of influence which one or two leading personalities exercise within each clique, and of the ramifications of that influence, following the general lines of Dr. J. L. Moreno's penetrating analysis of school children, *Who Shall Survive?* [12] To a considerable degree the value of specific news-items may depend upon the competence of the correspondents who were consulted. One or two men within each clique are the intellectual arbiters: their interpretation of events is followed by the others; their "tips" are treated with particular respect. Likewise, the striking influence of Eastern newspapers should be observed. Practically all correspondents in the capital read one or more of the following papers: the New York *Times*, the Baltimore *Sun*, the New York *Herald Tribune*, the Washington *Post*, and the Washington *Star*.* (Eastern newspapers are more influential in the capital because they can be read the morning they appear; mid-western papers are several days old by the time they reach Washington.) The news-columns of these journals are followed closely, day by day. A correspondent may plan his activities so as to develop angles on stories which he clips from one or another of these newspapers.

* See Chapter VII.

The influence exerted by the writers for the New York *Times*, for example, is thus very great: the facts in a New York *Times* dispatch will be copied widely and incorporated—in whole or in part—into news-accounts going to papers all over the country.

In the same manner, the columnists who are followed by the corps: Raymond Clapper, Paul Mallon, Arthur Krock, Messrs. Allen and Pearson, play a role in shaping opinion or inspiring stories. No method exists for testing the frequency with which correspondents use the materials made available under one or another of these "by-lines."

The "planted story" is an interesting co-operative device, used for purposes of self-protection rather than co-operation. Suppose a St. Louis correspondent has an important story involving New York politics. He will send it to his paper and then give a Blacksheet or a "withdrawal" (the original of his dispatch, which he gets back from the telegraph office for his records) to a New York correspondent with whom he is friendly. The story is published in New York, where it has greater effect because of its regional relevance. Had the story appeared only in the St. Louis paper of the original writer, it might have attracted minor attention.

The "plant" may serve another purpose. If the St. Louis correspondent wanted to "go out on a limb," he might "plant" his story with several colleagues. The wider dissemination of his point of view lends authenticity to it. If his home office questions the validity of his dispatch he can point to the fact that reliable newspapers in New York, Detroit, and Chicago printed it. The defense is impressive.

A more ingenious mechanism may be involved. Suppose a correspondent from Pittsburgh has received information in confidence from a Pittsburgh official. It is important information and would make a front-page story. But the reporter dare not print it and risk alienating his news-source or, possibly, embroiling him in a political controversy. The Pittsburgh correspondent may "plant" the story in a New York or Baltimore paper. The facts are thus made public. (His informant may have offered no objection to having the story come out in this roundabout way.) Then his newspaper will pick the story up, citing the New York or Baltimore paper as its authority. Or the Pittsburgh correspondent may send his newspaper the story himself, on the pretense that he was *forced* to pick it up once other newspapers had, "somehow," picked up the facts. This excuse is not difficult to defend if the story had a Washington angle.

V. "THAT'S RIGHT UP YOUR ALLEY"

Variations in news-markets and readers' interests and differences in newspaper policy account for the exchange of news. Many stories are offered to correspondents by other correspondents for the simple reason that, in a phrase well-known in Washington, "that's right up your alley."

A correspondent from Cleveland may run across a story concerning a possible government grant to a Houston project. This is probably of no great news-interest to him, and he will offer the story to a correspondent from Texas. In the same way, each correspondent runs across many angles to a story which, because they are not of direct relevance to his central theme or have no regional interest for his readers, he offers to correspondents from another section of the country.

The phrase "that's right up your alley" has another meaning. Newspapermen become expert in estimating the pleasure with which their home offices will welcome stories with a particular political emphasis or with particular political implications. One correspondent may be working for a newspaper which is violently anti-administration and has been running a series of articles describing the iniquities of the government's attack on, say, holding companies. If he runs across a story which exposes the undelectable practices of holding companies he may think twice before sending it—especially if his paper has not printed previous stories of a similar nature. There is a telling remark which newspapermen use on such occasions: "There's no point in wasting telegraph tolls." He will give the story to a correspondent for a newspaper which has featured dispatches hostile to the holding companies or sympathetic to the government's position. The laconic phrase is apt: "It's right up your alley."

The field of co-operation opened up to correspondents by variations in newspaper policies is very wide. One has merely to notice the striking differences in newspaper make-up—or in the editorial columns, the news-columns, or the cartoons—to realize that many papers do not give adequate prominence to dispatches the implications of which conflict with the preferences of publisher or editor. Each paper has its own conception of "what is news," molded to a great extent by the character of its owner and the political bent of its editors. Papers have different values, diverse schemes of judgment, different demonologies. And correspondents are aware of the precise outlines of their paper's policy: they must be, else they could not have come to Washington, or, once in Washington, they could not have stayed there very long.

The Hearst newspapers do not welcome dispatches which, in effect, advertise pacifistic, internationalist, or "liberal" activities. The St. Louis *Post-Dispatch* does. The New York *Sun* does not respond with interest to stories exposing strike-breakers or the seamier side of red-baiting. The New York *Post* does. An objective analysis of these organs will verify this. The dissection of newspaper policy and its influence upon newspaper correspondents must be left for later chapters.* At this point it is enough to indicate that a story which has not reached the stage of national importance can be "ducked" by a correspondent. (He has no fears about ignoring it because if his paper wants the item it can, presumably, get it from the press associations.) He offers it to another reporter because "it's right up his alley."

VI. "OFF THE RECORD"

Information offered "off the record" is intended to enlighten the correspondents and provide them with a richer background for the interpretation of events. "Off the record" information may involve an explanation of *why* an executive cannot discuss something for publication, why he will not make a particular announcement, or why he

* See Chapters X, XIII, and XIV.

intends to adopt a certain policy. It may contain information which is tentative; it may deal with matters still in a state of flux; it may entail facts which it would be premature or indiscreet to reveal at the moment; it may embody a point of view to which the informant does not wish to commit himself at the moment. "Off the record" remarks can be very valuable to newspapermen. They serve as points of orientation amid the half-truths of political controversy. Sometimes they serve as a check upon the authenticity of other information. Sometimes they illuminate future courses of action or point to probable changes in policy.

Some examples of "off the record" information will illustrate these comments:

1. A government official was asked to comment on an attack launched against his department by a well-known industrialist. The official replied with an answer, for publication, couched in polite language; then, "off the record," he explained that the industrialist's attack could be traced to the fact that the department was engaged in an investigation of certain irregularities in his corporation. Did such evidence exist? Yes—but the statement could not be published at the time, since the investigation had not been concluded.

2. An official explained, "off the record," that a bill was being fought by a group of Congressmen in alliance with a certain lobby. The issue could not be pressed because of a delicate political situation in the state from which a leading spirit of the opposition came; martyrization of the Congressman by the federal government would be inexpedient.

3. An official was asked if a large corporation's request for a federal loan would be granted. He replied that it would not; then, "off the record," stated that so far as the government could determine the organization was in a hopeless financial predicament.

4. A cabinet member, not wishing to dignify the attacks on him by a politician with overweaning ambitions, gave the corps enough information "off the record" so that they would not misinterpret his public silence.

One purpose of the "off the record" comment which is not ordinarily observed is this: information may be supplied with so perfunctory an admonition to "keep this strictly confidential" that it is clear that the informant *wants* the facts made public. What he means, in effect, is, "Print this, but don't quote me." Furthermore, if Democrat X and Republican Y are engaged in a public fight, X may be supplying newspapermen with information about Y for which he does not wish to be held publicly responsible and which, above all, he does not want Y to know he has offered the newspapermen. X generally discovers that Y has been resorting to the same tactics.

A great deal of unnecessary mystery has been attached to "off the record" remarks. Most information offered in this form finds its way into the newspapers in guarded form, particularly in the "gossip columns," within a few days. It may be couched in phrases beginning, "It was learned from reliable sources" or, "On the best of authority." Often a correspondent incorporates the implications, if not the substance, of the remarks into the general texture of his dispatch.

Many correspondents do not attend conferences precisely because they do not wish to be held to the "off the record" ruling. They believe that sooner or later they will get the information from their own sources; they do not wish to have a good story "sewn up." It has happened that an official has begun to offer information "off the record" only to be interrupted by a correspondent with these words: "Will you please not make that statement 'off the record'? I already have the information and intend to publish it."

The "off the record" comments at President Roosevelt's press conferences are not supposed to be communicated to anyone, not even to the correspondent's own home office. That at least was the form which the original ruling took.[13] But since newspapermen feel, quite correctly, that they are employed by their newspapers and not by the President, this stipulation is rarely observed with compulsive rigor. The visitor to the National Press Club can hear half a dozen stories an afternoon which fall into the "off the record" category. It has been said that the President knew that "off the record" remarks would ultimately find their way into press dispatches, in however disguised a form, and that he had hit upon a clever and deceptive kind of "trial balloon."[14]

To the Department of State a modified form of "off the record" remarks is a necessary and extremely valuable device. On Friday, March 22, 1935, Secretary of State Cordell Hull held a press conference with a large group of reporters; many correspondents for foreign papers were present. The tension of the European situation at the time (Germany had just announced her intention to rearm) was in the air. Several questions concerning our possible action

in Europe according to treaty rights were met by the statement that we would pursue "our normal course." Then
Mr. Hull offered some information "off the record" which
was a clear comment on the American attitude to Germany's rearmament program in violation of both the Versailles and the American-German peace treaty. Mr. Hull
went over a stenographic copy of his remarks with Michael
J. McDermott, Chief of the Division of Current Information of the Department of State, and later the correspondents had Mr. Hull's remarks read to them by Mr.
McDermott. The information was not to be quoted verbatim nor to be used as an official statement; it was
given to reporters for their own information. The statement was framed in the most guarded and general language; the most definite line was:

The United States has always believed that treaties must
constitute the foundation on which any stable peace structure
must rest . . . all who believe in peaceful settlements of international problems of all kinds have felt increasing concern over
tendencies to fail to live up to the letter and spirit of treaties.

The statement was intended to indicate to the country
what the general attitude of the government was, without giving any foreign government the occasion to object:
it was not an official memorandum nor an official statement from the Secretary of State. It served this interme-
diate purpose admirably. The news-dispatches on March
23 emphasized the government's stand on the "sanctity of
treaties" and stated that the State Department "disap-
proved of Germany's rearmament." They were careful to
use such lines as these: "Without mentioning the German
Government by name" (Associated Press); "It was evi-

dent from Secretary Hull's informal remarks" (New York
Times); "The American government today delivered
what was obviously intended as a mild rebuke to Germany
. . . While carefully avoiding direct mention of Germany
by name" (Universal Service); "Although Secretary Hull
did not say so, all indications were . . ." (New York
Herald Tribune); "Secretary Hull inferentially rebuked
Germany" (Washington *Post*); "Without mentioning
Germany or any nation specifically by name . . ." (United
Press); "In the form of 'Information to Correspondents'
Cordell Hull . . . today voiced the American Govern-
ment's protest" (*Christian Science Monitor*).[15]

In minor matters some correspondents, more cynical
than their colleagues, evade the strict letter of the "off
the record" law in an ingenious manner. Correspondent A
may communicate some "off the record" information he
has heard to Correspondent B, prefaced by the remark:
"*I* got this in confidence." If the proper rapport exists
between these gentlemen, Correspondent B will print the
information, concealing A as his source. Then Correspondent A may use the information in one of his own
dispatches. If A's informant protests that A has violated a
confidence, A has merely to say, "But I got the story from
B's paper. I couldn't ignore it after B had published it."
This delicate strategy represents the triumph of professional instinct over professional ethics.

VII. MISCELLANY

In addition to these sources of news there are more informal channels—particularly in Washington—by which
news is conveyed, leads dropped, "tips" communicated.

The correspondent does not and cannot draw a line of division between his professional and social activities. And in his social life it is more difficult to avoid than to get news.

We have seen that in Washington all conversational roads lead to politics. The better a correspondent "mixes," the more news he acquires. Lunches, dinners, cocktail parties, and formal receptions are fruitful sources of information for the socially active newspaperman and yield news of varying degrees of usability.

It would be a grave injustice to the corps to regard them as social scavengers. The newspaper correspondent is generally an acceptable person from the social point of view. He is married, a family man, moral,* a good conversationalist, and, of course, a "good fellow." He may be an asset to social functions because of either his personal graces or the exciting gossip he picks up in the performance of his duties. It is recognized that newspapermen know a little about everything and it is believed that *"none* of it ever gets into the paper, my dear." This makes newspapermen particularly attractive to hosts and hostesses in a city where one-half of the non-laboring energy is devoted to the pursuit of the "inside story."

Nor should one assume that the correspondent exploits his hostesses and his social contacts by unconscionable revelations of "what went on at the Ambassador's soirée." Most people in Washington are generous with the facts they know and are, indeed, flattered to see them appear in print. The illuminati who crowd the social functions of the capital are not reluctant to part with information; they

---

* The Bohemianism of newspapermen is outdated; it has never applied in Washington.

may merely prefer not to be identified as responsible for it.

The same motivations which lead Congressmen to talk during their office hours operate after their office hours. In the latter circumstances impulses of loquacity may be intensified by the lulling warmth of the liquor, the geniality of the group, the camaraderie of the occasion, and the absence of those inhibitions against confidential speech which are found in the formal press conference, the presence of a stenographer, or the vigilant portrait of George Washington on the wall.

The chief value of information which is social in origin lies not so much in its substance as in the clues which it offers and the lacunae which it fills. It is more valuable as a point of departure for further inquiry than as an end and a fact in itself. Some newspapermen pay lip-service to a curious code of ethics in treating information acquired in the informal atmosphere of social contact. One Washington correspondent heard a high official drop valuable facts about a certain political group, at a dinner party. He knew that the official's facts were authentic and of great value. But he did not intend to violate the strict morals of his profession, the social faith of the official, or the hospitality of the hostess. So, knowing what the facts were, he waited several days, then called up all of the persons involved in the official's remarks. By skillful questioning, and by giving the impression that he knew a great deal more than he did, he developed the story—and printed it. "Had the official tried to call me down for breaking the story, I could say, 'Hell! I got it from X, Y, and Z.' After all I didn't quote *him*—and I waited *three days* to break the story!"

There is grave doubt as to whether other correspondents, with more adamant consciences, would have followed this procedure. Many would have felt morally obligated to reject the facts learned at the dinner table sternly from their memories—a difficult and disturbing process for men whose memory must be excellent and who would be engaged in writing stories to which those facts were directly relevant. Other correspondents, no less cognizant of their social burdens, might have passed the story on to a colleague with the stipulation, (1) "You can't use this, but . . ." or, (2) "Don't quote me," or (3) "I can't vouch for its accuracy, but I heard. . . ." And some correspondents would feel that three days wasn't long enough to wait. . . .

RESTRAINTS

The Washington correspondent must maintain a reputation for discretion. He must be careful to remain *persona grata* with his news-sources. In the words of the trade, "he must keep his sources open." He may do this by repaying his informants in the currency of journalism: he may play up a story which casts glory on a good news-source and play down a story which is embarrassing. One veteran newspaperman in the capital has said that "almost every correspondent has special news-sources whose displeasure he consciously or unconsciously fears." [16] He complained that Washington correspondents are compelled to operate on a "commercial-friendship basis":

The Washington correspondent . . . wants to hold friendships and he believes that if he prints all the news and the truth he cannot do this. Friendships mean news. So the reporter becomes something of a servitor, a satellite—unknowingly. His truth is not his own; and, therefore, not the public's. The Washington correspondent today does his work as a business proposition. . . . If by printing a fact he will arouse the anger of a good news-source his decision is easy and immediate. For an angry friend means less news, more work, and a poorer record of stories.[17]

This point of view more validly applies to correspondents from small papers than to those from metropolitan journals, and for several good reasons. The representative of a large newspaper is interested in national news or news which, though "local" to him, is charged with national interest. (The news of New York, Chicago, Pittsburgh, or Detroit has a national market.) But the correspondent for a small paper, or a string of small papers, is interested primarily in news of interest to his locality alone. (The press associations supply his paper with news of the nation.) The correspondent for a metropolitan journal can get his information from a dozen sources. News about a large city, for example, breaks through half a dozen different Representatives, two Senators, federal agencies with projects in the city, the Republican and Democratic party organizations, and so on. Furthermore, the press associations and the several reporters in the capital from that city are constantly on the alert for news of metropolitan interest. But news about Siwash is "bottle-necked" at two points: the Representative of the district in which Siwash falls, and, to a lesser degree, the Senator from Siwash state. These men control the political jobs to be distributed in Siwash, and the pork-barrel appropriations. The reporter for the Siwash *Siren* is pretty much at their mercy. If they choose to "freeze up" on him he is in a difficult position because he has no alternative sources of information. The news involving New York or Pittsburgh may take the center of the political stage, and be subject to publicity, wide interest, and thorough press coverage; but news about Siwash has its birth and consummation in the Congressional wings, unspotlighted and unsung. Hence the small-fry Congressman achieves, in relation to such matters, a particular importance denied him in all others. And where a legislator or official will think twice before antagonizing the correspondent for a powerful and politically influential newspaper, he may be high-handed and peremptory with the reporter for a relatively insignificant organ. The correspondent for the small paper thus depends upon one or two men for his information and labors under the necessity of currying their favor.

What type of news will a correspondent play down or ignore because of the exigencies of "commercial-friendship"? Here are several examples of the kind of stories which Congressmen may try to have reporters keep out of the local papers:

1. One New England Congressman took a trip to the South during a session of Congress and pressed the newspapermen from his state to say he had been in Washington all along.

2. One Congressman fights to keep his West Point and Annapolis appointments and his pension awards out of the papers, not wishing to arouse the ire of those disappointed.

3. One Congressman threatened to give no more news to a correspondent who had prepared an article made up of extracts from a speech the Congressman had made.

4. A solon used every effort to keep his weekly trips to Pinehurst, where he played golf, out of the paper.

5. Another closed his office to a reporter who had sent a dispatch which mentioned the fact that the Congressman had returned to the capital after a four-week vacation.

6. Another grew perceptibly cold because a correspondent had said the Senate had listened to the Congressman's reading of a document with "a slightly ironic smile."

7. One correspondent wrote that a certain Senator had been criticized and his sincerity challenged on the floor of the Senate because of his vote on the bonus; the Senator warned the newspaperman that if similar "harmful" stories were to appear no more news-items would be forthcoming from the Senator's office.[18]

It will be observed that these items are of relative insignificance insofar as national affairs are concerned. But in the small field in which they operate they have considerable importance, for in the steady influence of repeatedly favorable or unfavorable dispatches there may lie the difference between a Congressman's re-election and his defeat.

The decision as to whether to print or not, and with what emphasis, entails a conflict between professional duty and professional discretion. The decision is generally made by calculating the returns. An insignificant item which involves a good news-source may be suppressed or written in so perfunctory a manner that it gets little attention. A correspondent dependent upon Representative Simeon O. Jones may not report the fact that the distinguished solon was arrested for speeding, or for striking a waiter at a night club while in a state of heroic inebriation. But if a story is big enough to overshadow the benefits of suppression, or if it is a story which may have national repercussions and will come to local notice anyway, then the correspondent will send it off. No correspondent would dare suppress the fact that Representative Jones will be tried for criminal malfeasance or was rebuked by the State Department for an insult to the honor of a foreign country. In the refreshing language of one correspondent: "There are stories you've *got* to print, even if they involve your own mother." In minor stories—"Well, it's foolish to sacrifice a first-rate news-source for a third-rate yarn." Newspapermen have told this writer that they did not mention such facts as these: that a Protestant Senator's daughter was being married in a Catholic church; the romance of a Congressman with a divorcée; the party "deal" which accounted for one Representative's change of vote on an appropriation measure. Several members of the press corps close an eye occasionally to minor stories about the political tactics of Postmaster General Farley or Attorney General Cummings—both decent fellows and good news-sources.

The newspaperman is not completely impotent against the threats of legislators. The correspondent can use publicity as a threat. A correspondent may frame a terribly damaging dispatch (composed of excerpts from a Congressman's oratorical effusions, for example), show it to him, and be "coaxed" into forgetting about it—with a piece of "hot news" as *quid pro quo.* Such bargaining is rarely explicit. It is not considered ethical by reputable newspapermen.

It is impossible to generalize about the extent to which news-coloring and news-suppression, based on personal obligations of the kind discussed in this section, thrive in the capital. It is no secret that some newspapermen are charged by the rest of the press corps as being sycophants to ambitious politicians on or off Capitol Hill; that others are won by the flattery of Representatives, Senators, or administrative officials who call them by their first names, slap them on the back, open the sacred portals of Washington Society to their wives, or ask them for advice on political matters. In any event, the degree to which a newspaperman becomes the henchman of a political personage depends upon his own character, the security of his position, and the orders or example of his publisher.

Fortunately, for every story which is killed another is dispatched; where some correspondent tries to play a story down, another may throw his energies into playing it up. In the intangible area of personal discretion, such factors as courage, vanity, asperity, or vengeance play cardinal roles. But this much can be said with assurance: (1) news is suppressed, colored, or played down in inverse proportion to its significance and national interest; (2) the smaller the paper on which a given locality depends for its information, the less independent of pressure can the Washington correspondent of that paper be, and the less *probability* is there that that paper will get complete and unbiased news from "our special correspondent." *

* Like all generalizations this is subject to qualification; some small papers have correspondents in the capital who are conspicuously resourceful and courageous.

Where the calculation of consequences has triumphed over the compulsion of conscience and a story is discreetly "forgotten," how is conscience then assuaged? The rationalizations are several:

"Well, let my paper pick the story up from the AP if they want it."

"I'm working for my paper and my job is to get news. I'll get more and better news if I soft-pedal this item. It is my *duty* to my paper to ignore it."

"It would be a dirty trick on Jones; he's given me too many hot tips."

"What the readers don't know won't hurt them. Why get them hot and bothered about a minor incident?"

The dialectic entailed in these psychic maneuvers should not go unnoticed. There are, of course, variations on these simple themes.

V. Covering Washington

THE layman may be excused for visualizing the Washington correspondent as a combination of master mind and detective, inexhaustible of energy, with devious techniques for getting facts, a genius for being on the spot when news "breaks," and with mysterious sources of information. As a matter of fact, there is neither mystery nor magic in the process of "covering Washington." It is a systematic routine. As practiced by the more brilliant newspapermen it requires energy, insight, resourcefulness, a wide fund of information, and friendships in official circles. As practiced by the more mediocre correspondents it is a pedestrian task, much like working on the city desk of a newspaper, but under less pressure, at a better salary, and with considerably more prestige. To these men the life of the reporter in Washington is "no more exciting than knitting." [1]

News is not gathered by any haphazard process, either in Washington or in Walla Walla. "News," a term about which there has been considerable debate,* is essentially the departure from the normal. And events depart from the normal at certain fixed points. In any city, police headquarters, the courts, fire stations, the city hall, the Bureau of Vital Statistics, are focal points at which unusual events become overt. [2] Newspapers station reporters at these points to "cover" such events.

* See Chapter XII.

In Washington the places at which events materialize are covered with great efficiency. The press associations have reporters stationed at each government department, each administrative agency, the White House, the houses of Congress, the Supreme Court, and so on. Reporters cover committee hearings and investigations regularly. The movements of high officials are followed. Hotel registrations are watched. The life of the President is, of course, followed with microscopic care and visitors to the White House are questioned. Congressional leaders are interviewed when news breaks. Party leaders are always open to questioning. Every major government agency issues press releases about its work. All important officials hold press conferences, sometimes twice a week. The representatives of private pressure groups ("lobbyists") are more than willing to supply information in their field of interest. There is, in short, a very definite and systematic method by which events and persons are covered for the newspapers of the country.

It is obvious that no one reporter can be responsible for covering Washington. For the purposes of analysis the Washington correspondents may be divided into four groups:

Reporters for the press associations. Reporters for the press associations are generally assigned to a definite "beat" and work exactly as men attached to the city desk of any newspaper. The press associations are organized much as a city room, with editors, copy writers, re-write men, "leg-men," telegraph editors, feature writers, etc.

Special correspondents. A special correspondent is the Washington representative of a single newspaper, or of a string of newspapers under the same ownership. Washington is his "beat." The special correspondent, unlike the press-association reporter, is not stationed at a fixed point. He has wide latitude in choosing the events which he will cover on any given day. He keeps in touch with his home office, whether it be in California or New England, and concentrates on news of particular interest to his newspaper, its readers, and its locality. He knows that the press-association service to which his paper subscribes will take care of all other news.

Free-lance correspondents. These are correspondents who send their dispatches to a number of small papers, no one of which can afford to have a special correspondent of its own in the capital. Each client pays a small weekly sum for the service, and may ask the free-lance correspondent to act as a "special" by covering a certain event or interviewing a certain official.

Columnists and commentators. These men are either independent (their columns being distributed through a syndicate), or employed by a newspaper chain or a press association. Columnists and commentators are editorial writers rather than reporters in a strict sense. They do not attempt to cover "spot news." They write up interesting political sidelights, interpret trends, analyze maneuvers, or purvey amusing anecdotage and gossip.

I. THE PRESS ASSOCIATIONS

The greatest responsibility for covering Washington falls upon the press associations. Any newspaper can get complete coverage on Washington if it is a member of the Associated Press, or if it subscribes to the United Press or the International News Service. These agencies serve

newspapers all over the world. The Associated Press has
1,376 clients in the United States, according to estimates in
1937; the United Press has about 1,100; International
News Service about 750. The Federated Press, a minor
service, confines itself to labor news; the dispatches of its
Washington correspondent go to about 115 papers. Central
News of America concentrates on financial news.[3]

THE ASSOCIATED PRESS BUREAU *

The Associated Press bureau in Washington had sixty-
eight full-time employees at the time of this study. This
included reporters, news editors, copy and re-write men,
feature writers, photo editors, and columnists. The bureau
sends out about 50,000 words of copy on an average day.[5]
The staff is divided into three classes: the General Staff
(reporters, news editors, etc.), the Features Staff (columnists, feature writers, sports, science, agriculture and finance
experts), and the Regional Staff.

The chief of the bureau operates as does the managing
editor of a daily newspaper. He is in complete charge of
personnel and policy. He is the point of contact between
the Washington Bureau and the New York offices of the
Associated Press, and, indirectly, between the bureau and
the 1,376 papers which it serves. Under the chief of the

* The Associated Press, unlike the other press associations, is a "non-
profit organization" which serves only its own membership. Members
of the Associated Press are admitted by a vote of the directors of the
organization. Contrary to common belief, no "franchise" is conferred.
New members are merely elected to receive the form of service desired
and for which they make payment. Daily news service may run from
a few hundred words for the smallest members to 75,000 words a day
in the large cities.[4]

bureau are three news editors, one for each of three shifts into which the General Staff is divided. All news-dispatches pass over a copy desk, where they are checked for accuracy, grammar, form, libelous material, etc. On the desk they are condensed, corrected, or cut down. They may be re-written by special re-write men. The news editor of each shift is the central intelligence, observing the total flow of news which is telephoned into the office by reporters stationed all over the capital. The news editor assigns a rough space length to stories according to his "news budget." He informs reporters about special angles to stories which have broken in other parts of the city. He may move his reporters around from place to place. Each day a "schedule" is filed, i.e., sent to New York, informing the New York office of the probable number of stories to be covered that day, and the probable length of each. This permits the New York office to tell papers all over the country approximately how much news will be sent from Washington that day, so that they may leave comparable space open.

Press-association reporters are stationed at a definite beat.* They keep in almost hourly touch with their news desks by a telephone wired directly to their offices. They call in as soon as a story breaks. It is the press-association reporter rather than the special correspondent who is under the incessant pressure of time. He often dictates his stories

* The reporters on the Day Staff are placed at the following beats: 1. Press gallery of the Senate (3 men). 2. Press gallery of the House of Representatives (3 men). 3. Department of State, War and Navy. 4. Treasury Department. 5. Interstate Commerce Commission. 6. Supreme Court. 7. Department of Labor (and American Federation of Labor headquarters). 8. Department of Commerce (and Federal Trade Commission, U. S. Chamber of Commerce, National Emergency Coun-

over the telephone to stenographers or re-write men. One reporter may be responsible for five or six related departments, no one of which supplies enough news to warrant being covered by a special man. Reporters are available for assignment to any place where an unusual quantity of news breaks suddenly.

The Features Staff of the Associated Press supplies services of a syndicate type. Special correspondents write columns, many of them signed (most Associated Press news dispatches are anonymous), on politics, finance, markets, agriculture, science. Byron Price, until recently head of the bureau, wrote a column entitled "Politics at Random" twice a week, and a column entitled "The Week in Washington" for Sunday papers. Kirke L. Simpson writes a daily column for morning newspapers called "A Washington Bystander." Herbert Plummer writes a similar column for evening newspapers. These columns are interpretative in nature; they do not attempt to cover "spot" news.

It is of interest to notice the technical method by which Washington dispatches are distributed by the Associated Press. News-dispatches are transmitted from Washington simultaneously over two trunk wires: one to New York and one to Kansas City. At these points the dispatches are

cil, National Association of Manufacturers, Bureau of the Census). 9. Department of Agriculture (including the farm lobbies, the Weather Bureau, Crop Reports, etc.). 10. Department of the Interior (and allied activities: Public Works Administration, Oil Administration, Civilian Conservation Corps, Works Progress Administration, etc.). 11. Post Office Department and Department of Justice (and Civil Service Commission, Veterans Administration, veterans lobbies). 12. Securities and Exchange Commission. Roving reporters, or reporters on general assignment duty, are shifted from place to place.

re-routed over three main trunk lines: North, South, and West. Thus, if a news-dispatch is sent from the capital involving a minor appropriation for a Public Works Administration project in Maine, the New York office will relay it to all New England newspapers on its North trunk line; it will not, however, send the news over the Southern wire, since the story will not interest readers of southern newspapers.* The Kansas City office re-transmits news-dispatches on a trunk line which runs to San Francisco. It may "kill" a story which is of no interest to the far West. Dispatches are often shortened along the line. A story starting as several hundred words in Washington may be cut to a few paragraphs in Kansas City and sent westward. The estimation of the probable news-value of any dispatch to newspapers located in different sections of the country enters into the transmission process at several points.

The dispatching of news is further complicated by procedures which resemble the buying and selling of commodities. A newspaper which is a member of the Associated Press may "order" a story, because of its particular interest in the subject matter. A California paper may want a thousand words about a debate in the House of Representatives on the Citrus Fruit section of a Tariff Bill. The Associated Press will supply the paper with such coverage, charging a fee for the service. Perhaps only seventy-five words on this story will be sent to newspapers in New England,

* From New York, news is also transmitted to Kansas City, on the Western wire. This trunk line runs through Chicago, for example, which is another center for the dissemination of news. Thus, if the New York office sends a story over its Western wire which is of interest to papers in Illinois, the Associated Press office in Chicago will shunt the dispatch over an auxiliary circuit serving papers in Illinois.

which are not particularly interested in tariffs on citrus fruits.

In 1934 an elaborate regional service was set up in the Washington bureau of the Associated Press. The nation was divided into twenty-one regions and a reporter was assigned to concentrate on each. These regional reporters augment the regular news-dispatches, which are written from a national point of view, with stories of more specific interest to each area. Thus, on a story involving a representative from North Carolina, the reporter whose region includes North Carolina will write a special dispatch. In the same way a Department of Labor statement involving a labor dispute in Illinois may be given 200 words by the Associated Press reporter at the Department of Labor, whereas the regional reporter may send 500 to 1,000 words to Illinois newspapers, using more background, local facts, and greater detail.

The regional service of the Associated Press has presented a challenge to the special correspondent by invading his area of specialization. Competition between the correspondent for a single newspaper and the regional correspondent for the Associated Press is a comparatively new phenomenon in the capital. Reporters for large metropolitan papers are not worried by this competition, but correspondents for the smaller newspapers are being pressed to the wall.[6]

Since the Associated Press serves 1,376 papers of differing political complexions, formally equal in status, and since each is free to complain of the bias, inaccuracy, or "color" of a dispatch, the news-accounts of the organization are marked by caution and conservatism. There is a fear of offending some member of the association. Stories are written, on the whole, with a calculated emasculation of tone. Adjectives are shunned and an effort is made to avoid any semblance of "bias." In recent years this standard has been relaxed somewhat. The competition of the younger, more vigorous, and more colorful press associations has led the Associated Press to "jazz up" its stories. Since 1921, "by-lines" (reporters' names) are permitted on some stories; the traditional policy was to observe the rule of strict anonymity.

A comparison of excerpts from an Associated Press dispatch on the return of ex-Mayor James J. Walker to New York and from the New York *Times* account for the same day will suggest the flamboyance which the Associated Press has come to tolerate on occasion:

Former Mayor James J. Walker and his wife returned to New York yesterday aboard the United States liner Manhattan and received a welcome from several thousand old friends and admirers down the bay and at the dock.

New York *Times*, November 1, 1935, p. 1

Amid tumultuous and riotous scenes of welcome by Broadway faithfuls, James J. Walker, strangely nervous and uncertain, came back from exile today to the town he deserted under fire three years ago.

The trip down the bay . . . was a noisy triumphal procession that verged into hysterical mob scenes at the Chelsea pier.

Associated Press dispatch, in Washington *Post*, Nov. 1, 1935, p. 1

THE UNITED PRESS BUREAU

The United Press Bureau in Washington consists of twenty-seven men, organized in a manner similar to that described for the Associated Press. The bureau sends out 30,000 to 35,000 words a day on an average. Originally founded as a press service for afternoon papers the majority of the clients of the United Press still fall into that category. Through its directors and personnel the United Press is affiliated with the Scripps-Howard newspaper interests. The cost of the Washington bureau to the United Press in 1933 was about $149,200 per year. This included salaries, travel expenses, light and power, stationery, telegraph and telephone charges.[7]

United Press dispatches are generally shorter and more compact than those of the Associated Press. They are usually written more freely and with more literary grace. The United Press, unlike its chief competitor, is a profit-making organization. It sells news to any buyer. It sells as attractive a product as it can. In newspaper circles it is recognized that the United Press is the most "liberal" press association. Its dispatches on labor stories, unions, civil liberties, big business, immigration, etc., are more forceful and aggressive than those of the Associated Press.[8] The United Press staff includes more competent experts on labor, the tariff, unions, than comparable men in other press associations. The United Press will carry such stories as the annual "honor roll" citations of the *Nation*, national liberal weekly, which other associations do not cover.[9] It will have articles on industrial spies, on labor problems, on the lobbies behind legislative action.

The United Press permits its correspondents a greater latitude of style and treatment than is found in the Associated Press. The atmosphere which prevails in the offices of the bureau is one of informality; the staff operates with a high morale. Many United Press dispatches are frankly interpretative and in some the "spot" character of news is missing. These dispatches may recapitulate the events of a week, and possess a quality whih some newspapermen consider to be "crusading." The United Press has a wage scale below that of the Associated Press; because of this, inexperienced men are often stationed at important beats.[10]

INTERNATIONAL NEWS SERVICE AND UNIVERSAL SERVICE

The International News Service (INS) and the Universal Service * are Hearst properties which sell their services to any newspaper, as profit-making organizations. The INS serves afternoon papers. It has a Washington staff of seventeen. It dispatches around 20,000 words a day.

Universal Service serves morning newspapers, most of them either in the Hearst chain or of a similar editorial bent. There are fifteen men in the Washington bureau, which sends from 10,000 to 15,000 words of copy a day. Universal Service correspondents are also listed in

---

* On August 14, 1937, while this book was being printed, the Universal Service was abolished by the Hearst organization. The International News Service absorbed its clients and was placed on a twenty-four hour basis.

the *Congressional Directory* as special correspondents for individual Hearst newspapers. Thus, the correspondent for the Chicago *Herald & Examiner* is a member of the Universal Service staff as well. It is not surprising, therefore, that recognizable Hearstian emphases are to be found in the news-dispatches of Universal Service.* This does not mean that all Universal Service dispatches are characterized by bias; many stories are accurate and impartial. But the total output of no other press association shows so high a proportion of news written for specific news-preferences.[11] The content of some dispatches are of a type which apparently no editors in the nation save those working for Mr. Hearst consider to be legitimate news; the treatment given to other materials suggests that, in the words of one Washington correspondent, "they are meant to tickle the Boss rather than enlighten the public."

It should be observed that the headlines which are placed over press-association dispatches often distort their content. In this respect, the news-accounts of INS and Universal Service are particularly subject to misinterpretation, since captions are placed over them by men in the offices of the individual Hearst newspapers. Hearst headlines are by tradition alarmist and hysterical.

On May 7, 1936, the New York *Daily News* facetiously suggested a Pulitzer Prize for propagandistic headlines for the following memorable effort from the New York *American:*

* On September 19, 1935, the New York *American* printed a Universal Service dispatch on page 1 which used the Hearst editorial expression "raw deal" (for New Deal) and referred to the Wagner Act as "labor's so-called Magna Charta."

MARYLAND VOTE
HITS NEW DEAL

———

Breckinridge Holds
Roosevelt Lead to
Only 6 to 1

Comment

The haste with which press association stories are turned
out, and the brevity with which important events must be
treated, operate against clarity, proportion—and fairness.
Often it is the length at which a complex event or political
conflict is described which makes the difference between
accurate and inaccurate reporting. A comparison of the
news-accounts in the New York *Times,* for example, and
the highly skeletonized reports in a "tight" paper like the
Cleveland *Plain Dealer* (which, with a high regard for
accuracy, sacrifices details to space requirements) will illustrate the point.

It is important to remember that news-dispatches from
the press associations are often the work of many men.
News editors, copy desk, and re-write men change, delete,
re-write, and shape stories prepared by different reporters.
They often combine reports from two or three different
beats and synthesize them into one dispatch. This is particularly true when a story breaks simultaneously in several different spots or when the same story has repercussions in different places. The head of one bureau in
Washington maintains that the relationship of the desk to

the news is quite as intimate as that of the reporter to the news.

The length to which press associations go to avoid charges of partisanship in political matters is illustrated by the rule laid down by the Associated Press during the last Presidential campaign. Reporters were told not to use adjectives in describing the ovations given the candidates, since Republican papers usually protest that Democratic candidates receive a "mild" rather than a "tremendous" ovation, while Democratic papers protest that the reception of Republican candidates is "luke-warm" rather than "warm-hearted." Reporters were obliged to state the length of the ovation in factual terms: "The crowd cheered for three full minutes." In the same way, press associations prefer "The auditorium, which seats ten thousand, was full" to "a tremendous and enthusiastic crowd."

The consequences of denatured press association dispatches are described in the following words of Paul Y. Anderson, Washington correspondent for the St. Louis *Post-Dispatch* and a Pulitzer Prize winner in 1929:

The necessity of serving thousands of newspapers of every shade of political opinion, with the aim of giving offense to none, has the effect of reducing every story to the lowest common denominator. The result is a colorless, euphemistic product with which few editors can quarrel, but with which many readers would quarrel violently, if they had any intimation of the exciting but untold realities. For this condition the press associations are hardly to blame, although there are instances when they lend themselves deliberately to official propaganda.[12]

II. THE SPECIAL CORRESPONDENT

Why should a newspaper assume the substantial expense of maintaining its own Washington bureau when it can receive swift and complete coverage from a press association? The difference in responsibilities and service between a special correspondent and a reporter for one of the press associations may be indicated by offering a sketch of the activities of a typical "special." The correspondent for the Des Moines *Register* and *Tribune,* for example, concentrates his attention only on those segments of the total stream of events which are primarily of interest to (1) Des Moines, (2) Iowa, (3) agricultural problems and the farmer, (4) The Middle West. The Des Moines *Register* and *Tribune* receives the dispatches of the Associated Press (and its regional service), the United Press, and International News Service. It has, apparently, more than ample national coverage. But it has a Washington correspondent to supplement this coverage.

The special correspondent for the Des Moines *Register* and *Tribune* is a man who has been trained on its staff, is familiar with the kind of reading public which it reaches, and is an expert on the news-requirements of his editors and the interests of his readers. He is a specialist on Iowan politics and agricultural problems. He sends his paper only such dispatches as he knows will interest his news-market. He will keep in close and constant contact with the Senators and Representatives from Iowa. He will interview Iowans of importance who are visiting Washington. He will get statements from farm leaders and offi cials of the Department of Agriculture and related agencies. At press conferences he will confine his interest, his questions, and his notes to matters of particular relevance to Iowa and farmers. He will make no effort to cover stories on the Securities and Exchange Commission, for example, on minor labor troubles in the textile industry, or on political moves which have their locus in the east.

Since the special correspondent has the confidence of his editors and is considered expert in estimating the value of news to his own paper, he is given greater space for his dispatches than a press agency would dare devote to similar stories. The dispatches of the special correspondent are also more interpretative, with more comment and more inferences.

Historically, the special correspondent began as an editorial writer and commentator writing from Washington, as well as a reporter.[13] But his function has changed until, more and more, he is becoming an extension of the city desk. Today a special correspondent is in daily contact with his home office, consulting his editor on the news he will cover. He may be assigned to stories just as if he were a reporter on the city staff. The degree to which a special correspondent is permitted freedom in choosing the stories he will cover, and in which he is emancipated from the guiding hand of the city desk, varies from paper to paper. But it is important to notice that the transformation of the special correspondent from the status of an editorial commentator to that of a reporter fulfilling assignments which originate in the home office, has led papers to rely upon syndicated columnists, rather than their own representatives, for articles concerning "the fate of the nation, the state of the Union, and what an unimpeachable authority said last night about the President's intentions towards the Island of Yap." [14]

A vivid picture of what a special correspondent is required to cover may be obtained from the following list of tasks which editors have on various occasions referred to their Washington offices:

1. A defaulting banker of high social standing and political influence in the city hall made fraudulent representations by publishing certain bank statements in a newspaper. It seemed clear that the banker's case would pass through the local courts, with the assurance of a pardon from the Governor. The newspaper got its Washington correspondent to "stir up" the Postmaster General's office in Washington. The banker was prosecuted and sent to a federal penitentiary.

2. The traffic arteries of a city were clogged by heavy motor traffic. A Washington correspondent was asked to get action from the proper government bureau.

3. When a locality suffered from an outbreak of typhoid because of diseased oysters, a Washington correspondent prodded the Public Health Service into action. [15]

With federal activity invading local life, with even crime and sex placed under federal law (the Mann Act and the Anti-Kidnaping Bill, for example), an increasing number of local stories develop a Washington end, "and the Washington bureau of any large newspaper gains importance and loses dignity." [16]

It is a fallacy to imagine that special correspondents in Washington are concerned exclusively with national news. With the exception of the metropolitan journals on the

Eastern seaboard, many newspapers are concerned with *local aspects of national events*. Their correspondents in Washington reflect this emphasis on regionalism. The geography of the United States does not permit timely national circulation. Attention-areas in the United States are localistic. We do not have the close integration of interests which characterize smaller and more homogeneous nations, less diversified in their economic resources and more centralized in their political structure. We have no national newspaper comparable to the London *Times* or *Le Petit Parisien*.

The President, his official activities, and his social life are, of course, news to every paper in the country, regardless of its location. Tax legislation is national in interest. But financial news originating from or directed toward Wall Street may not be of interest to papers west of the Mississippi.

Most Washington correspondents are interested either in national news so significant that it will interest readers equally in California or in Maine, or, more commonly, those facets of national news which are relevant to the claims and interests of the locality in which their newspapers circulate. A comparison of the content of newspapers in New York City with those in Topeka or Salt Lake City will indicate the contrasts in the content of news columns.

The home office uses its special correspondents to develop a "Washington angle" on local news. This is an important function. When automobile strikes break out in Detroit, for example, correspondents for the Detroit papers plunge into activity to get statements from the Secretary of Labor, the American Federation of Labor headquarters, the National Association of Manufacturers, Mr. John L. Lewis' Committee for Industrial Organization, etc. When a state Senator at Springfield, Illinois, charges that the Democratic machine in Chicago has injected graft into the administration of public relief services, correspondents for Chicago papers are instructed to get comments from Illinois Senators, federal relief officials, the Democratic National Committee, and others.

There are more varied and subtle reasons for the existence of the special correspondent in Washington:

1. Newspapers gain a distinct economic benefit by maintaining a Washingtou bureau. A special correspondent is an "exclusive" feature with circulation value. Since the dispatches of the press associations are available to a newspaper's competitors, and since these dispatches are identical in content, a newspaper which offers its readers the dispatches of its own correspondent in addition to press association services is providing an added attraction to the public. The Pittsburgh *Post-Gazette*, for example, invades the western and southern part of Pennsylvania and the north-eastern part of West Virginia. It tries to attract readers who have a choice of many other small local papers, which are served by a press association, by having a special correspondent in Washington.

2. Large newspapers prefer to have their own correspondent in the capital write the important news of the day in a more distinctive manner than is found in the reports of the press associations. The special correspondent is free to develop contacts and "inside" sources of information for which the association reporter may not have the time, the motivation, or the talent. The special corre-

spondent possesses greater mobility and freedom of interpretation.

3. The special correspondents write with only one paper
in mind, only one specific reading public, and only one set
of editorial preferences. The last point is extremely important. A press-agency reporter's consciousness of a mul-
tiplicity of censors results in a striving for literal accuracy
and the use of a colorless tone with inoffensiveness as the
prime desideratum. The association correspondent is generally required to confine himself to "the cold facts;" the
special correspondent may indulge in conjectures and prog-
noses. In the parlance of journalism, he can "go out on a
limb."

4. The special correspondent may have the important
function of writing "policy stuff." The publisher who
wants an interpretation of the news consonant with his
editorial policies or his personal biases is obliged to use
a Washington correspondent of his own. A certain proportion of the press corps is concerned with the problem
of giving a special "slant" to the news.* Raymond G. Carroll, a Washington correspondent of long standing, has
written:

> The ideal Washington correspondent is a good reporter
> who "knows his onions." That is, a writer who does his job
> faithfully according to the policies and wishes of the ownership
> of the newspaper or string of newspapers he represents.[17]

Objective evidence supports the thesis that some newspapermen in the capital have as their major responsibility
the delicate task of "giving the paper what it wants." The

* See Chapter X.

Chicago *Tribune*, for example, could get from no earthly source other than its own Washington bureau the type of dispatches which grace its pages. In reporting the investigation of the Senate Munitions Committee in 1936 a Chicago *Tribune* correspondent employed language of a type outlawed by the simplest canons of contemporary journalism.

There is no question that the atmosphere and background of the whole inquiry are pacifistic and socialistic. Senator Gerald P. Nye, North Dakota radical . . . Raushenbush is of German descent.

The following dispatch from the Washington bureau of "The World's Greatest Newspaper" (December 7, 1935) further illustrates the "policy" type of special correspondence:

In what was interpreted in some quarters as a bid for a cabinet post in the event of President Roosevelt's re-election, Senator George W. Norris, Nebraska radical, today announced that he would not seek another term in the Senate, because it would interfere with his campaign for Roosevelt.

His statement was the latest of an exchange of laudatory effusions between himself and the President. . . .

If his insistence not to run for re-election is really final this time (he has made similar announcements in previous campaigns) his reluctance may be based partly on the embarrassment of choosing a party label under which to run next year, some observers said.

The accounts of the Associated Press, United Press, New York *Times*, Baltimore *Sun*, or New York *Herald Tribune* gave a different version of the facts. There was no mention of the insidious bid for a cabinet post. Senator Norris was referred to consistently as an "independent" or, by the New York *Herald Tribune,* as "always an independent despite his titular Republicanism." Most revealing are these lines from the New York *Times* of December 7, 1935:

Little doubt is felt here that Senator Norris could win either the Republican or the Democratic nomination for the senatorship next year. . . . Some of his friends believe that he would like to give further impetus to a movement of Progressives away from formal membership in either major party, by coming back to the Senate as a Progressive or Independent.

5. The special correspondent gets a "by-line" and his name and dispatches may be of sufficient distinction to attract readers. Hence the value to the New York *Times* of the dispatches of Arthur Krock or Louis Stark, for example; or of J. Fred Essary or Paul W. Ward to the Baltimore *Sun.* In such cases the special correspondent is an "exclusive feature" with a following of readers.

6. A Washington bureau may help to attract advertisers to a newspaper. It enhances prestige. Some national advertisers and advertising agencies consider the existence of a Washington bureau when they wish to place their accounts in a selected group of newspapers.

7. A paper may be compelled to have a special correspondent in the capital because its competitor has one.

8. A special correspondent is of value in advising his editors on national political affairs and in helping to shape editorial policy. He serves as a funnel through which the vast and fruitful stream of Washington gossip may be

poured into his home office. This may enrich the substance of his paper's editorials and refine its political insights.

9. A publisher may use his special correspondent for extra-journalistic purposes. The correspondent may be obliged to entertain the publisher's friends who pass through Washington. He may introduce important advertisers to the social life of the capital. If the correspondent is a member of the Gridiron Club, a select fraternity of Washington correspondents limited to about fifty active members, then tickets to the famous Gridiron dinners (which the President and most of the important officials of the country attend) become social and business assets of considerable importance. The publisher's vanity, in short, may be gratified by having a special representative in the capital, and the Washington correspondent may be required to perform duties which place him in the category of a personal-service bureau. Publishers' wives enjoy the rarefied atmosphere of Washington's social circles and newspapermen have not been unknown to act as their social patrons. Publishers are flattered by invitations to dine at the White House. In the Hoover administration, many a newspaperman in the capital found himself obliged, by a hint from his superiors, to get his employer into the Executive Mansion. Being human, the publisher enjoys the sensation of being able to say to his dinner guests: "My Washington correspondent tells me that the President tried to get . . ."

A Washington correspondent may serve to aid the publisher in more material fashion, by supplying information on matters which affect the publisher's estate. Newspapermen have complained of the necessity of "running publishers' errands" around the time when income-tax schedules are due.

The Washington correspondent, in short, must be responsive to the wishes of his employer. In Raymond G. Carroll's words:

. . . and "wishes" is important, for those wishes may include the maintaining of an entente cordiale with the occupant of the White House . . . and in addition the performing of a score or more of tactful chores in other quarters.

Again this trusted Washington correspondent may be the custodian of certain vital friendships running from his employer to various members of both branches of Congress. There are matters of legislation in which a local newspaper is the chief bond between a community of business interests and the federal government.[18]

10. A special correspondent may be called upon to engage in informal pressure policies. If a politically active publisher is interested in an impending bill he may suggest that his correspondent see Senator So-and-So, who was elected through the support of the newspaper, and intimate to him that "Mr. Jones is interested in this bill and wants to know how you stand on it." If the publisher has a strip of land which will sky-rocket in value because of a PWA allotment he may suggest that, "in the interest of the city," the correspondent "talk to the right people." The activities of publishers as property owners, bankers, and corporation officials are not carried on in psychological compartments completely sealed from the publishing compartment. It is no secret in Washington newspaper circles that some correspondents were required to do their share in securing the repeal of the "Pink Slip Law," providing for publicity on income tax returns, to

which most publishers were vehemently opposed. Some correspondents added their influence, with varying degrees of innocence and indirection, in defeating the Tugwell Pure Foods Bill. Since this bill represented a direct and dangerous threat to advertising revenues, it was fought with fervor by advertisers and publishers.[19] Special correspondents have sometimes found it wise to get support in the capital for their publishers' ambitions to hold governmental posts. One reporter was given the task of persuading the army to send planes to a city for the dedication of a municipal airport.

In no sense is this an admission that Washington correspondents function as secret lobbyists. They are merely alert sentinels who sound the alarm when there is danger near to that which in the home office opinion affects the welfare and prosperity of local interest. They are also preparers of the atmosphere in which their employers do their contacting with the federal government. The clever Washington correspondent sets the stage, and adjusts the spotlights for the coming of his boss.

So it is that much of the value of the Washington correspondent to his newspaper is concealed, and not generally known.[20]

It is a little difficult to see where Mr. Carroll, author of the above remarks, draws the line between "preparing the atmosphere" and "lobbying."

III. COLUMNISTS AND COMMENTATORS

There are two kinds of daily "columns" issuing from Washington: editorial columns and columns of political "revelations," gossip, and anecdotage.* Journalists like Mark Sullivan or David Lawrence produce daily dispatches which are, in reality, editorial commentaries on political affairs. These dispatches make no attempt to cover news in the reportorial sense. Raymond Clapper, of the Scripps-Howard Newspaper Alliance, will analyze the factors which led President Roosevelt to present his plan for a reform of the Supreme Court. David Lawrence, familiar with constitutional law and history, will sketch the legalistic aspects of the plan, with unmistakable editorial opinions of his own. Arthur Krock (New York *Times*) will place current events in the larger configuration of American history, or will discuss the reasons which led the President to adopt a certain course of action. (Mr. Krock's column is distinguished by a severe impersonality and a more objective approach than is found in other columns.) Mark Sullivan, of the New York *Herald Tribune* Syndicate, comments on the politics of the day in a tone characterized by a vigorous conservative philosophy. The editorial columns, it is clear, are of a genre distinctly different from news-dispatches on the one hand, or "behind the scenes" columns on the other.

The second type of column, the so-called "gossip

---

* A distinction should be made between those columns which originate in Washington and those which come from New York. The daily columns of Walter Lippmann, Dorothy Thompson, Heywood Broun, or Westbrook Pegler are not, strictly speaking, Washington columns. They do concern themselves with political news, and they do editorialize; but their field of inquiry is not limited to the capital. By a Washington column one ordinarily means such features as "The Daily Washington Merry-Go-Round," by Robert S. Allen and Drew Pearson, or the columns of Paul Mallon, Raymond Clapper, David Lawrence, or Mark Sullivan.

column," is a phenomenon of recent years. "Gossip columns" sprang up during the Hoover administration as a necessary device by which correspondents could speculate about news which the government either refused to make public or presented in unreliable fashion. Paul Mallon estimates that no less than 125 columns of political gossip, purporting to give "the news behind the news" or "off the record," have been launched in the last four years.[21] These syndicated columns have soared into popularity largely because of the standardization of news-dispatches. There has been a natural demand for a humanized version of the news, for the "inside story." [22] Readers want to know not merely which official plans are being discussed and which Congressmen are voting for what measures; they have an avid interest in what Mr. Borah privately thinks of Secretary Hull, what Mrs. Roosevelt said to the wife of Senator X, how the beautiful wife of an Ambassador made a *faux pas* at the White House, what political "deal" is being consummated between Mr. Farley and a southern Democratic leader. The output of a Walter Winchell or a Mark Hellinger and the flamboyant columns about Hollywood and Broadway—these have whetted the public appetite for a similar type of news from Washington. In the search for a fresh "angle" on Washington politics, the columns have come into a vigorous vogue. The sensational success of *Washington Merry-Go-Round,* published anonymously in 1931 by Messrs. Allen and Pearson, marked the beginning of a new era in news-styles from the capital.

The striking growth in the popularity of columns which take the reader behind the political scene, giving the "low down" on current events, is seen in their extensive use by newspapers all over the nation. In "Middletown," (Muncie, Ind.), the "typical" American city which has twice been anatomized by a staff of sociologists under the direction of Robert S. Lynd the phenomenon has been recorded:

> The outstanding innovation in Middletown's newspapers is the increased share of signed syndicated features from Washington and New York in the news columns. Whereas Brisbane's column and David Lawrence's dispatches were the sole features of this sort in the politico-economic field in 1925, Middletown read in its morning paper in 1935 Brisbane's "Today," Drew Pearson and Robert Allen's "Daily Washington Merry-Go-Round," Will Rogers' daily paragraph, Leslie Eichel's "World at a Glance," and Kirke Simpson's "A Washington Bystander"; while the evening paper in 1935 had also entered this field with Walter Lippmann's "Today and Tomorrow," "The National Whirligig," Paul Mallon's Washington dispatches, and Frank Kent's "The Great Game of Politics." [23]

It is interesting to observe, in this connection, that many special correspondents are today required to meet this new type of competition by writing an informal column of their own, in addition to their regular news-dispatches.* Readers find a more varied and glamorous picture of Washington in these journalistic vignettes. They are given the pleasure of being offered "confidential news." They are regaled with tales of political motivation, drawing room intrigue, and the clash of colorful personalities.

How does the writer of a "gossip column" work? He

* See Appendix D, Table XXII.

is generally a man who has had long experience in the capital as a regular correspondent for a newspaper or a press association. Some columnists, indeed, function in both capacities. He has built up many valuable contacts in official, semi-official, and social circles. He has many friends and he "mixes" well. Information is supplied to him freely from a wide number of sources. Officials and lesser officials sometimes offer tips to columnists on news which has not yet matured into fact, or for which they do not wish to be held responsible, or which they do not care to publicize in a formal statement to the press or during a regular press conference. An imminent shake-up in a department or an argument between two political luminaries may receive the benediction of print in this way. An item in a column may thus serve as a "trial balloon," or may be calculated to embarrass someone against whom a grudge is held.

Newspapermen are probably the columnist's best aides, since they give him information which is suitable for a column and not for their own news-accounts. A reporter covering a committee hearing on a proposed munitions bill may overhear an amusing conversation between the wives of two of the witnesses. This is hardly appropriate for a dispatch on the day's events; but it makes a delectable tidbit for a column. Every correspondent runs into confidential or amusing episodes which he may pass on to a friend who writes a column.

Some columnists have one or two assistants whose business it is to scour the city for leads and gossip, with particular attention paid to stenographers, underlings, reception clerks. A humble porter in the Treasury building informed a newspaperman that he had seen Father Coughlin enter the office of the Secretary of the Treasury; this was an excellent clue to a big story which had not yet come to attention. A minor secretary in a large office may reveal that a high official is having lunch with a noted industrialist, giving a columnist a lead on possible developments concerning a bill which is pending. Little stories emanating from parties, receptions, and dinners—all these are grist for the columnist's mill.

There has been some complaint by correspondents that writers of columns and confidential news-letters (which are sent to private subscribers) utilize "off the record" material which the correspondents themselves are pledged not to print.[24] Some writers of columns do not attend press conferences because they do not wish to be bound by the "off the record" rule. They prefer to write with absolute freedom, making their own guesses; they receive "off the record" information from sources other than the official who has divulged the information only after binding his hearers to strict confidence.

Most correspondents read a daily column for their own information and interest; frequently they pick up illuminating leads from them. There have been some conspicuous "news-beats" in the columns. "The Daily Washington Merry-Go-Round," for example, has scored on the following events:

On December 22, 1935, the column predicted that President Roosevelt would present his budget to Congress in two parts: regular expenses and emergency expenditures. This happened fifteen days later.

On July 12, 1936, "The Daily Washington Merry-Go-Round" forecast the currency agreement between France,

England, and the United States, explaining the negotiations between Secretary Morgenthau, the Bank of France, and the Bank of England with reference to supporting the franc by a gold agreement. The story broke on September 26, two and a half months later.

On October 30, 1936, Robert S. Allen committed himself to the opinion that Roosevelt would carry all but three states.

On September 23, 1936, the column predicted that Eugene L. Vidal, Director of Air Commerce, would resign, along with his two Assistant Directors, and that they would be replaced by one man—Professor Fred Dow Fagg, Jr. Five months later, on March 1, 1937, the story was confirmed in complete detail by the events.

On January 28, 1937, Allen and Pearson reported that the President was determined to curb the Supreme Court's power and, in a surprise move, would ask Congress for the power to appoint six new judges. On February 5 the historic move was made.[25]

Paul Mallon has pointed to future political maneuvers on many occasions. Arthur Krock and Raymond Clapper have suggested provocative reasons for political moves and have anticipated developments on others. Mr. Krock's exclusive interview with President Roosevelt, printed in the New York *Times* on February 28, 1937, was a rare journalistic scoop.

Some of the Washington correspondents say that "gossip columnists" inflate the value of known—but as yet unconfirmed—possibilities by "making mysteries out of common knowledge."[26] No doubt several of the events cited above, from the Allen-Pearson column, were "in the air" in the capital, and did not completely surprise the press corps when they broke. But others represent first-rate "news-beats."

Special correspondents and press-association reporters are often barred from printing expected developments and *probable* political moves because the factual basis for these events has not been established in authoritative form. Columnists have the advantage of being permitted to operate in an area of speculation, hypothesis, and prophecy which other Washington correspondents are denied. Obviously, not all of the predictions made in columns are supported by subsequent events; a complete picture of the accuracy of prognostications would require balancing the successes with the "duds." There are many of the latter.

Some columns are published in as many as 400 papers, reaching an audience of 13,000,000 potential readers.[27] This does not mean, of course, that they are read by that many people. An investigation conducted and published by *Fortune*, in January, 1937, concluded that "nationally featured columnists are less influential than might be supposed; their opinions count little." The same analysis indicated that approximately thirty-five per cent of the nation's readers read a newspaper column; but Washington columns were far down on the list of popularity as compared to the contributions to culture of the late Arthur Brisbane, O. O. McIntyre, or Dorothy Dix.[28]

IV. W.C.N.S.

The teletype service of the Washington City News Service is an indispensable aid to the Washington correspondent. This is a subsidiary organization of the United

Press which reports news by electrical transmission over private wires to teletype machines in the offices of newspapers or special correspondents. The W.C.N.S. has its own staff of reporters, and operates exactly as a city news service.

The teletype machine runs almost without a stop, typing sixty to seventy words a minute. It supplies news efficiently and well-edited. It merely skeletonizes the events of the day, giving the correspondent a running digest of all that is happening. The "ticker" supplies a typewritten record of press conferences, legislation, votes in Congress, Supreme Court decisions, etc. Each morning it includes a list of hotel registrations so that a correspondent can keep informed about the arrival of important visitors, especially those from his own state or city.

The teletype service relieves the correspondent of much anxiety over being "scooped" on routine stories. He can take several hours off for lunch, secure in the thought that when he returns a complete record of all that has happened will be waiting for him. If the correspondent does not have a ticker in his own office, it is simple enough to drop into the office next door. The National Press Club, in the National Press Building, where most of the Washington correspondents' offices are located, has one of these invaluable machines.

PART TWO

Introduction

SO far we have discussed what the Washington correspondents do. Let us now turn to a consideration of who the Washington correspondents *are*. What are their social origins? What are their personal political preferences and their private economic beliefs? What is their educational background? Which newspapers do they—expert newspaper men and women—read? Which magazines? Which newspapers do they credit with reliability in the treatment of news? Which papers do they regard as prejudiced? Why did these men and women enter journalism as a career, how did they get to Washington, and what did they bring to their post? How much do they earn? What complaints do they voice about their work, their editors, their publishers? What impulses characterize them as persons compared to, say, professors, merchants, or acrobats?

These questions strike at the very heart of this study, and are relevant to any understanding of journalism in a democratic society. It has been suggested earlier in this book that the Washington correspondents form a professional skill group with a community of responsibilities and talents; that a profession attracts certain personality "types" by its very nature, and stamps the perspective of its members with a characteristic identity. Since absolute objectivity in journalism is an impossibility, the social heritage, the "professional reflexes," the individual temperament, and the economic status of reporters assume a fundamental significance. The correspondent who makes $1,500 a year may assign a different emphasis to a story on minimum wage legislation than one who gets $25,000 plus a free automobile and chauffeur. The reporter who was raised in the tenderloin district of an industrial city may seize upon different "facts" in a housing story than one who spent his adolescence in the environs of Newport. The newspaperman whose publisher has a phobia about income taxes may communicate a different version of a Congressional debate than the reporter whose publisher is crusading for government control of profits and unearned increment. However unaware the reader in Keokuk may be of these factors, they may have entered—whether consciously or unconsciously—into the dispatches he reads each night.

The first five chapters have been concerned with journalistic methods. The next five chapters deal with journalists. They are concerned with the sociological anatomy of the Washington correspondents as a group. They present facts which identify the semi-anonymous persons who are our eyes and ears at the capital. They form what may be called the biography of the press corps.

The information is drawn from facts supplied by 127 Washington correspondents, who answered two lengthy questionnaires submitted to them by this writer in 1936.* Statistics and tables have been reduced to a minimum; where they are included it is simply because they are exciting in themselves, and because they give sharper outline and precision to the material. Readers who wish to explore the data further will find figures and tables reproduced in complete detail in Appendices D and E.

* The questionnaires are reproduced on the following pages.

BIOGRAPHICAL QUESTIONNAIRE

Filled Out by 127 Washington Correspondents

Name_____

Birthplace_____ Year of Birth_____

Number of years in journalism, in any capacity_____As a Washington Correspondent_____

Do you write a column?_____How often_____Length_____ words

Kind of news you send from Washington (National, agriculture, relief, White House, etc.)
_____

How did you get into journalism? (Accident? Choice? Desire to write? Through a
    school of journalism? Personal contact with first employer? Etc.)
_____

List the jobs you have held in newspaper work, giving names of papers and your age
    at the time:

List the jobs you have held besides newspaper work. Give your age at the time.

Number of years in grammar school?_____ Where? (List cities)

Number of years in High School?_____ Where?

Number of years in College?_____ Where?
Specialization in college (Journalism, economics, liberal arts, etc.):_____
College degrees_____ Honors? (Varsity, debating, scholarships, ΦBK)_____
_____

At what age did you begin contributing to your support?_____
At what age did you begin supporting yourself wholly?_____
At what age did you leave home to live elsewhere?_____

Father's occupation_____ Father's political bent _____
Number of younger brothers_____ Younger sisters_____ Older brothers_____
        Older sisters_____

Were you given religious training?____ Mild or strict?_____ Church_____
Do you go to church today?_____ Regularly, rarely, occasionally, never?_____
Which denomination?_____

Check father's income-level yearly:	$1000-2500	$2500-5000	$5000-10,000	Over $10,000
1-While you were in grammar school				
2-While you were in High School				
3-At college, or between 16-21				

How old were you when you married? _____ How many children have you had? _____
Please check: Single?____ Married?_____ Divorced? ___ Number of times married _____
What was your wife's occupation before marriage?_____

Which newspapers do you read regularly besides your own?

Which magazines do you read regularly?
To which magazines have you contributed articles?

List your clubs, societies, patriotic organizations, etc.

What is your hobby or favorite recreation?

Sketch travel, study or work outside of U.S., giving your age at the time:
    (Use other side if necessary)

BIOGRAPHICAL QUESTIONNAIRE FILLED OUT BY 127
WASHINGTON CORRESPONDENTS.

If you agree with a statement, check it .... ✓
If you disagree, mark it .... O
If you are uncertain, mark it .... ?

***

___"I believe that 'rugged individualism' is the best economic philosophy today."
___"I favor government operation of mines, public utilities and railroads."
___"If European nations can afford to arm they can pay us the War Debts."
___"The U.S. should cooperate more energetically with the League of Nations."
___"The U.S. should enter the World Court, with reservations as to its jurisdiction."
___"I favor higher taxes on the upper income brackets, on huge profits, etc."
___"Some form of government regulation over big business has become imperative."

***

I prefer the stories of (check one): ___AP ___UP ___INS ___US
... because they are: ___better written ___more reliable ___more liberal
The three U.S. newspapers which give the most fair and reliable news are:
1.
2.
3.
The three papers which are least fair and reliable are (Don't give more than one from
any one chain): 1.
2.
3.

___"The press devotes too much space to trivialities: scandals, sensations, divorces."
___"In general, news columns are equally fair to big business and labor."
___"Comparatively few papers give significant accounts of our basic economic conflicts."
___"The publishers' cry of 'Freedom of the Press' in fighting an NRA code was a ruse."
___"Most papers printed unfair or distorted stories about the Tugwell Pure Foods Bill."

***

If salary and security were no consideration, for which three U.S. papers would you
most prefer to be a Washington correspondent? (In order of preference.)
1.
2.
3.
Which one of the following posts would you most prefer to fill (ignoring salary):
___editorial writer ___foreign correspondent ___daily columnist
___managing editor ___Washington correspondent ___business dept.
___editor-in-chief ___head of Washington bureau ___roving reporter

If you had your choice over, would you choose journalism as a profession?_____
Which field, other than journalism, would you choose today? _____
Of the current candidates for President, who is your choice? _____
Whose daily column do you consider most significant, fair and reliable? _____
Ignoring salary, what is the worst part of the Washington Correspondent's job:
_____

***

(Note: The following statements have been made to me by different correspondents. This
is an effort to discover how widely these views are held or denied. -- L.C.R.)
___"I often feel the need of knowing more economics for my job."
___"It is almost impossible to be 'objective'. You read your paper, notice editorials,
get praised for some stories and criticized for others. You 'sense policy'
and are psychologically driven to slant your stories accordingly."
___"I am not aware of any definite, fixed 'policy' of my paper."
___"My orders are to be objective, but I know how my paper wants stories played."
___"Correspondents try too hard to please their editors. If they had more independence
they would discover that they really have more freedom than they assume."
___"I have given good stories to other men because my paper wouldn't welcome them."
(This does not mean for geographical or regional reasons.)
___"In my experience, I've had stories played down, out or killed for 'policy'reasons."
___"In general, I agree with my paper's political point of view."

___"I favor a Newspaper Guild to improve salaries, contract and bargain collectively."
Apropos a Newspaper Guild, I feel that:
___"newspapermen are individualists and craftsmen, not in a class with labor."
___"it is unethical for newspapermen to organize into unions."
___"I have nothing to gain by joining a Guild."
___"a Guild would make reporters partisan in treating labor and union news."
___"newspapermen should not strike, nor use the threat of strike."
___"a good newspaperman doesn't need a Guild: it is organized for the lazy,
the incompetent or the mediocre."
___"it would become too radical."

***

(Finally: Many correspondents have urged me to discover the average salary of the
corps. They have offered to state theirs in this anonymous form. It will be a
very great help to this research, and deeply appreciated, if you would give your
annual salary below. If you handle several papers please state your total net
salary. Thank you.) Salary (per annum): $

ANONYMOUS QUESTIONNAIRE SUBMITTED TO THE 127 COR-
RESPONDENTS WHO HAD FILLED OUT THE AUTOBIOGRAPH-
ICAL QUESTIONNAIRE. 107 RETURNS WERE RECEIVED.

VI. The Social Composition of the Press Corps

WORDS are the journalist's tools and it would seem a defensible hypothesis that newspapermen are drawn from a psychological environment which placed a premium upon articulateness. One would expect more reporters to be the children of parents who handled ideas rather than things: teachers, clergymen, lawyers, or editors, rather than farmers or industrial workers.[1] One would expect newspapermen to have been exposed to the attraction of talk, particularly talk about social and political affairs, in homes with literate preoccupations. And one would expect them to have middle-class origins, rather than stemming from the ranks of manual labor, since deference for verbalization and a drive to achieve facility in it would be more pronounced in the former than the latter.

In the light of this approach it is not wholly fortuitous that out of 123 Washington correspondents who supplied information on this point, ninety-seven (76.3 per cent) are children of Professional, Proprietary, or Clerical groups, according to the occupational categories of Professor William F. Ogburn, the so-called "white-collar" class.[2] Fifty-five (44.7 per cent) correspondents' fathers were members of a profession. Of the professional group, fourteen (11.3 per cent) were editors or newspapermen, thirteen (10.5 per cent) were lawyers. The labor population, including

153

skilled, semi-skilled, and unskilled workers, contributed only fourteen men to the corps, exactly the amount contributed by newspapermen alone. The farmers of the country produced but 9.7 per cent of the group.*

The press corps ranges in age from 23 to 70 (as of 1936). Over one-half of the 127 correspondents (51.1 per cent) are between 30 and 40 years of age; over one-fourth are between 36 and 40. The arithmetical average age for the group is 41.7. The median line, dividing the older from the younger one-half, falls between 37 and 38. Twenty-two correspondents (17.1 per cent) are over 50 years old; twenty (15.7 per cent) are 30 or younger.

The data on the social origins of the press corps, showing the high proportion whose fathers were members of a profession as compared to farmers and laborers, gain significance from the fact that in 1900, the date closest to the average year of birth of the newspapermen studied, the professions formed only 4.3 per cent of the country's population, whereas the farm population was 35.6 per cent, and the labor population totaled 48.4 per cent.[3] If we tabulate these figures side by side the emphases become sharper:

TABLE I †

OCCUPATIONAL GROUP	PER CENT CONTRIBUTED TO PRESS CORPS	PER CENT OF POPULATION IN 1900
Professions	44.7	4.3
Labor (skilled, semi-skilled, unskilled)	11.3	48.4
Farmers	9.7	35.6

* Complete tables on all the facts used in this and succeeding chapters are in Appendix D.

† For 123 correspondents. The Proprietary and the Clerical group are omitted from this table.

Compare these figures to those of Robert F. Harrel, who conducted a study of 505 American editors, editorial writers, department managers, managing editors, and special writers, called *Factors Making for Success in Journalism.*[4] Out of his cases 32.0 per cent had fathers of a professional status, as compared to our 43.3 per cent. 8.3 per cent of the fathers were journalists, as compared to 11 per cent among the Washington correspondents. By this comparison about 11.3 per cent more of the fathers of the Washington press corps were in the professions than a sample of other journalists in the country, and about 2.7 per cent more were newspapermen themselves. Both studies demonstrate the high percentage of journalists whose fathers were members of a "white-collar group."

The economic strata from which the press corps came are basic in interest. 57.5 per cent of the correspondents' families had incomes of $2,500 or over while the newspapermen were in grammar school; 62.1 per cent, while they were in high school; 64.4 per cent, while they were in college, or of college age. For the same three periods of education, the family incomes *under* $2,500 accounted for 42.3 per cent, 37.7 per cent, and 35.4 per cent respectively.

The significance of these figures may be suggested by the fact that according to the analysis of income stratification upon which economists still depend, the 1918 estimates of the National Bureau of Economic Research, 92 per cent of the gainfully employed in the United States earned less than $2,500 a year. Only 2 per cent earned $5,000 or over.[5] The average annual-earning figures for employed wage-earners as compiled by Paul H. Douglas and F. T. Jennison shows that in 1910 the *average* annual earning (per wage-earner) was $573; in 1918 it was $997; and in 1920 it was only $1,337. As late as 1928 it was only $1,405.[6] It is safe to conclude that the correspondents came from families which had incomes considerably above those of the averages for the country's wage-earners as a whole.

The size of the communities in which the correspondents were born, raised, and in which they received their elementary education, is of relevance as an index to their earliest environment. 38.5 per cent of the corps were born and raised in towns which had a population under 2,500 in 1900.* Almost exactly one-half (49.6 per cent) come from communities under 10,000; 62.2 per cent from those under 25,000. The number who were born and raised in cities of 100,000 or over totaled only 16.6 per cent of the group.[7]

It has often been remarked that Indiana contributes a surprisingly high proportion of journalists to the nation. An analysis of the states in which the Washington correspondents were born supports this. Indiana ranked first with 10.2 per cent of the corps (distributed evenly between the ages of 28 and 63). Illinois was second with 9.4 per cent. The pre-eminence of Indiana is increased by

---

* Where a man received his education in a locality different from that in which he was born, the place in which he received the first six years of his education was used. There were so few of such cases that they do not affect the general results markedly.

The reasons for using 1900 as a date of reference are discussed in the Appendix on Reference Notes, under note 3 of this chapter.

the fact that (a) only seven Indiana papers were included in the study (3.7 per cent of the 186); (b) in 1930, Indiana had only 2.6 per cent of the population of the nation; in 1900 her population was approximately 3 per cent.[8]

The reasons for Indiana's curious position as an incubator of literary and journalistic figures have never been fully explained. Professor Harold D. Lasswell has suggested one stimulating hypothesis: symbol manipulators and handlers may sprout in areas of political conflict. Indiana has long been a "balance of power" state, a strategic lever in national elections.[9] This fact may account for the political consciousness and talents of Indianans, and the attraction of politics and allied fields as a career. It seems possible that the intelligences of the middle class rather than going into law, finance, or business, as would be the case in metropolitan centers, are drawn to those occupations which confer prestige upon the felicitous use of words: politics or writing.*

Reporting is, at bottom, a career compact of an essentially antagonistic attitude to the inertia, log-rolling, and ineptitude of orthodox political action. Scratch a journalist and you find a reformer. To what type of political consciousness were the Washington correspondents exposed in their impressionable years? The political identification of their fathers shows that 72.7 per cent were either Democrats or Republicans (44 were Republicans, 41

* This would not, of course, explain why the same phenomenon is not to be observed in Iowa or Kansas.

Democrats), 13.6 per cent were Independent, and the rest were distributed in categories described as Liberal, Social-ist, Progressive, Radical, Labor, or "no party." Since the combined Republican-Democratic vote from 1896-1912 was approximately 98 per cent of the total vote cast [10] (1896-1912 may be taken to encompass the most impres-sionable formative years of the majority of the correspond-ents), the 30 per cent of the correspondents' fathers who were not affiliated with one of the two major political parties represents a marked divergence from the general political pattern of the country. The large proportion of teachers, lawyers, doctors, and journalists among the fathers of the correspondents makes this plausible.

The future will probably see a larger percentage of journalists drawn from the ranks of liberals, independents, socialists, and third-party sympathizers. The intensification of social crises precipitates discontent with the circumlocu-tions of "respectable" political parties in the intellectuals of the middle class, caught between the hammer of in-dustrial capitalism and the anvil of proletarian violence. Dissatisfaction is communicated to the sons of intellec-tuals in the atmosphere of homes characterized by the rising insecurity of middle-class men who handle sym-bols for a living. The sons of lawyers, clergymen, jour-nalists, and teachers may well be possessed of heightened reformist energies to embark upon a career which throws them into vital contact with the organs of the body politic, and which opens the possibility of "tearing away the veils of pretense and hypocrisy," exposing politics and politi-cians in the disenchanted light of "hard-boiled" jour-nalism.

Journalism is often called a "game" in the argot of its practitioners. But many newspapermen like to embellish their status by insisting upon the designation of their trade as a "profession." Since the first requisite of a profession is the exclusion of the unfit, "the profession of journalism" is chiefly a convenient term of reference. Newspaper work requires a congeries of skills and techniques. But it is a profession with no professional standards, no professional discipline, no examining or accrediting bodies, no agreement upon norms for testing competence. From this point of view the educational background of the Washington correspondents is particularly interesting.

Out of 127 members of the press corps, sixty-five (51.1 per cent) are college graduates in possession of a four-year degree from an accredited institution of higher learning. Thirty-six correspondents (28.3 per cent) attended college, but received no degree. Twenty-two of these thirty-six (17.3 per cent of the total of 127) went to college for only one or two years. Twenty-three correspondents (18.1 per cent) had no college work at all (eight attending high school for less than four years). Two did not have any high-school education.

The academic record of the Washington correspondents cannot, obviously, be compared to that of other professional groups—since all lawyers, doctors, teachers, or engineers are, *ipso facto,* college graduates and have earned a higher degree. But the record is more impressive than that of a sample group of American editors, managing editors, and feature writers. The analysis of Robert F. Harrel to which we have referred shows that in 1931 only 40.8 per cent of 505 successful journalists in an editorial position were college graduates (as compared to the 47.2 of the capital press corps), and that 67.4 per cent attended college at all (ninety-two Washington correspondents would fall into this category—72.4 per cent of the entire group). Whereas 8.4 per cent of Harrel's cases did not attend high school, only 1.5 per cent of our group were spared secondary school education.[11]

The record of the Washington correspondents who finished their academic work is auspicious. Sixteen were awarded the Phi Beta Kappa degree.* Ten won scholarships. Two were graduated *magna cum laude*. Eight members of the press corps received a higher degree—the M.A. Of these, four were Rhodes Scholars, completing their university careers at Oxford. Four of the men included in this study have been awarded the honorary LL.D.

Much more suggestive for our purposes is the *kind* of education which was chosen by the Washington correspondents. The newspaperman in the capital is today faced by the necessity of reporting news which is a compound of economics, political science, monetary problems, constitutional and international law, public administration, social service. The activities of the New Deal range from the field of public works to the esoteric art of encouraging piscatorial copulation. Such responsibilities require intellectual poise, if not specialized competence, in the face of intricate events. A *systematic* approach to the hectic cosmos of Washington would necessitate sophistication in the field of political economy, in all its ramifications; an *impres-*

* According to the Phi Beta Kappa Association, about ten per cent of college students are awarded the key.

sionistic approach, which is the approach of journalism, would profit by at least a limited experience in the disciplines of the social sciences.

The curricular specialization of those correspondents who received a university education shows a pronounced Liberal Arts and Humanities emphasis, with a corresponding lack of contact with the formal areas of economics, political science, or sociology. 19.6 per cent of the college men and women of the press corps chose "Liberal Arts" as their field of major application; * 10.2 per cent were chiefly concerned with Journalism; * 9.4 per cent did most of their work in English and in pre-legal arts and humanities. Only four correspondents majored in Political Science; only three in Economics. Thus, only seven of the newspapermen studied, 5.4 per cent of the total, may be credited with more than a cursory academic contact with the social sciences.†

Now the meaning of these figures is deepened by remembering that men who are burdened with the duty of recording the events of the contemporary political scene would seem to be in need of a disciplined frame of reference within which to orient themselves, and by which to appraise the significance of men, measures, and goals. Without some framework within which competing plans and theories (whether of prices, slum clearance, or industrial unionization) can be related to an inclusive system, or without some analytic viewpoint from which to place social

* Chiefly correspondents under 37 years of age. The first school of journalism was not founded until 1908.

† This may be qualified by the recognition that some colleges require students majoring in Journalism to take a minimum number of social science courses.

phenomena in a perspective of time and totality, the observer is left with little but an unsystematized bundle of preferences and an incoherent mélange of impressions. He can do little more than interpret acts and issues according to emotional impulses and affective hopes. His insights may be keen and his sensitivity high, but his ability to understand is limited to the one-dimensional sphere of distilled facts.

This is not merely an academic gauge, the validity of which newspapermen challenge. It was tested in the anonymous questionnaire submitted to the same Washington correspondents who supplied data on their educational background. The following statement was contained, to be checked "Yes," "No," or "Uncertain":

"I often feel the need of knowing more economics for my job."

86.6 per cent of those who answered said "Yes." This was a higher degree of agreement than on any other question but one. 10.6 per cent checked "No"; 2.6 per cent were uncertain.* Extensive interviews and contact with over 150 members of the press corps lead this writer to the conclusion that a majority of the correspondents often feel inadequate to cope with the bewildering complexity of the news they are assigned to cover.[12] Complaints were often heard that "my college work is a dead loss today," and many correspondents regret that they did not have a more thorough training in Economics or Political Science, rather than Journalism, Ancient History, or the Elizabethan Sonnet.

* Note that the statement was, "I often feel the need of knowing more economics *for my job.*"

It may be objected that the newspaperman is not required to be an economist or a social scientist, that his job is to report facts, that his talents should be those of getting news, that his energies should be devoted to accurate and interesting writing. The well-known aphorism of Lionel C. Probert, former head of the Associated Press bureau in Washington, may be cited to challenge the argument: "The Washington correspondent has got to write news for the milkman in Omaha." The objections are not relevant. What concerns us at this point of the analysis is the attitude of the newspapermen themselves to their own adequacy for their tasks. It is the degree of intellectual security with which they can regard the multitude of matters which they are supposed to describe and, in however small measure, clarify to their readers. For men without "a frame of reference" and with an uncontrolled impressionistic (rather than analytic) approach to issues are driven to a surface interpretation of events. They cling to normative words of ambiguous content: "liberty," "Americanism," "justice," "Democracy," "socialism," "communism." And words are unstable points of anchor in a world of changing words.

Newspapermen evidence a marked insecurity in the presence of social theories or political conceptualization. In this light the caustic reportorial reaction to "New Deal professors," "crack-pot theories," "The Brain Trust," "Frankfurter's bright young men," etc., suggests the projection of doubts of personal adequacy upon those who have increased personal and professional insecurities. Many newspapermen compensate for their inner uncertainty (or inner conviction of incompetence) by lusty deprecations of those whose intellectual equipment they vaguely fear. They soothe their injured sense of self-esteem by the oblique device of irony about those whose respect they would in actuality prefer to enjoy.

These comments are germane to an understanding of the thinking and the non-conscious drives of the newspapermen in the capital. They are especially applicable to the corps since 1933, when the character of Washington news changed, for better or for worse, from news of political personalities and party intrigues to news charged to a high degree with socio-economic content. There were not many professors in the capital before 1933, nor was there a deluge of governmental activity in fields where academic competence was imperative.

There is a supporting insight into the attitude of the Washington correspondent in the following excerpts from conversations with various members of the press corps:

"I used to get into a cold sweat when I had to write up Roosevelt's money policy."

"Going off the gold standard was a story that gave me a headache I never want to have again."

"The news has taken a crazy turn. We're used to giving the dope about how Jim Farley cracks the whip, or why the Chamber of Commerce fought the Zilch bill. Now we've got to write about hogs, unemployment, the price of copper, and the interstate commerce clause in the Constitution."

One correspondent sheepishly confessed to this writer that when Professor Warren's theories of prices had the ear of the man in the White House, he dutifully read through the treatise of Warren and Pearson on gold. "I got more confused than ever, so I dropped it. I write the stuff up as I understand it. That's more than 99 per cent of my readers will understand anyway."

During the period when monetary problems were the hottest news in the capital many correspondents consulted Dr. E. A. Goldenweiser of the Federal Reserve Board, or members of the staff of the Brookings Institution. To these reporters there was a compensation of the kind found in the remark of one veteran newspaperman:

"To do the job, what you know or understand isn't important. You've got to know whom to ask. I didn't understand most of what Goldenweiser told me, but I took careful notes and wrote it up verbatim. Let my readers figure it out. I'm their reporter, not their teacher."

And there is a triumphant prop for self-reassurance in this last comment:

"I'd like to see the Tugwells or the Frankfurters try to write up the stories they're making—for the big girls and boys who read Little Orphan Annie. That would be a laugh. No matter how low I get to feeling I always know I'm doing a better job than *they* could."

One of the popular conceptions about newspapermen is the supposed uncongeniality of their domestic relations. It is generally suspected that the character of newspaper work, with its irregular hours, tensions, and stimulation to the imbibing of alcohol, does not encourage domestic felicity; that reporters are temperamentally restless and "not the marrying kind;" or that their private lives are characterized by discord and a high percentage of divorces. The evidence of the Washington correspondents does not confirm these fancies. Admitting that success, relative security, and high salaries would tend to make the journalists in the capital atypical of other reporters (e.g., police reporters, or the war-horses of city rooms), the evidence is nevertheless revealing.

One hundred and eight out of 127 Washington correspondents are married today. Seventeen are single and have never married. Two have been married but are single today. According to the estimates of Professor William F. Ogburn in *Recent Social Trends in the United States*, 60.5 per cent of the population fifteen years of age or over is married; [13] 85.0 per cent of the Washington correspondents fall into that category, a considerably higher proportion.

Twelve correspondents have been divorced, 9.4 per cent of the total group. If the divorce rate of the country be taken as one for every six marriages, as is estimated by Professor Ogburn,[14] then 9.4 per cent of the corps is a figure below that of the average for the nation.

Thirty of the correspondents' wives had no occupation prior to their marriage; eighteen were secretaries or stenographers; seventeen were teachers. This distribution is to be expected; American girls of marriageable age are distributed along the same general lines. (The four married women correspondents are married to newspapermen.) The rest of the wives were clerks, students, social workers, in the fine arts (five), etc. The middle-class and "white collar" character of the corps extends to their marital choices.

It is sometimes suggested that newspapermen tend to evade the responsibility of having and raising children, because of their temperamental instability or the conditions of their work. This, again, is not supported by our evidence. Sixty-seven of the 110 correspondents who are or have been married are parents. Since about one wife out of five in the United States had no children in 1930,[15] a higher proportion of the correspondents had children than the citizens of the nation as a whole. The average number of children, per married correspondent, is 1.02. The average family size for the corps is 2.89, a figure slightly lower than the 3.01 persons per family found to prevail in the professions in 1930.*

The conclusion to be drawn from these figures is obvious: the Washington correspondents are fairly representative of other professional groups in their marital relationships and, if anything, are more "domestic" than the country as a whole, as pictured by average figures.

Newspapermen are not church-goers by reputation. The famed cynicism of journalists arises only partly from the "disillusionment" inherent in their tasks; the seeds for much of it are to be found in the psychological protest formations which made journalism attractive to begin with. The antiseptic view of the universe which characterizes reporters is reflected in their indifference to formal religion. Out of 122 Washington correspondents, 116 received religious training—designated by thirty-six as "strict," and

---

* The family estimate is for parents and children, and single persons. In this case, to get the average family size, the number of correspondents married was doubled (except for two cases, where both husband and wife are correspondents included in this study), and the total number of children and single correspondents was added. The sum was divided by 127.

by seventy-eight as "mild." This training was experienced in the Methodist, Presbyterian, Episcopalian, Roman Catholic, Congregationalist, and Baptist churches by 74.1 per cent of the group. (The churches are listed in order of frequency.) The remaining 25.9 per cent of those exposed to religious training were distributed in twelve other sects, varying from the Mormons to the Church of Christ, Scientist. Four correspondents (3.1 per cent) are Jewish.

How many of these men and women attend religious services of any kind today? "Never," sixty-five (51.1 per cent). "Occasionally," thirty (23.6 per cent). "Rarely," seventeen (13.3 per cent). "Regularly," twelve (9.4 per cent: nine Roman Catholics, two Christian Scientists, and one Episcopalian).

It is of interest that only 9.4 per cent of the correspondents attend a church regularly, that 51.1 per cent never do and that 13.3 per cent rarely do. 64.4 per cent, almost two-thirds, are either never or "rarely" within a sacerdotal institution. These figures are markedly below the best estimates for the religious membership of the country as a whole.*

The personalities who enter journalism are often men who revolt against the authority symbols of their youth; newspaper work fosters iconoclasm, or buttresses it; most newspapermen are not church-goers.

---

* In 1926, 59 per cent of the adults living in cities of 25,000 and over were church members. Half of the American people thirteen years of age or over are on church rolls today.[16]

VII. What Do They Read?

NEWSPAPERMEN are also newspaper readers, and in their case the reading of a daily paper has a magnified significance. Newspapers supply a reporter with information which he incorporates, consciously or not, into his own dispatches; they influence his political dispatches; they influence his personal political attitude and his professional activity. Most newspapermen in the capital read, first, the paper which competes with their own, in order to keep *au courant* with the activity of their competitors in the capital. Practically every correspondent reads one or more Washington dailies (because they cover the events of the capital thoroughly and because their local news is national news) and either the New York *Times*, the New York *Herald Tribune*, or the Baltimore *Sun*. Papers from the middle and far West are not followed closely because they arrive in the capital several days after publication. One reporter known to this writer scans six papers each morning before making his rounds. He clips half a dozen stories a day for reference, either using their substance in his own news-accounts or using them as a point of departure for his own investigations.

Which newspapers do the Washington correspondents read regularly, besides their own? The table which follows gives the twelve leading papers as indicated by 110 members of the press corps.*

* The average number of newspapers read regularly by each correspondent is 4.7.

TABLE II

NEWSPAPERS READ REGULARLY BY 110 CORRESPONDENTS,
NOT INCLUDING THEIR OWN

	NUMBER MENTIONS	PER CENT OF 110 *
New York *Times*	100	90.9
N. Y. *Herald Tribune*	72	65.4
Baltimore *Sun*	71	63.6
Washington *Post*	65	59.0
Washington *Star*	59	53.6
Washington *Daily News*	48	43.6
Washington *Herald*	30	27.2
Washington *Times*	11	10.0
Wall St. *Journal*	7	6.3
Chicago *Tribune*	5	4.5
Philadelphia *Record*	4	3.6
N. Y. *World-Telegram*	4	3.6

This table lists only those papers specifically named. But since twenty-seven correspondents wrote in "all Washington papers," or "all local papers," without designating any by name, it appears advisable to correct the list by adding twenty-seven to each of the Washington papers. There is no doubt in this writer's mind that more correspondents read Washington papers than the table above suggests.

* The percentages do not add up to 100 because each correspondent was permitted to list as many papers as he chose. The percentages refer to the *number of mentions* for any one paper, divided by 110, the number of correspondents who answered this question.

What Do They Read? 171

TABLE III

NEWSPAPERS READ REGULARLY BY 110 CORRESPONDENTS,
NOT INCLUDING THEIR OWN

(Corrected with reference to papers in Washington, D. C.)

	NUMBER MENTIONS	PER CENT OF 110
New York *Times*	100	90.9
Washington *Post*	92	83.6
Washington *Star*	86	78.1
Washington *Daily News*	75	68.1
N. Y. *Herald Tribune*	72	65.4
Baltimore *Sun*	71	63.6
Washington *Herald*	57	51.8
Washington *Times*	38	34.5

Both tables demonstrate the extraordinary circulation of the New York *Times* among the Washington press corps. Over 90 per cent of the correspondents who devote their time to covering the capital read the *Times* regularly for information or as a point of departure for their own work. The political influence of the *Times* is clearly greater than its circulation figures would indicate: certainly the "angle" which the *Times* may take on a story, or the facts which its seventeen-man bureau in the capital may unearth, affect the news-dispatches of correspondents for journals all over the United States. It is to be expected that the Washington *Post*, as a morning newspaper in the capital, would have a wide circulation among the press corps. The fact that the Washington *Star* and *News*, along with the *Post*, are read by far more correspondents than read either the Washington *Herald* or *Times*, the morning and afternoon

Hearst papers, is of considerable interest. Lastly, the wide circulation among the press corps of the New York *Herald Tribune* and the Baltimore *Sun* should not go unnoticed.*

Second in interest only to the newspapers which newspapermen read, are the magazines to which they turn each week. The following table lists the magazines specifically mentioned by ninety-seven correspondents in answer to the question, "Which magazines do you read regularly?"

TABLE IV

MAGAZINES READ REGULARLY BY 97 CORRESPONDENTS †

MAGAZINE	NUMBER MENTIONS	PER CENT OF 97
Time	57	58.7
Nation	33	34.1
Harper's	33	34.1
Saturday Evening Post	33	34.1
Collier's	28	28.8
New Republic	26	26.8

* In Chapter IX the press is rated by the correspondents according to reliability and fairness of news treatment. It should be repeated that some papers which are held in high esteem by the correspondents, such as the St. Louis *Post-Dispatch* or the Kansas City *Star*, are not read regularly because they cannot get to the capital for several days, and because their local news, unlike the local news of New York, is of limited national interest.

† The following magazines are not included in the table, having received only two mentions each: *American, News-Week, Yale Review, National Geographic*. One mention was made of each of the following: *Annalist, Annals of the American Academy of Political and Social Science, Ballyhoo, Business Week, Cosmopolitan, Liberty, Living Age, London Sphere, House Beautiful, London Economist, Manchester Guardian, Outlook, Parents, Popular Mechanics, Red Book, Round Table, Stage, Story, Survey, Vogue*.

MAGAZINE	NUMBER MENTIONS	PER CENT OF 97
New Yorker	24	24.7
Atlantic Monthly	19	19.5
Fortune	18	18.5
Reader's Digest	16	16.4
Scribner's	16	16.4
Esquire	9	9.2
Today	8	8.2
American Mercury	5	5.1
Current History	5	5.1
Forum	5	5.1
New Masses	5	5.1
Foreign Affairs	5	5.1
Literary Digest	4	4.1
Review of Reviews	4	4.1

It is revealing that *Time* magazine, which attempts weekly syntheses of political developments in a dramatized fashion, has a striking popularity with the press corps.* Newspapermen are not attracted to sustained analyses of technical questions, nor to technical treatments of political affairs, as this list shows. They read to get useful information in swift, unweighty form. In any profession a high percentage of the practitioners read organs which approach professional problems in a non-popularized fashion. But newspapermen show no reading habits of this type. *Time,* the magazine which is most popular with them, is subtitled, appropriately enough, "The Weekly Newsmagazine."

There is a reason for this. Newspaper work, with its

* Partly because *Time* often mentions the names of correspondents, and has a section on the Press.

emphasis upon the accumulation of brute facts, precipitates anxiety in newspapermen about the hazard of "missing something" or "overlooking something." This drives the reporter into a sustained preoccupation with the factual materials which it is his duty to record. He is an inveterate reader of newspapers and magazines with contemporary news content.* The large number of correspondents who read the *Nation* and the *New Republic* is worth noticing. Here they find weekly syntheses of news and interpretations of events of a pronounced "liberal" color. The *Nation* and the *New Republic,* to which some of the members of the press corps contribute, provide a corrective balance and an integrating perspective to the news of the daily press. They also emphasize news which newspapers do not always feature. It would be interesting to evaluate the influence which the *Nation* and the *New Republic,* with numerically small circulation figures, exert upon public opinion by virtue of their influence upon writers, reporters and other symbol specialists.

The search for "news" and the obsessional fear of missing out on a story, making an error, or failing to exploit a sequence of facts, dominate not only the newspaperman's professional but his private life. The amount of "shop talk" in which Washington correspondents indulge, at lunch, at dinner parties, in their homes, was particularly conspicuous to this observer. Professional gossip and the

* The limitations inherent in using the questionnaire method made it impossible to obtain objective evidence about the type of *books* which the correspondents prefer. Such information would of course be important.

exchange of political information and "leads" occupy more of the Washington correspondents' time than comparable fields of interest do in the social conversation of doctors, lawyers, or teachers. In many occupational groups meeting socially there is a desire to "forget shop"; in newspaper circles there is a ubiquitous tendency to discuss it. The complaint that "they never stop working" is heard from many Washington correspondents' wives, who refer to themselves, in amused despair, as "newspaper widows."

VIII. The Professional Composition of the Corps

THE Washington assignment represents a degree of journalistic success which is surpassed by few editorial positions. The members of the press corps have prestige and a security of tenure considerably above that of other newspapermen. A special correspondent generally leaves the capital only to become an editor, managing editor, or editorial writer.* Many newspapermen in the capital have preferred to remain in Washington rather than accept a position nominally more important.

Sixty correspondents have at one time or another held full-time jobs outside of newspaper work. The press corps contains nine former teachers, five publicity men, four who were in advertising, a former diplomatic representative, two magazine editors, two lawyers, two printers, two ex-secretaries to governors, one ex-secretary to a Vice-President, a private detective, an acoustical engineer, a rancher, a United States War Relief Administrator, a surveyor, a movie director, a junior accountant, two bookkeepers, a tutor, a newsreel supervisor, an insurance agent. The oc-

* The following one-time Washington correspondents, for example, have become editors or publishers: A. J. Sinnott (Newark *Evening News*), Roy Roberts (Kansas City *Star*), the late Charles G. Ross (St. Louis *Post-Dispatch*), Lee Miller (Detroit *News*), Arthur Kirchhofer (Buffalo *Evening News*), Grafton Wilcox (New York *Herald Tribune*), Ludwell Denny (Indianapolis *Times*), Henry Suydam (Brooklyn *Eagle*), Lowell Mellett (Washington *Daily News*).

cupational record of the group is obviously more varied
than that of a group of doctors, lawyers, or teachers; the
professional disciplines of the latter generally lead in an
unbroken line from academic preparation to professional
duties. This is not true for journalists.

It may be more revealing to inquire: How many members of the press corps changed careers, leaving journalism and then returning to it? Twenty-three of the correspondents (18.1 per cent) have had full-time jobs some-
time *after* their newspaper careers had begun, taking work
which either paid better or seemed more attractive at the
time. This shifting of occupation is less frequent in professions such as law, medicine, or teaching. The jobs to
which the newspapermen were drawn were chiefly advertising, publicity work, or related fields. Two occupied
positions in the newsreel end of the movie industry. One,
Jesse S. Cottrell, was American Minister to Bolivia from
1921 to 1927. One correspondent was private secretary to
a former Secretary of the Interior. One was secretary of
a city commission. One correspondent broke his journalistic
career to teach, and one to serve a short apprenticeship in
law. Of all the non-journalistic jobs held by members of
the corps after they had had contact with newspaper work,
only one pertained to business.

The complete record indicates the dominant preference
of the press corps for work somehow related to journalism—work concerned with the handling of symbols,
rather than persons or things.

The professional equipment of the members of the press
corps suggests that these men and women have demonstrated their competence and reliability, to their superiors

at least, in long and varied experience in journalism. The average number of years of newspaper experience for the 127 Washington correspondents who form the subject matter of this study is 18.8. The median number is 16. This includes their entire experience in journalism. The average number of years the newspapermen have served as Washington correspondents is 9.7. The median falls at 8.

An analysis of the number of years of journalistic experience *prior to promotion to the capital* shows the average to be 9.2 and the median 7.* It is interesting to compare the average body of pre-Washington experience for correspondents of different ages. The one-fourth of the newspapermen above 48 years of age had 12.4 years of newspaper work before assignment to the capital. The one-fourth who are 38 to 47 years old today had an average of 10.2 years. The one-fourth between 33 and 38 had 7.6 years. The one-fourth from 23 to 33 had only 5.5 years.

It is clear that less journalistic experience is required by editors today than was once the case. The figures may be interpreted in this way:

1. The oldest fourth of the press corps (ages 48 to 70) averages over twice as much training before coming to Washington as the youngest fourth (23 to 33).

2. The older half (38 to 70) averages almost twice as much pre-Washington experience as the younger half (23 to 33).

---

* Analyses of years of journalistic experience exclude nine correspondents, who were born in Washington, D. C., and began their newspaper work in the capital, since their experience and careers are different from those of newspapermen who were promoted to Washington.

3. Correspondents over 38 years of age average more than twice as many years of journalistic experience prior to assuming their present duties as do correspondents under 33.

The actual ages at which newspapermen were appointed to cover Washington places these same facts in bolder form. The average age of appointment is 30; the median is 29. 57.2 per cent of the correspondents were sent to the capital between the ages of 21 to 30. But:

1. The oldest fourth of the press corps (48 to 70 years of age) was appointed to Washington at an average age of 36.8.

2. The fourth between the ages of 38 to 47 was appointed at an average age of 31.2.

3. The fourth between 33 to 38 was appointed at an average age of 29.02.

4. The youngest fourth (23 to 33) was appointed at an average age of 25.7.

The figures show a steady, graduated decline in the ages at which different age-groups of newspapermen were promoted to the capital. The oldest fourth of the press corps averaged eleven years more of journalistic experience per correspondent (prior to promotion to the capital) than the youngest fourth.

These are obviously gross quantitative standards and should be discounted accordingly. The *type* of experience classified as journalistic and the contemporary competence of different age-groups of correspondents are not considered here. But this much is clear: the Washington post was once treated as a stage in the career of a newspaperman which he achieved by competitive effort, and with which he was rewarded for his superiority over his colleagues. Seniority played a great role. (Until recent years the Washington correspondent, in addition to his regular news-dispatches, sent editorials on national affairs to his home office.[1]) Today this is patently less true. Younger men, men with less experience, are being sent to Washington.*

The steady growth in the size of the press corps, the greater concentration of coverage in the capital, the increase in the number of papers having a special Washington correspondent, and the increase in the *size* of the bureaus which individual newspapers maintain, all suggest reasons for the demand for younger correspondents.† Today newspapers seem to favor the practice of sending their brighter young men to be trained under the older Washington correspondents and to develop, in this way, an earlier and more intense specialized training in national political reporting. Many newspapers regard the Washington post as a proving ground for future editors, editorial writers, or foreign correspondents.

The older correspondents in the capital sometimes complain about the influx of "the fair-haired boys," implying that with the Washington assignment no longer awarded for competence and seniority, a new type of newspaperman is being sent to the capital: a "pet" of the publisher or managing editor, marked for a swift career back in

---

* Perhaps the larger proportion of young men in the press corps indicates the value of training in schools of journalism, which were not available to the older men, and which may be a substitute for longer practical apprenticeships.

† See Appendix G.

his home office, and especially sensitive to the kind of news his superiors will receive with most pleasure. In several cases known to this writer these charges seem to be applicable; but it is doubtful whether they apply to a sufficiently large proportion of the younger men in the capital to give them great credence.

The increased value of younger correspondents today, as against twenty-five years ago, may be found in the fact that since the younger men have been educated and trained in a society more conscious of socio-economic problems, they have had to disembarrass themselves of less of the "old-school" type of reporting which regarded politics as a simple personality-party struggle, void of deeper social forces, charged with the melodrama of surface maneuvers, one-dimensional in meaning. This writer has heard many older correspondents confess the difficulties of re-adjusting themselves, after a long career in orthodox political reporting, when President Roosevelt and the complex purposes of the New Deal tore national politics from its traditional path. The younger correspondents had greater flexibility. Many of them came to Washington fresh to record and interpret a new type of news unhampered by encrusted news-stereotypes.

Publishers often complain that their representatives in the capital become possessed by an insulated "Washington viewpoint"; in the enthusiasm of 1933 they seemed eager to have a new type of political correspondence which would keep step with the march of a new day. Thirty-nine correspondents and press association reporters out of our group of 127 have come to the capital since the advent of the New Deal. Several of these men followed Mr.

Roosevelt from Albany to the White House, having developed an acquaintanceship with his personality, methods, and staff which it would have been pointless for editors not to put to use. Several had gained a certain right to take up Washington correspondence because they had covered Roosevelt, rather than Hoover, in the 1932 campaign. Some had distinguished themselves as journalistic experts on labor, finance, or agriculture and, with these spheres of national life destined for dramatization, it was natural that editors send them on to the capital.

The record of the last four years leaves little doubt that some of the most independent and intelligible reporting on national affairs has been contributed by men who have been Washington correspondents for a comparatively short period. The dispatches of "newcomers" in the bureaus of the New York *Times*, the Baltimore *Sun*, the New York *Herald Tribune*, the Scripps-Howard, United Press, and Associated Press organizations, the St. Louis *Post-Dispatch*, the Des Moines *Register* and *Tribune*, the St. Paul *Pioneer Press*, to name the more conspicuous examples, have been distinguished for competence and insight.

The pre-Washington experience of the press corps may be suggested by the following facts, listed at random:

Nineteen Washington correspondents have been city editors.
Thirteen have been managing editors.
Twelve have been foreign correspondents.
Ten have been editorial writers.
Fifteen have been wire (telegraph) editors.
Twenty-two have served on the copy desk.
Sixteen have had experience in the business or mechanical

end of newspaper work: four telegraph operators, two type-setters, three advertising salesmen, three circulation agents.

Nine correspondents began their journalistic service as copy boys.

It is valuable to estimate what may be called the "professional mobility" of the press corps: the number of papers for which correspondents have worked during their careers, and the number of non-journalistic jobs they have held. It is generally felt that newspapermen "knock around," since journalism is not distinguished for either security or permanence of tenure. The record of the Washington correspondents is relevant to such conceptions, even though the press corps represents a group of journalists who have been more successful, hence more "stable" in their occupational record, than most of the newspapermen in the country.

The ninety special correspondents included in this study have worked for an average of 3.4 papers each. The twenty-seven press association reporters have worked for an average of 2.1 newspapers each. The special correspondents have worked for their *present* paper for an average of 12.5 years. (The median is 10.) The press association reporters have worked for their present organization for an average of 11.3 years. (The median is 10.) Although individual members of the press corps have worked for as many as nine or ten newspaper organizations, the figures suggest a comparative stability of employment by the standards of journalism.

How many Washington correspondents entered upon a journalistic career by deliberate choice, by accident, through personal contact with their first employers, through "pull"? These facts are of interest in understanding the general motivations which characterized newspapermen at the beginning of their careers.

REASONS FOR ENTERING JOURNALISM

REASON	NUMBER	PER CENT
Choice (or "desire to write")	96	75.5
Accident	15	11.8
Personal contact	13	10.2
Fathers' "pull" *	3	2.3

These figures may be compared to those of Harrel, who discovered only 49.6 per cent of his 505 cases as having entered journalism by "deliberate planning," and 26.5 per cent by "chance opportunity." [2] Clearly, the Washington correspondents represent a considerably higher proportion of men who chose to make newspaper work their careers, and a lower proportion who drifted into journalism by accident.

It is interesting to observe that the non-accidental nature of the methods by which the members of the press corps entered journalism is supported by their answers to the question, "If you had your choice over would you choose journalism as a profession?" One hundred and six answered: eighty-seven (82 per cent) said "Yes"; fifteen (14.1 per cent) said "No"; four were uncertain. The degree of satisfaction with newspaper work which this indicates is pronounced.

* Fathers' "pull" was written in by three correspondents; the category was not suggested.

How do the correspondents rate their own assignment? Do they prefer the post in the capital to other journalistic responsibilities? Would they rather be managing editors, foreign correspondents, editorial writers? To test their preferences in this matter the following question was asked: "Which one of the following posts would you most prefer to fill (ignoring salary)?" Eight categories were listed in random order. The answers follow, in order of preference:

Washington Correspondent	52	Managing Editor	6
Roving Reporter	16	Editor-in-Chief	3
Daily Columnist	13	Business Department	2
Foreign Correspondent	10	Editorial Writer	1

Thus, of the 103 who answered, fifty-two chose the Washington assignment. The moral is obvious.

One point of marked interest is the relatively low proportion of correspondents who indicated a preference for a position involving greater responsibility: only six out of 103 would care to be managing editors; only three, editors-in-chief. Obversely, newspaper work with a high degree of freedom of movement, and freedom of choice in the subject-matter of dispatches, ranked second only to the assignment in the capital. Hence the positive attitude towards work in which independence from routine and from office responsibilities are maximized: the jobs of "roving reporter," daily columnist, or foreign correspondent. The significance of this and related aspects of the psychological structure of the Washington correspondents will be discussed later.*

* Chapter XI.

What is the salary of a Washington correspondent? The report of the Treasury Department on salaries over $15,000 in 1934 mentioned figures running as high as $22,000 for Arthur Sears Henning of the Chicago *Tribune*, or $18,000 for Arthur Krock of the New York *Times*.[3] Several correspondents are known to earn $25,000 or more a year. These are, obviously, salaries considerably larger than those of the majority of the press corps, and they are paid to chiefs of Washington bureaus, functioning in a semi-executive capacity. There are newspapermen in the capital who make as little as $1,500 a year.

Eighty-seven Washington correspondents were generous enough to supply this writer with salary information. Because these returns were anonymous the salaries of special correspondents, press association reporters, columnists and syndicated writers cannot be treated separately to point out differences between the groups.

TABLE V

ANNUAL SALARIES OF 87 CORRESPONDENTS *

$1,550-2,400	8	$6,500- 7,400	12	$12,000	1
2,500-3,400	11	7,500- 8,400	6	13,000	1
3,500-4,400	11	8,500- 9,400	5	15,000	1
4,500-5,400	15	9,500- 9,900	1	16,000	1
5,500-6,400	11	10,000-11,000	2	18,000	1

The average salary for the eighty-seven correspondents is $5,987.56 a year. Like all averages, this tends to obscure the extremes. The median salary is $5,400. 21.8 per cent of the group receive less than $3,500 a year; 36.7 per cent

* For a more itemized table see Appendix E.

fall into the salary range under $5,000; 41.3 make between $5,000-7,000 a year; 21.8 per cent earn $7,500 or over a year.

The average salary for the corps is raised sharply by the salaries of several widely syndicated columnists and the heads of press associations and bureaus. It should also be borne in mind that several free-lance correspondents, representing half a dozen or more newspapers each, are included. Undoubtedly, the average salary of press-association reporters in Washington is lower than $5,987.56 a year. But, with whatever qualifications, the salaries of the Washington correspondents compare favorably with those of other professional groups. Surely they are far above the general salaries of newspaperdom. In the fall of 1934 the average weekly salary for the editorial employees of thirty-one representative newspapers (including those in executive positions) was only $41.81 (about $2,184 a year). 17.7 per cent earned from $20 to $30 a week; 19.6 per cent earned between $30 and $40 a week; only 28 per cent had salaries as high as $50 a week ($2,600 a year).[4] Only 11.4 per cent of the Washington correspondents received $2,600 or less a year.

IX. The Attitudes of the Washington Correspondents

BEHIND the depersonalization of a news-dispatch there is a man with a scale of preferences, however undefined, and a philosophy of politics, economics, and society, however unarticulated. What do the Washington correspondents themselves think about the value of the legislation which they cover, the politicians they observe, or the state of the union about which they so often write? There are many articles published each year which suggest "what the corps thinks," but they are the contributions of persons predisposed to favor one side or another of the issue under discussion, or else the evidence is limited to a small number of witnesses.

The 127 correspondents who gave this writer autobiographical information dealing with their education, experience, and professional training were presented with a second questionnaire (see p. 152), designed to get objectified evidence about the *opinions* of the press corps on political and economic matters. Because of the nature of the questions, the questionnaire was *anonymous*, and mailed both from and to this writer. One hundred and seven of the 127 correspondents filled out the questionnaire.

The information which follows supplements the biographical and professional analysis of the Washington correspondents by delineating their personal attitude to

some of the problems which face the society in which they
live.

I. POLITICS

In 1936 the United States was the battleground of
competing interpretations of the Constitution and the role
and power of the President. In a deeper sense, it witnessed a conflict between opposed philosophies of government and opposed principles concerning the degree to
which economic life might be controlled or implemented
by federal action. The Washington correspondents were
at the storm center of the controversy. They interviewed
party and business leaders on both sides of the election
fence, and were exposed to the daily flood of claims,
charges, and affirmations. The press corps has had, by
and large, more concrete and extended contact with the
men and methods that control the political structure than
any other group in the country. Their personal conclusions
concerning contemporary issues take on a singular validity
because of this.

How "radical" is the press corps? Only 21.7 per cent
of them "believe that 'rugged individualism' is the best
economic philosophy today." * 66.3 per cent are opposed
to "rugged individualism" as an economic norm of guidance; 11.8 per cent are uncertain.

A much higher proportion feel that "some form of
government regulation over big business has become imperative." 80 per cent expressed their agreement with

* Statements indicated in quotation marks represent the exact language used in the anonymous questionnaire. See Appendix E.

this statement; 17.1 per cent opposed it; 2.8 per cent were uncertain. Oddly enough, twelve of the twenty-two correspondents who support "rugged individualism" also believe that some degree of government regulation over big business *is* necessary. Apparently, the inescapable contradiction of the two preferences did not occur to them. An effort to get a more specific indication of *how much* "government regulation" the corps thinks desirable showed that 38.4 per cent "favor government operation of mines, public utilities and railroads." 53.9 per cent were opposed to this type of regulation; 7.6 per cent were uncertain. More of them, by 41.6 per cent, favor government regulation to government ownership—even in the sphere of public utilities.

There is a greater amount of agreement on the question of equitable taxation. 67.3 per cent of the press corps "favor higher taxes on the upper income brackets and on huge profits." 23 per cent do not. (9.6 per cent were uncertain.) The annual salary range of those who opposed higher taxes on the upper income brackets was from $2,400 to $9,000; their average salary was $5,494—which is, curiously enough, lower than that of the corps as a whole. Obviously there was not a significant relationship between personal emoluments and convictions about taxation.

The formal political allegiance of the corps is suggested by the votes of eighty-five correspondents on Presidential candidates, as expressed between February and May of 1936. Fifty-four (63.5 per cent) were for Roosevelt; twenty-six (30.5 per cent) were for a Republican candidate.* (Governor Landon had not yet been nominated; the correspondents wrote in their choice for the Presidency.) Norman Thomas received four votes; Earl Browder, one.

It is interesting to observe how the Washington correspondents' choice of a candidate differed from that of the country as a whole during approximately the same period. The American Institute of Public Opinion poll ("the Gallup poll") for February 16, 1936, showed that the voters were favoring Mr. Roosevelt against the field by a narrow margin.[1] A comparison is illuminating:

	GALLUP POLL PER CENT	85 CORRESPONDENTS PER CENT
Roosevelt	50.3	63.5
Republican	43.0	30.5
Socialist	2.1	4.7
Third Parties	4.6	1.1 (Browder)

The press corps was at this time significantly more pro-Roosevelt than the country as a whole, less pro-Republican, and slightly more pro-Socialist.

II. FOREIGN AFFAIRS

Newspapermen do not like to fill our questionnaires. The limitations of space and the necessity of sparing the correspondents' time in the unexciting business of filling out a long, mimeographed, cross-examination of attitudes

* Landon—8; Vandenberg—8; Borah—4; Hoover—2; Knox—1; Wadsworth—1; Robert Taft—1; "The Republican candidate"—1.

made only three questions on foreign affairs possible. The questions chosen were those most conspicuously in the focus of attention in Washington at the time.

Forty-seven out of 105 correspondents (44.8 per cent) believe that "The United States should enter the World Court, with reservations as to its jurisdiction." Only one less, forty-six (43.8 per cent), are opposed to participation in the World Court. Twelve (10.4 per cent) were uncertain.

30.4 per cent agree that "The United States should co-operate more energetically with the League of Nations;" but 55.2 per cent do not.

43.8 per cent feel that "if European nations can afford to arm they can pay us the War Debts"; 40.9 per cent, recognizing the fallacy in the statement,* disagreed.

The Washington correspondents, it is clear, are closely divided in their attitude concerning American entry into the World Court; but a majority oppose further co-operation with the League of Nations. Since the wording of the questions was broad and mild, stating "with reservations as to its jurisdiction" in the case of the World Court and suggesting no more than "more energetic co-operation" (not membership) in the case of the League of Nations, it may be concluded that a majority of the press corps favors American isolation from these two central international bodies. The Washington correspondents are hardly "international" in their attitudes on foreign affairs. They

---

* The War Debts must be paid either in gold or U. S. dollars; but the indebted nations can buy munitions from their private industrialists with their own currency. Payment of the War Debts involves the problem of the international transfer of funds.

are drawn from communities with emphatic isolationist opinions; they have been inculcated with the symbols of our traditional Isolationism. They represent newspapers the majority of which pay deference to the "no entangling alliances" of Thomas Jefferson (and attributed to George Washington). Their vote on the question of paying the War Debts suggests a lack of information about the foremost *bête noire* of our foreign relations. The 43.8 per cent who accept the cliché, "If European nations can afford to arm, they can afford to pay us the War Debts," betray a lack of familiarity with the economics of the situation.

Since the overwhelming majority of the correspondents treat American news, and news often of interest largely to the city or state in which their newspaper is published, they do not achieve much sophistication in the realm of foreign affairs. They leave State Department coverage to the press associations and the correspondents from foreign journals. Most of them are not expected to become adept in writing stories on world affairs. And most of them make no pretenses of confidence amidst the complicated, technical, and deceptive details of international relations.

III. JOURNALISM

The opinions of the correspondents on matters pertaining to journalism are of obvious interest and significance. Which newspapers and which press associations do they regard as most fair and reliable? For which papers would they today choose to work, disregarding salary and security considerations? What do they think of the press in its wider setting: its capital-labor emphases, its treatment of the economic conflicts which underlie contemporary events, its standards of what makes news?

NEWSPAPERS

The members of the press corps were asked to state "the three newspapers which give the most fair and reliable news," in order of their estimation. Out of ninety-nine returns, eighty-nine mentioned the New York *Times* for either first, second or third place; forty-eight named the Baltimore *Sun;* eighteen gave a Scripps-Howard paper. Assigning an arbitrary value of 10 for the first choice, 5 for second, and 3 for third, the results may be listed according to the score:

The New York *Times,* which is read most widely among the Washington correspondents, as we have seen, is also rated "the most fair and reliable" newspaper by a striking plurality. The Baltimore *Sun,* in second place, far outdistances other newspapers. In close succession follow the *Christian Science Monitor,* the Scripps-Howard papers, and the St. Louis *Post-Dispatch.*

As significant as the newspapers voted the fairest and most reliable are those which the correspondents designated "least fair and reliable." The results are equally emphatic. Out of ninety-three returns, no less than eighty-seven cited a Hearst newspaper for the dubious honor of being one of the three most unfair and unreliable papers in the country. Seventy-one named the *Chicago Tribune;* twenty-five the Los Angeles *Times.*

TABLE VI *

TEN NEWSPAPERS CONSIDERED "MOST FAIR AND RELIABLE"
BY 99 WASHINGTON CORRESPONDENTS

PAPER	1ST CHOICE	POINTS	2ND	POINTS	3RD	POINTS	NUMBER MENTIONS	TOTAL POINTS
N. Y. *Times*	64	640	16	80	9	27	89	747
Baltimore *Sun*	14	140	21	105	13	39	48	284
Christian Science Monitor	3	30	9	45	5	15	17	90
Scripps-Howard Papers †	4	40	6	30	5	15	15	85
St. Louis *Post-Dispatch*	2	20	8	40	8	24	18	84
Washington *Star*	2	20	8	40	4	12	14	72
N. Y. *Herald Tribune*	0	0	8	40	9	27	17	67
Washington *Post*	3	30	2	10	0	0	5	40
Phila. *Record*	2	20	3	15	0	0	5	35
Kansas City *Star*	0	0	1	5	6	18	7	23

Using the same 10-5-3 scoring scale, the correspondents'
poll shows:

The unchallenged position of the Hearst papers in the
dishonor roll of professional newspapermen needs little

* This table gives only the ten newspapers which were mentioned
most often. A complete list of this and succeeding tables is in Appendix E.

† Some correspondents wrote "Scripps-Howard"; others named a
Scripps-Howard paper. It was thought advisable to combine the votes
in one group.

comment. The Chicago *Tribune* and the Los Angeles *Times* occupy a firm place in the unenviable second and third places. It is interesting that almost as many corre-

TABLE VII

TEN NEWSPAPERS CONSIDERED "LEAST FAIR AND RELIABLE"
BY 93 WASHINGTON CORRESPONDENTS

PAPER	1ST CHOICE	POINTS	2ND	POINTS	3RD	POINTS	NUMBER MENTIONS	TOTAL POINTS
Hearst news- papers *	59	590	20	100	8	24	87	714
Chicago *Tribune*	24	240	37	185	10	30	71	455
Los Angeles *Times*	2	20	7	35	16	48	25	103
Scripps-Howard	4	40	5	25	4	12	13	77
Denver *Post*	0	0	4	20	6	18	10	38
N. Y. *Herald Tribune*	0	0	4	20	4	12	8	32
Washington *Post*	2	20	1	5	2	6	5	31
Phila. *Record*	0	0	3	15	5	15	8	30
Daily Worker (N.Y.)	1	10	1	5	2	6	4	21
Phila. *Inquirer*	1	10	1	5	2	6	4	21

spondents voted the Scripps-Howard papers "least fair and reliable" as voted them "most fair and reliable." This springs from the fact that these organs, distinguished for an aggressive news and editorial policy of "liberal" tone,

* Fifty-six correspondents wrote "Hearst papers," thirty-one mentioned a Hearst paper by name. As in the case of the Scripps-Howard chain, it was considered advisable to combine the results under the one group "Hearst papers."

are considered to violate strict "objectivity" by indulging in that most heinous of journalistic sins—crusading. Almost as many correspondents consider the Philadelphia *Record* and the Washington *Post* unfair and unreliable as the reverse. (The Philadelphia *Record* follows the tone and format of the New York *Post;* both are published by J. David Stern.*)

We have, thus, objective evidence of which newspapers the Washington correspondents read and how they rate the papers of the land, in order of both reliability and unreliability. Insight into the journalistic norms of the press corps is enriched by seeing for which newspapers the Washington correspondents would choose to work, if they had complete freedom of choice. The anonymous questionnaire asked: "If salary and security were no consideration, for which three papers would you most prefer to be a Washington correspondent? (In order of preference.)" Eighty-seven correspondents answered. Again alloting 10 points for first choice, 5 for second, and 3 for third, the order is:

By this standard, too, the New York *Times* is far ahead of the other newspapers of the country. It is the journal read most widely in the press corps, considered most fair and reliable by them, and would be the one for which sixty-eight out of eighty-seven of the correspondents in the capital would work if they had their choice. These facts are a striking tribute to the reputation of the *Times* and an indication of the prestige it occupies among a body

* One vote placed the New York *Post* as the second "least reliable" paper. That would add three points, if the J. David Stern papers were combined in our rating, moving them up one place in the order.

of experienced and skilled newspapermen. The position of the Baltimore *Sun* is second only to that of the New York *Times*. The St. Louis *Post-Dispatch* is third, and fourth according to the rating of fairness and reliability.

TABLE VIII

NEWSPAPERS FOR WHICH 87 CORRESPONDENTS WOULD PREFER TO WORK

PAPER	1ST CHOICE	POINTS	2ND	POINTS	3RD	POINTS	NUMBER MENTIONS	TOTAL POINTS
New York *Times*	31	310	16	80	21	63	68	453
Baltimore *Sun*	11	110	19	95	32	96	62	291
St. Louis *Post-Dispatch*	6	60	8	40	17	51	32	151
N. Y. *Herald Tribune*	4	40	12	60	8	24	24	124
Scripps-Howard	9	90	3	15	6	18	18	123
Phila. *Record* or N. Y. *Post*	5	50	6	30	1	3	12	81
Christian Science *Monitor*	4	40	0	0	3	9	7	49
Hearst papers	2	20	1	5	1	3	4	28
Kansas City *Star*	1	10	0	0	5	15	6	25
Chicago *Daily News*	1	10	1	5	1	3	3	18

The New York *Herald Tribune* is read second only to the New York *Times* and the Washington papers, is rated as the fourth most desirable paper for which to work, but is placed as the seventh "most fair and reliable" paper and is sixth in the list of papers considered "least fair and reliable." The *Christian Science Monitor,* which is not read widely among the Washington newspapermen, is rated the third most reliable newspaper in the country, but is not that high on the list of desired employers. This is no doubt due to the fact that most reporters are not attracted to the policy of the *Monitor* on news of illness, death, and violence—whether political or human. (For many years the *Monitor* did not use "death," "Santa Claus," or "died" in its news columns and it shows a tendency to emphasize amicable international relations as against crises and war threats.*) More men would like to work for either the Scripps-Howard or the Hearst papers than consider them "most fair and reliable"—which suggests a point observed by this writer: that some reporters have no illusions about the "objectivity" of their newspapers or their own dispatches but would enjoy the chance to indulge their own preferences and hostilities under the protecting aegis of a paper with whose biases they agree.

PRESS AGENCIES

The rise of the press agencies, serving hundreds of newspapers all over the nation, has been one of the dominant characteristics of twentieth-century journalism. The universal coverage of these organizations and the efficiency with which they dispatch and collect news from every corner of the world is a marvel of synchronous operation and news-gathering methods. Modern journalism depends

* One correspondent suggests that the name *Christian Science Monitor* does not elicit professional approval: "were it named just *The Monitor* I think there would be a different attitude."

upon their services to an increasing degree. Nearly all newspapers are spared the expense of having special correspondents in news-centers outside of their city either by being affiliated members of the Associated Press, or by buying the services of the United Press, International News Service, or Central News of America. There are smaller press agencies in different regions of the country.

The power and importance of these organizations makes the opinions of the Washington correspondents about them especially interesting. Since special correspondents in Washington compete against reporters for the press agencies, read their stories, and follow their activities, the press corps is peculiarly competent to pass judgment upon the relative merits of the dispatches of the several associations.

Ninety-seven Washington correspondents expressed their choice of press agencies *and* the reasons for that choice. They made a check opposite the name of one of the four leading associations, in answer to the question: "I prefer the stories of (check *one*); AP —, UP —, INS —, US —." The tabulated results show:

PRESS ASSOCIATION	NUMBER OF CORRESPONDENTS	PER CENT OF 97
United Press	48	49.4
Associated Press	44	45.3
International News Service	4	4.1
Universal Service	1	1.0

The question was followed by the dependent clause: "because they are: better written —, more reliable —, more liberal —." The correspondents were free to check as many of these reasons as they felt to apply to the press association they had selected. The results are illuminating:

PRESS ASSOCIATION	"BETTER WRITTEN"	"MORE RELIABLE"	"MORE LIBERAL"
United Press	42	19	27
Associated Press	5	43	..
International News Service	3	4	..
Universal Service	1	..	..

Several striking conclusions may be drawn from the evidence. The United Press dispatches are slightly more popular with the Washington correspondents than those of the Associated Press.* International News Service and Universal Service are not regarded highly. But the men who selected the United Press dispatches were more impressed by their style, their structure, and their liberalism than by their superior reliability as against those of the Associated Press. Whereas forty-two out of the forty-eight newspapermen who preferred the United Press stories felt that they are better written, and twenty-seven felt that they are more liberal, only nineteen would commit themselves to the view that they are "more reliable." The correspondents who chose the Associated Press dispatches were almost unanimous in agreeing that they were "more reliable" (forty-three out of forty-four). Only five felt that the Associated Press news accounts are better written. None felt that they are more liberal.

These figures achieve significance from another point of view. It is of some consequence that professional newspapermen prefer the dispatches of an organization which

* Nine Associated Press reporters were included in the 127 correspondents to whom the questionnaires were submitted, seven from the United Press, five from International News Service, two from Universal Service.

permits latitude of style, which "makes" news by exploration, inquiry, and its own initiative, and which encourages a liberal as against a conservative spirit, to those of an organization which emphasizes expository rather than attractive writing, does not try to create stories, and fosters a dominantly non-committal or conservative tone. Despite the value placed on "objectivity" in journalistic circles more newspapermen prefer to *read* news which is interesting and liberal than news which is generally reliable but dull—and "conservative."

In psychological terms it appears that the professional obligation of observing caution and detachment injects a certain frustration into newspapermen who also have preferences and hopes about the political materials which they handle; and that many of them prefer the news which buttresses their own preferences to the news which, however much more they are conscious of its reliability, is more dispassionate, less revealing, and less consoling.

GRIEVANCES

The complaints of a professional group are an excellent index to the working conditions which affect them negatively. To what aspects of their work do the Washington correspondents object? Ninety-four answers were received to the following question:

"Ignoring salary, what is the worst part of the Washington correspondent's job?"

No categories were suggested; space was allowed for a description of grievances. Many newspapermen described more than one complaint; each was recorded separately. The results fell into thirteen categories.

COMPLAINTS OF 94 CORRESPONDENTS

	NUMBER MEN
Hours ("long," "uncertain," "no home life," "few vacations," "on call 24 hours a day," etc.)	21
Home Office Queries ("ignorance of editors," "covering unimportant local news," "poor co-operation from home office," etc.)	18
Routine ("daily grind," "checking facts," "covering third-rate events for protection," "getting trivial details," etc.)	13
Politicians, Congressmen ("covering petty and ignorant men," "enforced association with Congressmen," "reporting hypocrites," "treating insincere, self-minded men seriously," etc.)	12
Publishers' Interference ("running publishers' chores," "lobbying for the boss," "requests to use influence," "pleasing the publisher," "writing what is wanted, not what is important," etc.)	11
Subject Matter ("range of stories," "complexity of news," "difficulty of interpreting events," "covering too many stories in limited time," etc.)	6
Government Routine and Officials ("red tape," "government agencies' handling of news," "bureaucracy," "dumb press relations men," etc.)	5
Tension ("inability to relax," "tension of work all the time")	5
Propagandists ("spotting propagandists," "handling too many government handouts," "fighting off special pleaders")	5

	NUMBER MEN
A Daily Story ("having to produce one story a day, whether important or not," "pressure to produce daily")	5
Boredom ("keeping from being bored in the capital." "ennui")	2
Personal ("doing someone else's proselytizing instead of my own")	1
Social Life ("artificial circles to mix in")	1

The correspondents' complaint against the long and irregular hours during which they work or are obliged to be on call is not unexpected. It is a grievance common to newspapermen everywhere. What is more revealing is their irritation with the queries rained upon them by their home offices: questions of fact, inquiries on stories which have been dispatched, suggestions for future stories. The necessity of covering petty events which seem more important to the editors on the desk (who retain a local perspective) than to the Washington correspondents (who are plunged into news with national outlines) creates wide discontent. The "stupidity of the office," the "ignorance of the editor," "poor co-operation in sending leads," the "interference of the desk," are common topics of commiseration among newspapermen who would prefer to assess and treat news without concession to the provincial restrictions of the home office. As the Washington correspondent becomes more completely an extension of the city desk, compelled to operate as if the capital were a "beat" rather than a large field in which freedom of movement and choice should exist, he chafes under the tightened reins which rob him of much of his independence. Irritation with the home office is evidenced in the laments against routine, much of which consists in covering events of negligible importance for the sake of "protecting" the newspaper.

Newspapermen thrust into daily contact with Congressmen develop a profound dislike for many of them. They see the solons without benefit of public "front." They are cynical once they have grasped the ignorance, pettiness, and ineptitude which some politicians bring to the chambers of Congress. More important, the correspondents are compelled, by circumstance and the traditions of political journalism in the United States, to gild the lily of reality —reporting chicanery without indignation and clothing the nonsense of demagogic oratory in the undisturbed language of news dispatches. This creates a sense of both frustration and guilt. Congressmen often assume an irritating conception of their status: newspapermen with years of experience in the capital may have to cool their heels in the anterooms of men for whom they have little respect. Sometimes they have to "play up" for the sake of getting a story, or have to wait in impotence until a political hack deigns to enlighten them on matters of public interest. The inability to "let off steam" and "expose" political charlatans intensifies hostility.

The complaints against publishers and publishers' interference is left for extended discussion in Chapter X. The displeasure with the complexity and range of the news for which the press corps is held responsible, with government red tape, private propagandists, the necessity of turning out a story a day and the unrelieved tension which that precipitates—these are obvious once the duties of the correspondents are visualized. The fact that two correspondents find the seemingly romantic job of covering the capital a bore is worth notice. And a silent tribute is due the hardy soul who confessed his or her unhappiness with the necessity of doing "someone else's proselytizing—instead of my own." The comment shows psychological insight.

A NEWSPAPER GUILD

The growth of the American Newspaper Guild, a national trade union organization affiliated with the American Federation of Labor, has been a salient feature of the journalistic history of the past four years. It was a guild case, that of Morris Watson against the Associated Press, which was used to test an important phase of the National Labor Relations Act (the Wagner Act) before the Supreme Court—meeting the claim that federal regulation of employer-employee relations in newspaper work challenged the constitutional freedom of the press. By June of 1937 the American Newspaper Guild had 11,112 members in over 250 local chapters,[2] and had made striking gains in concluding salary, contract and other arrangements with publishers.

The natural seeds for a guild movement are familiar to anyone who is aware of the low salaries, the inadequate vacations, and, above all, the impulsive hiring and firing which have always characterized newspaper employment. Reporters have found contracts a luxury confined to high-salaried men, columnists, and feature writers.

The Washington correspondents are in a favored position as newspaper work goes. Their salaries are high, their security is much greater than that of local newspaper men, they enjoy prestige in their home offices.* Above all, they have the consciousness of success and the knowledge that they are marked for either a long and undisturbed career in the capital or for further advancement in their organization. Members of the press corps who have been discharged by one newspaper have found little difficulty in being hired by another; others have discovered that, upon severing their relations with a paper, their experience and contacts in the capital open lucrative posts to them in the public relations sections of private pressure groups or the government. Many correspondents guard against emergencies by keeping their "contacts" alive.

In this light, the attitude of the press corps to the American Newspaper Guild takes on a unique significance. The answers to eight questions in the anonymous questionnaire offer a cross section of the attitude of the press corps to a labor organization of newspaper men and women.

"I favor *a* Newspaper Guild to improve salaries and contract and bargain collectively." †

Of 103 correspondents who answered, fifty-eight (56.3 per cent) agreed; thirty-eight (36.8 per cent) disagreed;

---

* Generally, they know their publishers and have a friendly personal rapport with them: they are thus spared the corrosive anonymity of ordinary reporters.

† The indefinite article was italicized because what was wanted was the press corps' reaction to unionization rather than the Newspaper Guild. Some correspondents do not approve of the leading personalities in the American Newspaper Guild, or the more energetic guild members in Washington.

seven (6.7 per cent) were uncertain. Those who favor a guild have a salary range of $1,500 to $16,000; those who do not, $1,500 to $18,000. The median salary for both groups is $5,000. The average salary of those who support a guild is $4,919.61; of those who oppose— $4,907.64. Obviously the salary range, average, and median is strikingly close for both groups: apparently there is no significant relationship between present income and opinions on a newspaperman's union.*

But the single attitude to a reporters' union is not enough for our purposes. It is in an exploration of related issues that results pertinent to the psychology of the press corps are found.

"It is unethical for newspapermen to form into unions." Only 16.1 per cent (of 93 answers) felt this statement to be true; 74.1 per cent disagreed with it, defending the ethics of organization—a point vigorously challenged by publishers; 9.6 per cent were uncertain.

53.6 per cent deny that "newspapermen should not strike, nor use the threat of strike." 29 per cent hold to this view. But 17.2 per cent were uncertain, a high proportion as compared to other returns. On this question, it is clear, the press corps has less certainty. The professional taboo on newspapermen striking is still strong enough to explain the relative indecision.

* Ten of the thirty-eight who oppose a guild did not give their salaries, to six of the thirty-eight who favor it. Assuming that the higher-salaried men hesitated to state their annual income, the salary range and average for guild opponents would be higher than our figures indicate.

Would a guild "make reporters partisan in treating labor and union news"? Opponents of the labor movement, especially newspaper proprietors and the American Newspaper Publishers' Association, stand or fall by this argument. What do the Washington correspondents think? 37.2 per cent hold that a guild would create partisanship by reporters in handling news in which, as union members, they would have an emotional vested interest; 46.8 per cent believe that it would not; 16 per cent, again a high percentage, are uncertain. The figures show that when faced with the problem of partisanship, as with the problem of the strike, the press corps shows relative uncertainty. This appears to reflect the uncertainty of newspapermen in general on these two aspects of guild organization.

Would a reporters' union tend to "become too radical" and does that worry newspapermen, with their traditional suspicion of radicals? 51 per cent of the press corps do not believe that a guild would become "too radical"; 22.8 per cent do; 26 per cent were uncertain. Since the question involves an unknown fact in the future, the high degree of uncertainty is explicable.

"A good newspaperman doesn't need a guild: it is organized for the lazy, the incompetent or the mediocre." This acidulous conception is denied by 61 per cent of the press corps and defended by 29.4 per cent. (9.4 per cent are uncertain.)

Lastly, there is great interest in the replies to two other questions. "Newspapermen are individualists and craftsmen, not in a class with labor." 60 per cent of the Washington correspondents agree with this distinction. Oddly enough, out of the fifty-eight members of the press corps who are in favor of a guild, twenty-one believe that newspapermen "are individualists and craftsmen, not in a class with labor." Of the thirty-eight who oppose a guild, thirty-five hold to this view, which is consistent and understandable.

How many correspondents in Washington, given the salary, status, and security advantages they enjoy, feel that "I have nothing to gain by joining a guild"? 56.9 per cent agree that the statement represents their personal position. One-third of the press corps (33.3 per cent) believe that they do stand to gain by membership; 9.6 per cent are uncertain. Of the fifty-eight who believe in the guild, twenty-two testify that they have nothing to gain by joining; twenty-eight recognize possible gains. But of the thirty-eight who are against a guild, thirty state that they have nothing to gain. One feels that he has something to gain. (Three were uncertain; four did not answer this particular question.)

The salary ranges of those who feel there are or are not personal benefits for them in guild membership show a direct relationship between income and attitude on the point.

1. The average salary of the twenty-nine men who favor the guild and feel that they have something to gain by joining it is $5,525.18.

2. The average salary of the twenty-two correspondents who favor the guild and feel they have nothing to gain by enrolling in it is $6,637.22.

3. The average salary of the twenty-nine who oppose

the guild and also believe that they can expect no gain from joining it is $7,010.50.*

THE AMERICAN NEWSPAPER GUILD

In contemporary society, the ideal of status has been replaced by the concept of class.[3] This poses a distasteful problem to intellectuals and members of the professions, who prefer the earlier and more flattering system of prestige values. The professions are today split within themselves, between the pious Haves and the impious Have-Nots. Corporation lawyers have identified themselves with a different social level than lawyers without clients or lawyers engaged in defending civil liberties. The birth of the American Lawyers' Guild is an overt indication of a bifurcation within the legal ranks. In medicine, the specialists and the fashionable doctors are faced with the growing discontent of doctors who have no patients, or physicians who look towards socialized medicine. Among teachers, actors, architects, writers, engineers, and now newspapermen, the movement towards trade unionism has challenged the philosophy of conservative professional associations.

Since newspapermen, unlike lawyers or doctors, are employees, conscious of an employer relationship, they are more receptive to trade union organization. They have received less deference than men of true professional stand-

* Not all the men stated their salaries. The averages are computed from twenty-seven salary returns in group 1, twenty-two in group 2, and twenty in group 3. The differences would probably be larger if all had given their salaries.

ing. Their security is subject to the whims and moods of city editors and publishers. During the depression they saw dismissals, lay-offs, and salary cuts effected with cold-blooded efficiency. Where a physician or attorney might blame "the depression" or "society" for his depleted income the reporter fixed his grievances squarely on a boss. The excessive hours, low pay, inadequate vacations, and incessant tensions of newspaper work have produced a natural desire among newspapermen for better working conditions, greater security and collective contractual agreements.

The Washington correspondents, on the whole, have retained fewer illusions about publishers than reporters elsewhere. They have witnessed the tactics of high-minded press magnates in fighting an NRA code, a Child Labor Amendment, and the Wagner Act. They are cynical of the nobility of purpose of the American Newspaper Publishers' Association or the American Society of Newspaper Editors—both of which oppose the guild movement. They have seen their employers meddle in politics and have sometimes been required to aid in the meddling. They know the pecuniary calculations for which publishers have fought tariffs on news pulp and paper while they supported tariffs on other commodities. As employees they have been compelled to recognize the concrete meaning of labor's relation to "capital." But with reference to trade unionism the corps is split within itself, as the figures on the seven questions pertaining to the American Newspaper Guild show.

The older Washington correspondents, heads of bureaus in a semi-executive capacity, are an élite in their own profession. They have access to the semi-aristocratic levels of society and politics. Many are home owners. They send their children to universities or finishing schools. They live in Chevy Chase or Virginia. They are consulted by their superiors on matters of policy. They are friends of their editors and publishers. They may become editors themselves. Their personal identity is not robbed by anonymous reporting or impersonal orders. These men exist in a different material and psychological environment than the reporter who makes under $3,500 a year and is unfamiliar with dinners in full dress.

From this point of view, there is a definite cleavage in the press corps. The Gridiron Club, for example, is not distinguished for welcoming certain men to its fraternal bosom. It is composed of the respected and respectable elders of the press corps, and those younger correspondents whose clothes, manners, and politics give no cause for social anxiety. The Gridiron Club has many points of characterization which suggest an exclusive college fraternity. It is not surprising, then, to find that many newspapermen in the capital speak of it with less than reverence. This writer heard many charges that the organization is used by correspondents to flatter their publishers (in the form of invitations to the annual Gridiron dinner) and by publishers to flatter their advertisers. The value of membership in the Gridiron Club is very great to a Washington correspondent, since it enhances his prestige with his employer. Raises in salary sometimes coincide with initiation into the order. The expenses involved in membership in the Gridiron Club are not negligible.*

* Initiation fee, the cost of the annual dinner, entertainment for out-of-town guests to the dinner, etc. Some publishers help foot the

Many correspondents have a happy rapport with their employers. They are well paid, treated well, and speak with liking of "the boss." Such men as "Joe" Patterson of the New York *Daily News*, J. David Stern of the Philadelphia *Record* and New York *Post*, Colonel Robert R. McCormick of the Chicago *Tribune*, or Roy Howard of the Scripps-Howard organization, to name a few, are regarded with genuine personal affection by their Washington correspondents. "They treat the boys right." This does not prevent the boys from joining the Guild as a matter of principle, as a form of reserve protection, and—more commonly—as an expression of a desire to strengthen the newspaperman's position against *publishers* rather than a publisher. The Washington Newspaper Guild is composed of different units of organization. It consisted of 507 members, as of May 28, 1937. Forty-three Associated Press reporters were affiliated with the AP unit, the United Press section had forty members, the Scripps-Howard Newspaper Alliance eight, Central News of America eight. There were sixty-seven special correspondents (i.e., out-of-town correspondents) in the Correspondents' unit. Some special correspondents are affiliated with the Guild through membership in home-office units rather than in the capital. The Washington *Star* unit had seventy-one members, the Washington *Post* fifty-three, the Washington *Times* forty-nine, the Washington *Herald* thirty-seven. The Guild units of papers published in the capital include local re-

bills of rooms at the Willard Hotel, where the correspondents dispense cocktails and highballs, before and after the dinner, for guests and friends. The cost of "these shindigs" has been estimated at $100 by one correspondent.

porters, re-write men, desk men, etc.—not included in this study as members of the press corps.*

The events of the past four years have deepened the press corps' "labor consciousness." In this they reflect the wider formations of the times. Sympathy for the social legislation of the New Deal created a psychological schism, between many correspondents and their employers, for which there had been no occasion in the days of more conventional political action in the capital. The Washington Newspaper Guild, in a sense the aristocracy of newspapermen, is less radical than the journalistic "proletariat." In July of 1937, the Washington organization opened an attack upon the leadership of Heywood Broun, President of the American Newspaper Guild, for his official support of and identification with John L. Lewis and the CIO movement. A year earlier the Washington newspapermen had tended to support industrial unionism, but the succession of sit-down strikes, violence, and confused leadership precipitated opposition in the ranks of the press corps.

THE PRESS

What is the testimony of the Washington correspondents on the more conspicuous criticisms of American journalism which have been made by educators, clergymen, liberals, and the laity? Five questions were put to the press corps which throw a light on their attitude to the more common charges against the fourth estate.

"The press devotes too much space to trivialities: scan-

* All figures were supplied by the Secretary of the Washington Newspaper Guild on May 28, 1937.

dals, sensations, divorce stories, etc." 60.5 per cent of the 104 correspondents who answered, agreed; 29.8 per cent disagreed; 9.6 were undecided.

"Comparatively few papers give significant accounts of our basic economic conflicts." One hundred and five correspondents answered this statement: ninety-one agreed (86.6 per cent—the highest degree of unanimity in thirty-eight questions), twelve disagreed (11.4 per cent), two were uncertain.

But there was far less agreement when this general statement was narrowed down to a sharper one: "In general, news columns are equally fair to big business and labor." At first glance it would seem that approximately the same number who felt that the press does not give significant accounts of the basic economic conflicts of our society would hold that news columns are *not* equally fair to big business and to labor. But 43.8 per cent of the press corps held the second statement to be true—that is, holding that big business and labor are treated with equal justice. 48.5 per cent declared this to be false. (7.6 per cent were uncertain.)

The apparent contradiction may be explained in this way: most correspondents agree that newspapers do not offer meaningful accounts of the nation's economic conflicts; but they disagree that this is the consequence of partisanship with reference to news about industry and labor. It may be, as was suggested to this writer, that they feel that the press does not devote enough space, enough detail, enough prominence, or enough emphasis to news with a predominant social-economic content—but that when it does, the capital and labor components of the news are treated with fairly equal justice. 43.8 per cent of the press corps seem to defend this position.

Many correspondents are convinced that labor news which originates in the capital is given wide dissemination and a fair "play" in the newspapers today. They point to the striking amount of front-page labor news since 1933. They maintain that the lobby of the American Federation of Labor and the informal pressure of the Committee for Industrial Organization represent a power as effective as any in the capital. They believe that the press which these and other national labor groups get might well be envied by the Chamber of Commerce or the Iron and Steel Institute.

The press corps was in the thick of the fight of the newspaper publishers against the NRA code. Some of the correspondents acted as agents for their publishers in getting information, sounding out opinions, suggesting to Congressmen what the preferences of the publishers were. Many were under an obligation to sound the "Freedom of the Press" alarum. Many believed the code was bad. How did the correspondents themselves feel about the publishers' stand on the issue? The question was put to them:

"The publishers' cry of 'Freedom of the Press' in fighting an NRA code was a ruse."

One hundred and five answered. Sixty-seven (63.8 per cent) agreed. Twenty-six (24.7 per cent) disagreed. Twelve (11.4 per cent) were uncertain.

On a related question, 46.2 per cent of 106 correspondents agreed that "most papers printed unfair or distorted stories about the Tugwell Pure Foods Bill." 21.6 per cent disagreed with this statement; 32 per cent, a very high proportion, were uncertain.* The discussion of publishers, correspondents, and social legislation is reserved for a later chapter. At this point it will suffice to point out that when 63.8 per cent of the press corps believe that the "freedom of the press" was a red herring in the publishers' fight against an NRA code, and when 46.2 per cent feel that newspapers in general printed unfair or distorted stories about the Tugwell Bill, the famed objectivity of the press on at least two important issues is open to serious challenge.

* There were complaints that the statement was worded too broadly to permit a definite reaction. The complaints seem justified by the large number of "uncertains."

X. "Policy" and the Washington Correspondents

THE question about which there is most curiosity and argument, in Washington newspaper circles, in the discussions in liberal journals, and among the reading public at large, is, "How *free* is a newspaperman to write up the news as he honestly sees and understands it?" The question was asked of this writer more than any other. Sometimes the question took the form of dogmatic statement: "Everyone knows they have to write what the publishers want;" or was couched in a sedulous assertion: "They'd be fired if they didn't cater to their home offices;" or appeared as a leading question: "Why are they sent to Washington, and why are they kept there?"

Any answer unsupported by objective evidence is properly open to the charge of generalization from isolated cases or subjective biases. In an effort to gain objectified evidence, the Washington correspondents were asked seven questions (in the anonymous questionnaire) which approached this problem from several points of view. Seven typical statements, which had been made to this writer by various newspapermen, were presented to the special correspondents, to be checked with symbols for "Yes," "No," or "Uncertain." The statements were omitted from the form which was sent to syndicated writers, columnists, and reporters for the press associations, because these men do not work for a single employer and would not be as sharply subjected to a restrictive "policy" as newspapermen responsible to only a single publisher. The results have greater validity because of this selection of witnesses. Of the 107 questionnaires returned, eighty contained the statements which we now consider.

First, are the special correspondents in the capital *aware* of a defined "policy" on the paper for which they work? The question was put in this form:

"I am not aware of any definite, fixed 'policy' on my paper." *

Seventy correspondents answered. Twenty-three (32.8 per cent) agreed with the statement. Forty-two (60 per cent) disagreed: i.e., they testified that they *are* aware of a definite policy. Five (7.1 per cent) were uncertain.

The point was approached from another angle. This writer had heard correspondents say: "My orders are to be objective, but I *know* how my paper wants stories played." The statement was included in the questionnaire in exactly this form. Out of sixty-six answers, forty (60.6 per cent) agreed. Twenty-three (34.7 per cent) disagreed. Three (4.5 per cent) were uncertain.

Now newspaper "policy" means several things. It does

* The negative statement, while undesirable as a questionnaire method, had specific advantages in this instance. If the question had read "I *am* aware of a definite, fixed 'policy' " it would have aroused psychological resistance and suspicion; it would have seemed a "loaded" question. In the negative form this danger was minimized. Tested reactions to both forms of the question, made before the questionnaire was mimeographed, indicated the superiority of the form finally used.

not mean that all the correspondents in Washington are the "tools" of their publishers. A correspondent who sincerely holds to a Democratic or Republican philosophy of politics or tends to favor a "conservative" or a "liberal" point of view may be working for a newspaper with whose editorial and journalistic policy he honestly agrees. He does not slant the news to curry favor with "the Boss"; he sees the news pretty much in the way his editors or publisher see it. Policy is rarely enforced by "policy orders" from the home office, telling a correspondent to "lay off" a certain case, or "play up Jack Robinson's testimony in the investigation."

The policy of a newspaper is maintained through less conscious and more subtle channels: through a choice of personnel, through subjective adjustments on the part of reporters, and through the institutionalization of a scale of values within the organization. A newspaperman who has worked for seven or ten years on the Oswego *Bugle* may have been attuned to the general policy of his paper by temperament, or has incorporated the perspective and the standards of the *Bugle* into his own thinking. He has developed a skill in evaluating and interpreting events in a manner which will give him the most favorable response from his superiors. He has learned that, whether by unconscious preference or calculated design, his editors find stories of a certain type "good" or "bad," cut some news-accounts and kill others, place certain dispatches on the front pages and others on the back pages. As a human being the reporter adjusts himself to the tastes of other human beings who pass judgment upon his work. The personal equation is true of journalism in Moscow or

Rome as well as in New York. Critics of the "capitalistic press" are inclined to forget this.

These comments take on weight when considered in the light of the answers which eighty correspondents made to the following question:

"In my experience I've had stories played down, cut or killed for 'policy' reasons."

Forty correspondents (55.5 per cent) checked "Yes." Thirty (41.6 per cent) checked "No." Two (2.7 per cent) were uncertain.

By the time the reporter for the *Bugle* is sent to cover the capital as a special correspondent, he has demonstrated a type of journalistic skill which arouses no anxieties in the minds of his editors or publisher. The reporter whose dispatches displease his superiors, who is thought to be a "crusader," a "radical," or a man with one bias or another, may simply not get to Washington.

The degree to which the individual correspondent has absorbed the philosophy of the newspaper into his own thinking may be seen in the following incident. The writer was interviewing a correspondent for a newspaper in the Middle West who stated, with considerable firmness, that he had never received a "policy order" and was absolutely free to interpret the news as he saw fit—short, of course, of editorializing, or an infringement of the libel laws. In the course of the conversation the correspondent was asked: "How would you handle the Committee hearings on the Guffey Bill?" (The Guffey Coal Bill, then in the committee-hearing stage, was a topic of major interest in Washington.) His answer was given without hesitation:

"Well, if a mine operator was attacking the bill I'd give the story a ride. If a union representative was defending it I'd fold up my note-book and walk out—his testimony is no story for my paper."

Extensive conversations with Washington correspondents for papers of diametrically opposed points of view have convinced this writer that many newspapermen (certainly not all) find their true journalistic level, and work for organizations in whose values and ethics they believe. One Washington representative of a Hearst newspaper devoted almost an hour to passionate comments on the dangers of the present administration, the infiltration of Communist influences in the schools and churches, the need for a larger navy and army, and the dangers of revolution and of a workers' dictatorship. That newspaperman was scarcely a robot for Mr. Hearst. He was in a perfectly sympathetic milieu and, if anything, found the columns of the Hearst paper gratifyingly "free" in permitting him to report the political scene as he honestly, if extravagantly, saw it.

But how many members of the press corps work for newspapers with whose political point of view they do not agree? In the questionnaire filled out by Washington correspondents for newspapers of every shade of political color and professional integrity, forty-nine out of the seventy-five correspondents who answered the following question (65.3 per cent) checked it "Yes":

"In general, I agree with my paper's political point of view."

Nineteen (25.3 per cent) testified that they did not. Seven (9.3 per cent) were uncertain.

What of the 25.3 per cent who do not agree with their paper's political inclinations? Not all of them find their journalistic duties onerous: a Free Trader may be working for a newspaper which is staunchly high tariff in its editorial columns; but the paper may confine its economic preferences to the editorial page and the correspondent may, if he fulfills his journalistic responsibilities conscientiously, write tariff stories which show no bias one way or the other. The "catch" here is that if his dispatch contains implications favorable to a low-tariff policy his superiors may suspect him of being prejudiced, whereas they will consider stories the effects of which tend to support a high-tariff position eminently "reasonable," "fair," and "objective." In conservative circles, for example, there is a pronounced tendency to identify the conservative point of view automatically with "truth," "facts," and "objective evidence." Radical groups are no more self-conscious.

Those correspondents who disagree with their newspapers and do feel it necessary to slant their news stories to reflect the wishes of their superiors are in an unfortunate position. They are well paid; they are treated with gentlemanly consideration. They must make a living. The labor market, in journalism as in other enterprises, is not wide enough to permit freedom in choosing employers. In a society where "freedom of choice" is a pretty concept delimited by economic reality, a clear conscience is a luxury confined to those with the economic means to refuse compromises with personal ideals.

Newspaper policy is perpetuated by non-authoritarian devices. Every Washington correspondent reads his own paper: if he reads nothing else he looks to see how and where his story was "played," i.e., what prominence was given to it. It is the dominant motivation of every newspaperman to get as good a play for his stories as possible—it is the barometer of his success. And by observing the play given to stories from day to day the correspondent is, in effect, estimating the values which his editors have assigned to his output from the capital. One Washington correspondent told the writer:

Policy orders? I never get them; but I don't need them. The make-up of the paper is a policy order. Suppose I've written a story which, I notice, is shoved back to page 18. No big local story has forced it off the front pages, and the story is worth a big play. But it's shoved back. Well, suppose I reverse my 'slant' —and *that* story makes page 1. I follow that line and keep on making page 1 or 2. I give them what they want, and I can tell what they want by watching the play they give to my stories.

A paper's editorials, cartoons, features, and make-up influence its employees by the persistent processes of suggestion.

In this connection the reactions to the following statement are of great interest:

"It is almost impossible to be objective. You read your paper, notice its editorials, get praised for some stories and criticized for others. You 'sense policy' and are psychologically driven to slant your stories accordingly."

Seventy correspondents answered: 60 per cent (42) agreed; 34.2 per cent (24) disagreed; 5.6 per cent (4) were uncertain.

The correspondent becomes skilled in selecting those events, or those aspects of events, which will get the most positive response from his editors. On papers which pursue a journalistic practice of integrity and play news according to the news-values inherent in the stories, the correspondent's estimations are merely those of any good reporter applying judgment to the total stream of events. On papers which are infused with an extra-journalistic bias, stemming from the publisher's extra-journalistic purposes, the correspondent examines his news for angles which will gratify his superiors and further his own career.

It is sometimes charged that newspapermen use the cry of "Policy!" as a shield behind which to hide their own lack of fortitude. This point is often raised in the capital. It is asserted that some of the correspondents writing colored stories do so of their own volition, using the excuse that their publisher demands that type of news. This point of view was tested by getting the correspondents to check their reactions to the following statement:

"Correspondents try too hard to please their editors. If they had more independence they would discover that they really have more freedom than they assume."

Out of seventy-four answers, forty (60.6 per cent) agreed with the statement. Twenty-three (34.7 per cent) disagreed. Three (4.5 per cent) were uncertain.

Editors, too, sometimes complain of the journalistic phenomenon of "trying too hard to please the boss." A. R. Holcombe, then managing editor of the New York

Herald Tribune, told the 1930 convention of the American Society of Newspaper Editors:

Our experience has been, in controversial matters, where the paper takes a stand editorially, it is very difficult for the reporter to believe that the paper wants its news columns free from partisanship; so that we have never been able to attain complete non-partisanship in our news columns, although we want it, and we want it very sincerely.[1]

It is not difficult to understand why this is so. It would be expecting a superhuman opaqueness to reality to charge reporters with the task of maintaining an objectivity which their superiors violate, and with the burden of clinging to a journalistic ethic which their publishers discard. The record of newspaper proprietors in the 1936 Presidential campaign is close enough to make extended discussion of this point superfluous. The managing editor of the Buffalo *Evening News,* Mr. Alfred H. Kirchhofer, was associate director of publicity for the Republican Party in 1928 and was in charge of Republican publicity in 1936. In neither instance did he resign from his journalistic post. In 1936 he merely divided his time between his two functions. It is known that the Buffalo *Evening News* sent an order to its staff informing them that despite Mr. Kirchhofer's political activity and despite the editorial opinions of the newspaper, the news was to be treated impartially. But it would betray a simplicist conception of the human personality to assume that correspondents working under such conditions could seal their minds to the fact that their immediate superior had allied himself with one side of a political issue and would return to his duties after election day.*

In the same way it is difficult to see how employees for the Hearst chain or the Chicago *Tribune* could defy their sense of discretion by fighting against the political atmosphere in which they worked. The Detroit *Free Press* issued a full-page statement on "Americanism," in paid advertisements, which included such hyperbole as this:

As President he [Roosevelt] has gathered around him a nebulous collection of half-baked theorists, some Communistic, some Fascist, in their leanings. He has imported to this Country warring ideas from the conflicting schools of thought that dominate dictator-ridden Europe.[2]

Were the employees of the Detroit *Free Press* expected to reject these thoughts sternly from their memories?

There are, of course, instances in which newspapermen are given explicit instructions concerning the treatment they are expected to give to specific news events. The following cases illustrate sample types of pressure. They were given to this writer by different Washington correspondents and, as such, merit the journalistic cliché, "on the most reliable authority."

1. During the 1928 Presidential campaign one Washington correspondent was ordered to tour several Eastern states and write a series of dispatches analyzing public

---

* On the other hand, although Mr. Roy Roberts, managing editor of the Kansas City *Star*, was virtually campaign manager for Governor Landon, the news columns of the *Star* maintained an admirable degree of impartiality. For further examples see Chapter XIII.

opinion. His editor's telegram ended with the jocular phrase: "And don't forget we are backing Al Smith."

2. During the fight for the repeal of the Pink Slip law on income taxes, a fight in which newspaper publishers took an active part, several Washington bureaus were informed, by telephone, letters or in conversation that: "Mr. X [the publisher] is very anxious to have the Pink Slip law repealed." Stories with implications favorable to the Pink Slip law were not welcomed.

3. The Tugwell Pure Food and Drug Bill was treated with extraordinary delicacy by the press, and eight separate Washington correspondents have told the writer that "they wrote around the story" or ignored it, because of the intense opposition of their publishers to the measure.

4. When the Veterans' Bonus Bill was under discussion a correspondent sent a dispatch for a Sunday feature story analyzing the measure. He reviewed the history of bonuses after previous wars in which the United States had taken part. He pointed out that history showed that the payment of a bonus was by no means the end of veterans' pressure, that a demand for a pension law generally followed. He cited the number of widows and orphans still receiving pensions from the government for the War of 1812. His article was supported by facts, figures, dates, and historical evidence. And it was returned with this laconic comment: "You seem to forget that we are supporting the payment of the Bonus." The correspondent re-wrote the article, changing it to this slight extent: the argument concluded that a study of history showed that a veterans' bonus was "clearly in the American tradition." This triumph of casuistry was printed.

5. A correspondent was telephoned by his home office and told to find out whether certain facts in regard to a Senate bill "are true." He said that so far as he knew they were not true, but he would investigate. Investigation confirmed his opinion. The next day he told his office of his findings. He was asked if he was *sure* the facts were not what the home office implied. This process was repeated for several days until the correspondent concluded that the home office "was damned eager to get the story the way they wanted it—so I strained the facts and wrote it."

6. One correspondent was warned "not to crusade" after he had written a story with pro-labor implications: his managing editor said that the story was not "spot news" Some time later, the correspondent was told to interview a certain Senator (whose record indicated that his comments would support the newspaper's stand on another matter). Although the subsequent story was not "spot news" it was printed. This was not considered "crusading."

7. The writer has seen a long letter to a Washington correspondent from his home office explaining why a certain dispatch had been killed. There was no complaint that the story was either untimely, untrue, or unimportant. There was no effort to deny that it was a good story, well written and supported by ample evidence. The explanation merely stated that according to the newspaper's policy on the matter, it was "unwise" to print it. "It would just make unnecessary trouble."

8. The most amusing reason advanced for not printing a correspondent's dispatch occurred in the following case:

while covering Europe, a newspaperman for a large newspaper in the Middle West wrote an account of the Hungarian crisis and the role which Communism played in it. His dispatch was carefully worded and well documented. It was a judicious and thoughtful analysis. He received the following reply from his office: "Your story was great. However, we do not think it advisable to print it because it does not reflect Mid-Western opinion on this point." He did not forget these delectable words when he was assigned to cover Washington.

9. Several correspondents wrote up a report of the Consumers' Division of NRA on the properties and value of ethyl gasoline, in which the Standard Oil Company was named. The dispatches were killed by two papers and printed by a third, but the name of Standard Oil was deleted.

Newspapermen may be well aware of what is expected of them without policy orders. There is an institutional atmosphere which communicates the official point of view to the personnel with precision. At the height of the "Red scare" initiated by the Hearst newspapers, a New York reporter was sent to interview Professor George S. Counts of Columbia University. Hearst reporters in other cities had interviewed professors of political science and education, had distorted their remarks, and, in one case, had deliberately set out to "frame" a university figure. Professor Counts, profiting by experience, had a stenographer present to take down every word of the interview. And the reporter confessed:

Mr. Hearst is engaged at present in conducting a Red Scare. . . . You realize of course that because of my assignment I will have to select the most sensational statements from the interview in order to make out a good case. This is what Mr. Hearst is expecting.[3]

The influence of an institutionalized "sense" of policy may be illustrated by several examples. When Mr. Eugene Meyer, banker, financier, and former head of the Federal Reserve Board and the Reconstruction Finance Corporation, purchased the Washington *Post* in 1933, he expressed an intention to make the *Post* an accurate and impartial newspaper. In speeches throughout the country and in conversations with his editors and political staff this purpose was emphasized.[4] But Mr. Meyer discovered that for months his news columns and the general make-up of his paper betrayed a pro-Republican bias. Despite his formal instructions many members of the *Post* staff persisted in writing stories of the type which they *felt* he would like. They could not believe that Mr. Meyer's instructions were to be taken literally. They were experienced newspapermen.*

A curious and unprecedented interest in monetary stories swept through the *Post's* personnel. Mr. Meyer, as a banker and an ex-government finance officer, was of

* Some members of the press corps have criticized this interpretation of Mr. Meyers's intentions. At the time Mr. Meyers purchased the *Post*, in 1933, it was widely believed that he intended to make it a staunch Republican organ. The June 12, 1933, issue of *Time* (p. 47) suggested that Mr. Meyers's motive was to promote a Republican comeback in 1936. There is considerable disagreement in Washington newspaper circles concerning Mr. Meyers's policy, but this writer inclines to the interpretation expressed above.

course interested in stories dealing with monetary problems. He would suggest to his editors: "The Federal Reserve Board is meeting today. Don't you think it would be a good idea to have a man cover it?" And the reporters for the *Post* swiftly arrived at the conclusion that "the Boss likes money stories." Stories on gold, money, discount rates, and government finance began to blossom out in the pages of the *Post*. The editors assigned them prominence. Every reporter on the paper was eager to write money stories, or play up monetary angles in other stories, in order to catch the eye and win the approval of the publisher. "The place went mad on money," one reporter said.

Another example of the psychology which may sweep through an organization regardless of the formally expressed attitude of the publisher or editors is to be found in the consistent prominence given to silver stories by the New York *Times*. The facts, so far as this writer can determine, are illuminating. Mr. Adolph Ochs, late publisher of the New York *Times*, spent an evening several years ago in asking the man who was then head of his Washington bureau, Richard V. Oulahan, many questions about monetary problems—particularly about silver. So great was Mr. Ochs' interest that Mr. Oulahan, on returning to Washington, began to contribute dispatches pertaining to silver. These stories were given the usual "play" assigned to his output. Other correspondents for the *Times*, sensing a new pattern of interest in their newspaper, came to believe that silver was big news for their organization. They felt that such dispatches would "get a big break" in the paper. The New York office, receiving stories with an emphasis on silver in greater proportion than ever before, began to feel that the subject was more important than *they* had imagined. Something in the nature of an office tradition grew up and the columns of the *Times* gave a priority to silver stories which became the subject of curiosity in newspaper circles.

Lyle Wilson, head of the Washington bureau of the United Press, was touring the country in the fall of 1936; he specialized in a series of chatty, informal stories on his impressions. The articles were featured in many newspapers. And within the next weeks dozens of United Press correspondents over the country began to submit stories in the same light genre, imitating Mr. Wilson's angle. An order had to be sent out to stop this contagious practice.

The whole process of journalism reduces itself to a successive series of anticipations. The reporter fashions his facts into a story which he hopes will catch the attention or merit the praise of the city editor. The minor editors try to perform their deeds in a manner which will elicit praise from the editor-in-chief. He, in turn, is subject to the will, the caprice, and the preferences of the publisher. Now the publisher is not necessarily an insidious, calculating figure who conspires with industrialists and pollutes the news.* He may be determined, as some publishers are, to offer no *conscious* interference with the unprejudiced presentation of news. But this is not enough. Regardless of his expressed intentions there is a subtle ordering

* He may, of course, confuse his convictions with the truth. See Chapter XIII.

implicit in the employer-employee relationship. Newspapermen say that a good newspaperman can "sense" policy, that he knows, by professional "instinct" and experience, what kind of story or what treatment of a story will win the praise and pleasure of his superiors.

Nelson A. Crawford has described the point in the following passage, from *The Ethics of Journalism:*

Fear in journalism begins with the reporters and permeates every part of the newspaper organization up to the publisher. Conversation with many reporters has convinced the writer that the vast majority are fundamentally honest. It likewise has convinced him that the vast majority are either liberals or radicals, though in many cases unintelligent ones. If, however, one picks up the average newspaper today and reads the stories written by these men one will find a certain bias toward conservative and reactionary policies and against liberal and radical policies. Presumably, if these men unconsciously varied from strict objective truth in writing their stories, they would vary in the direction of their own conviction. . . . What is the explanation of their varying in exactly the opposite direction?

All, or nearly all, the newspapers that the reporter has seen, including the one on which he is working, have exhibited a conservative bias in handling the news. He believes that the publisher wants only stories with a conservative bias and that if he writes an important political or economic story showing no bias or showing radical or liberal bias, the story will not be printed and he may be fired. If nothing more, he feels that the story will be so altered by the copy desk as to maintain the conservative bias. The statements of the managing editor [urging reporters to be objective] have not removed his fears. . . . He is perhaps encouraged in his beliefs by the city editor and the copy-readers—men who have grown old and cynical

in the newspaper office. . . . There is instilled into the young
newspaperman's mind the feeling that the publisher is involved
in various capitalistic enterprises, that his business and social
associates are all capitalists, and that he is publishing a newspaper in the interests of capitalism. . . .[5]

It cannot be forgotten that for all his prestige the
Washington correspondent is an employee. As an employee it is only natural for him to strive to perform his
work in a manner satisfactory to his employers. And it is
the latter, rather than the former, who, in the final
analysis, set the standard of the news from Washington.
A newspaper whose policy it is to get accurate, impartial
news will not tolerate a correspondent who does not fulfill this primary requirement and will, by its conduct,
encourage him to send that kind of news. A newspaper
whose policy it is to prefer news slanted to coincide with
the political faith of its editors or publisher, will not
keep paying a correspondent who does not "give it what
it wants" and will, by the very nature of its format,
compel him to depart from accuracy and judiciousness.
Newspapers get the type of Washington correspondence
which they deserve and which they, and they alone, make
possible.

PART THREE

XI. The Psychology of the Correspondent

MAX WEBER has said, in *Politik Als Beruf*, that journalists, like lawyers and artists, have no clear-cut social classification.[1] The social origins and allegiances of most journalists are, by and large, middle class. Their antagonism to big business is acute. Their discontent with the status quo is greater than their agreement upon alternatives to it or methods for re-casting it. They reflect the indecision of the larger social stratum from which they come.

Most Washington correspondents have a strong faith in individualism and individualistic effort. Their work entails a maximum of competition between persons and it confuses them to attempt a reconciliation of individualism with the contemporary forces of monopoly and neo-mercantilism. Many members of the press corps are opaque to a recognition of the social conditions which delimit and constrain individual success. Some believe that a firm "trust-busting" campaign will restore genuine competition, preserving the advantages of laissez-faire and the democratic freedom which arose with it. Others prefer a profit economy with social checks and benevolent governmental services.

Most of the correspondents believe in democracy. But having seen it operate at close quarters, with its cargo of demagogues, pressure agents, political careerists, and red tape, they are both bitter about the uses to which democracy is put and confused about legitimate controls over it. They are unsentimental about the persons who occupy democratic posts but sentimental in their conception of the kind of persons who could, ideally, occupy them. In this they are no different from most intellectuals.

The correspondents are intellectuals insofar as their primary function is to handle ideas and interpret social events. But their thinking rotates around the concrete rather than the abstract. Their adjustment may be said to be that of persons to persons, rather than persons to ideas. In interpreting current affairs they analyze them in the context of contemporary trends rather than against the configuration of historical movements or within a frame of depersonalized reference. This makes for greater "realism" in their dispatches but less depth in their evaluations.

Unlike other middle-class groups, the press corps has seen "politics in the raw." They have had their faith in politicians and orators destroyed. Hence they are less susceptible to the Utopian claims of demagogues. Their approach to such virtuosos of the larynx as Huey Long, Dr. Townsend, Father Coughlin or the Reverend Gerald L. K. Smith is one of skepticism. They are trained to identify movements led by such leaders as "rackets."

Most correspondents are "liberal" in their antagonism to authoritarianism, whether from the left or the right. They have a sincere and deep conviction about the license of free speech. And, like liberal groups, they become confused when free speech is used to threaten the structure of the state or to articulate political aims incompatible with democratic society. Hence their theoretical defense of the right of Communists to have access to the soap boxes and the radio, and their personal antagonism to "agitators" when the privileges are exercised too energetically.

The Washington correspondent lives in a twenty-four-hour cycle of time. He must make "snap decisions." This tyranny of the immediate makes it difficult to achieve perspective, or apply what Vincent Sheean has eloquently described as "the long view." Each day the newspaperman is faced with new challenges and fresh sensations. Each day presents a deadline which must be met. This telescoping of crises into a daily cycle stamps tension and obsession into the behavior pattern of the journalist.

There is a curious sequence in the day of a Washington correspondent. The morning papers greet him with half a dozen promising stories for investigation. Messages from his home office demand answers to questions of fact or urge him to cover stories of particular interest "back home." There are press conferences to attend, committee hearings to visit, "visiting firemen" to corral. There is lunch at the Press Club with other reporters on the alert for a "story," or at the Cosmos Club with voluntary or involuntary news-sources. There are telephone calls to make and illuminati to interview. There may be a debate in Congress which he should witness, a tea at an embassy, or a formal reception by a cabinet member. Above and around all, there is the iron moment of the deadline. No matter how lackadaisical the reporter, how dull the day, how complete the co-operation of his colleagues or the comprehensiveness of his Blacksheets, the meeting of a deadline involves the crisis of an internalized drama. The concentrated fury with which reporters pound out their dispatches is best described as the rape of the typewriter. After the catharsis, there is relaxation in the bar of the Press Club or the coffee shop of the Willard.

Journalists are caught in the remorseless vitality of the moment. They are hyperactive persons. In the exhilarating chase after the Now there is refuge from the restraining past and the disturbing future. The most striking affective feature of recent autobiographies like Webb Miller's *I Found No Peace* (the title of which is sufficiently illuminating), Negley Farson's *The Way of a Transgressor*, Vincent Sheean's *Personal History*, or the less personal *Inside Europe* of John Gunther, is the picture of overreaction against the passive parts of the personality, the flight from self-understanding in the narcotic pursuit of things outside the self.* If this seems unnecessarily "psychological" one must still ask why men choose a career which promises no great material rewards and little public recognition, which demands a subordination of private life to professional duties, which offers "no peace" to the personality.

Newspapermen like to romanticize both the impulses which led them to embark upon a newspaper career and

* Modern psychology emphasizes the dynamic character of the personality. Within the emotional structure there are patterns of impulse and inhibition which conflict with or neutralize others. In "psychopathic" personalities the entire energy is utilized in such internal struggles. Our society nourishes and sets a premium upon the externalization of impulses in the form of active behavior and active relationships. It fosters inter-personal competition. This requires personalities which can adjust to reality and participate in it—as distinguished, for example, from Oriental cultures which stress the internalization of energies in the form of contemplation, fantasy, or religious preoccupation.

the pleasures to be found in it. Gerald W. Johnson of the Baltimore *Sun*, whose writings are not ordinarily characterized by effusiveness, wrote the following description of the reporter's life:

There are men predestined from their mother's womb to regard this world as a garish, outlandish and somewhat bawdy, but infinitely amusing and thrilling show, yet without ever being stage struck. They delight in portraying it, but feel no urge to participate in the action. . . .

Some of them are cynical . . . some are pessimistic . . . but vast numbers of them are thoroughly ingenuous, squealing with delight at each melodramatic climax, hissing the villains heartily, and rapturously applauding each successive hero, real or bogus. . . .

Suppose they are not rewarded with much money, or dignity or fame; suppose they are debarred from living the life of a normal man; suppose they wield no power while they last, and cannot last long? What of it? They each yell more, sweat more, hiss more, start more tears and goose flesh in the course of their lives than a dozen normal and ordinary men. They have a helluva good time.[2]

But the energies which lead men into newspapers are more specific than this passage suggests: the desire to startle and expose; the opportunity to project personal hostilities and feelings of injustice on public persons under the aegis of "journalistic duty"; inner drives for "action," plus inner anxieties about accepting the consequences of action. The last is particularly important.

There is a sense of invulnerability attached to newspaper work. Journalism represents a world within a world. Reporters derive a vicarious pleasure in experiencing the excitment of events as observers, not participants, without personal risk in the outcome of those events. The newspaperman is a socially insulated figure. He covers riots, civil wars, or financial cataclysms with professional indifference. His value as a journalist depends, in most cases, upon his maintenance of an unaffected point of view. Hence the equanimity with which photographers take pictures of drowning men, or with which newspaper veterans interview the condemned. Theirs is the same secure feeling that movie audiences find in looking at newsreel pictures of a flood.

The Washington correspondent outstays Presidents and cabinets. He is, as it were, self-sufficient in the small world of his newspaper organization. His first vested interest is his status as a privileged observer. He can attack Senators at their most vulnerable point—the reading public. Not even the President can claim immunity from his pen. One member of the press corps told this writer: "I watch Congress wrangle over labor unions and old age pensions—and I'll still be paid to watch them when the shooting's over. I see the politicians worrying about whether the Republicans will be elected—and I know there will be reporters to cover a Republican administration too. I'd hate to see a war—but if the suckers stand for it . . . they've got to have war correspondents at the front, too—reporters, not soldiers." There is consoling security in such a position.

The withdrawal from participation means not merely a uniquely privileged identity but also a stifling of periodic urges to act, advise or take a hand in political affairs. The renunciation of personal action creates tension despite the preferences of the ego (the calculating, rational part of the personality), and, in a time of crisis, precipitates guilt. There is a strong drive to jump into the fight. Some newspapermen contribute to weekly or monthly magazines where they find an outlet for the animus outlawed from their dispatches; others turn to press agentry; others begin to advise Congressmen, officials, or lobbyists. Some members of the press corps function, in Ray Tucker's phrase, as "part-time statesmen."

Nor do they limit their advice and action to their writings. Their newspaper careers are an amateur sport by comparison with their unknown and unwritten activities in cloak rooms, corridors, and committee rooms on Capitol Hill.

They initiate and conduct Congressional investigations, suggest policies and procedures and appointments, write speeches and interviews, promote publicity stunts, dominate some public officials and influence less aggressive and articulate members of the corps.

It is almost impossible to exaggerate their backstage influence.[3]

The press corps became conscious of its political power during the battle over the entry of the United States into the League of Nations. Ray Tucker asserts that it was a small group of correspondents, working with Alice Longworth, who:

conspired hourly with the "irreconcilables" and performed service far beyond the call of newspaper duty. They tipped off most of the Congressmen to Wilsonian statements and maneuvers, and started Senatorial counterattacks before the War president could unlimber his orators. They wrote philippics for the Borahs, Johnsons, and Reeds, cooked up interviews . . . carried on independent research into the League's implications, dug up secret material. Their dispatches bristled with personal hostility to the League, and the carbon copies which they distributed to pro-Wilson writers affected even the latter's supposedly favorable articles. The Covenant was defeated by the Senate press gallery long before it was finally rejected by the Senate.[4]

The role of reporters for the Hearst newspapers in defeating our entry into the World Court is a case of more recent relevance. It was several correspondents who resuscitated Teapot Dome, and supplied Thomas J. Walsh with the more devastating questions in the Senate Committee hearings.[5]

Ruth Finney of the Scripps-Howard Newspaper Alliance, an expert on the subject of power, played an important and continuous role in the fight for the construction of Boulder Dam. She published a damaging report of the "teller vote" taken in the House of Representatives on the Utility Holding Company Bill.[6] A Washington correspondent revealed the amount of the Vare "slush fund" in the 1926 Pennsylvania Senatorial campaign, which led to an exposé of the methods of a powerful political machine.[7] Paul Mallon and Raymond Clapper, then reporters for the United Press, published a secret Senate roll call on the confirmation of a Presidential appointment and forced a change in the practice, so that committees began to conduct their public duties publicly.[8] M. Farmer Murphy, then of the Baltimore *Sun*, wrote memorable stories on the trading and chicanery which accompanied the 1930 Tariff Bill through the Senate.[9]

It was a group of Washington correspondents who initiated the historic attack on the confirmation of Charles E. Hughes's nomination for Chief Justice of the Supreme Court. Richard V. Oulahan suggested that certain Senators agreed to take up the newspapermen's campaign in consideration of front-page stories which would benefit their political fortunes.[10] When the Supreme Court declared the AAA unconstitutional, two young newspapermen, J. R. Wiggins of the St. Paul *Pioneer Press* and Felix Belair, Jr., of the New York *Times*, suggested to Secretary of Agriculture Wallace and Chester A. Davis that the purposes of the AAA could be achieved under the Soil Conservation Act, if that measure were slightly revised. The Department of Agriculture gave full credit to these men for pointing out the potentialities of the statute.[11] Ashmun Brown of the Providence *Journal* revealed that Postmaster General Farley's proud departmental "surplus" in 1935 was no more than a rearrangement in bookkeeping. In newspaper circles it is freely charged that President Hoover tried to get the so-called Pecora investigation to concern itself only with the "short selling" phase of stock exchange activities. But the Senate Committee extended their jurisdiction to stock market operations in general. A number of experienced correspondents insist that Mr. Hoover and several Senators tried to devitalize the investigation on several occasions. Because of changes in counsel before Ferdinand Pecora was brought to Washington, the investigation had died several times. It was a group of energetic newspapermen who revived the story, did a little investigating of their own, wrote new angles and hot leads, and created enough public interest and news-value to inject new life into what became one of the most important Senatorial investigations of the century. The La Follette Committee investigation of Civil Liberties, or the Nye Committee hearings on munitions manufacture, owe much to the energy and co-operation of newspapermen.

But many Washington correspondents are cynical, if not disappointed, over the lack of public response to their work: several have remarked to this writer that the public reads the comic strips and the sport pages but scarcely pays any attention to their dispatches. Many have spoken ironically about the fact that their importance is exaggerated. One of the most aggressive members of the press corps remarked, with irritation, that although his articles had been appearing on the front page of his paper regularly, under a "by-line," friends would greet him with the annoying question: "Say, are you still with the *Clarion?* I haven't seen any of your stuff for ages." These same friends were quite conscious of the fact that the *Clarion* carried the daily wisdom of Beatrice Fairfax or the cultural homilies of Dick Tracy.

One of the most seductive phases of the reporter's life is the sanction which his calling receives from society. He is above the law, in a sense; he flashes police and fire passes; he is admitted to official hearings; he is given a box seat at trials and investigations; he is granted the immunity of priests and lawyers, in some states, with regard to information obtained confidentially; his minor transgressions against speeding laws, his presence in gambling joints, etc., are excused.

Silas Bent tells of the time he signed the name of another person in order to get a telegram which would give him an exclusive story. He experienced no anxiety about this hardly moral act:

As the child of God-fearing parents . . . I had a strict sense of private property. I would not have pilfered ten cents or ten dollars. But my conscience was wholly untroubled about the message, because I had done the conventional thing. I was living up to the standards of my fellows. . . . I was exultant, not ashamed.[12]

It was not merely the exultance of having scored a journalistic triumph; it also contained the pleasure of breaking a taboo serene in the knowledge that society forgives reporters much "in the line of their duty."

The reporter's business is often to get secrets and tell them. Any vestigial guilt about this practice is defended by the statement "that's the job of a newspaperman." Sometimes there is a direct conflict between the newspaperman's professional and private motivations: as a reporter he should tell; as a friend he should not. Professional guilt is created by withholding facts which private conscience inhibits him from divulging; private guilt is produced by his revealing facts which his professional conscience demands. Hence defenses are required to support either the telling or the suppressing: "I *had* to write that story, Pete. It was my duty;" or (to his editor) "I didn't see any reason to put Pete on the spot." The ideal reporter would have no friends who could be damaged by newspaper dispatches; but since the most valuable information is often obtained from friends in the thick of events, there is a contradiction of relationships which makes the ideal condition impossible in fact.

It is interesting that so many newspapermen react negatively to "gossip columnists." * Actually, the gossip column, whether in Washington or New York, merely extends the journalistic license, by exploiting rumor, inference, and innuendo. It is journalism pushed to the marginal area. Why, then, should the press corps, like other newspapermen, regard gossip columns with distaste? Partly because "the key-hole boys" are permitted freedom from the caution required in orthodox reporting, but also because their practices reactivate feelings of moral culpability in other newspapermen. In this context, the antipathy of reporters for gossip columnists may be said to be an over-reaction against murmurs of personal guilt. It is significant that newspapermen, whose trade requires a good deal of prying, were hostile to the activities of prohibition agents and are not captivated by the high-handed performances of the G-men.

The cynicism of newspapermen with regard to politics and politicians is a self-protective device. There is a saying that every cub reporter is an idealist and every veteran is hard-boiled. The "hard-boiled" eidolon is a kind of professional stereotype, a cherished *persona*, in Jung's meaning. Actually it is a compensatory idealization. Truly "hard-boiled" gentlemen do not crowd their walls with pictures of ex-Presidents, Vice-Presidents, and Senators, inscribed "To Charley—a real friend." The anatomy of many correspondents' glorification of President Roosevelt

---

* Many correspondents resented the publication of *Washington Merry-Go-Round*, especially because of the chapter on the press. Their hostility was expressed in the phrase, "It's befouling your own nest."

in 1933 and 1934, their disillusionment in 1935, and their active iconoclasm in 1936 illustrates a significant affective process.

In the first two years of the administration, critics complained that Mr. Roosevelt had charmed the correspondents and "prostituted" them to his ends. This is naive. Mr. Roosevelt did not hypnotize the press corps. He used every means at his disposal to strengthen his position, politically and psychologically. He tried to inspire news most favorable to himself and his goals. But this any executive will do—if he can get away with it. Where the practice was absent in Mr. Roosevelt's predecessors it was more because of a lack of adroitness than force of scruples. We have seen that, in 1935 and 1936, the high expectations of the press corps turned to "disillusionment." It will be valuable to analyze the change in attitude.

The technique of newspaper writing necessitates overstatement. *Competition, in journalism, has been raised from the plane of speed in transmission to the plane of originality in interpretation.* This competition, concentrated upon the interpretation of a common body of subject matter, places a premium upon spectacular judgments and bold "angles." In Washington this is particularly true: mass press conferences, handouts, departmental information services, and the excellent overall coverage of the press associations—these drive correspondents into an emphasis upon original insights and interpretive acrobatics. Real "scoops" in Washington are uncommon. The struggle for the front page revolves around different "angles" extracted from the same general body of information, or the utilization of private news sources. The necessity of writing a story a day, even in the dullest periods, has pernicious consequences.

Competitive journalism, like competitive advertising, ends in the asseveration of impossible claims. But journalists, unlike copy-writers, are preoccupied with persons, not commodities; they are directly exposed to the influence of their subject matter. Reporters often come to believe in the fictional qualities which they assign to public figures during that professional delirium which characterizes the daily meeting of deadlines. Newspapermen are driven to overstatement because they are competing against overstatements. And men who operate in the realm of words unconsciously assign to the words they use a reality which transcends their intentions. In this context it was not Mr. Roosevelt who hypnotized the Washington correspondents: it was the Washington correspondents who hypnotized themselves.

The one measure of value which most newspapermen possess is the rod of success. Ashmun Brown has stated that, for the Washington correspondent, "The man who gets away with it is a good politician." [13] This empirical standard does not create analytic judgments which have validity beyond the immediate day and the successes thereof. The press corps vested a great deal of emotional faith in Mr. Roosevelt; as long as he was a politician "getting away with it" that faith was justified. But when he began to meet formidable opposition from the Supreme Court, Congress, the Republicans, the elders of the Democratic Party, and the wide front of private groups who fought the President tooth and nail, when he began to meet with a series of defeats or temporary setbacks, some of the Washington correspondents began to falter. The corps had greeted Mr. Roosevelt with frenzy in 1933; in it there was a will-to-believe which, because it ignored future possibilities and past experience, would end by tearing down the myth it was creating.

The "disillusionment" with the President by newspapermen represented an externalization of guilt. For the Washington correspondents were naive, rather than hard-boiled, in the adulation which, upon their own initiative, they showered upon Mr. Roosevelt. Having "betrayed" the objective function which they felt they must observe, the conscience of the correspondents acted with doubled vigor. Newspapermen added to a situation for which they held the President responsible, those discontents which might more legitimately have been directed against themselves. This was improper, for in inter-personal relations as in commerce the admonition *caveat emptor* throws responsibility upon the gullible. A healthy proportion of the antagonism to Mr. Roosevelt was over-reaction by reporters who would have preferred that their earlier exaltations of the man might be removed from the record. They could not wipe out the emotional commitments of the past, but they intensified their efforts to compensate for them.*

The emotional affect of the Washington correspondents travels along cyclical lines. It has happened so often be-

* The correspondents who yielded to anti-Roosevelt pressure from their home offices should not be ignored. This pressure both buttressed and sanctioned the psychological pattern analyzed above, where it did not initiate an anti-Roosevelt point of view by itself. It has been estimated that 85 per cent of the American press opposed Mr. Roosevelt in the 1936 campaign. It can hardly be denied that the editorial stand, and its intensity, influenced newspapermen-employees, where actual "policy orders" did not. See Chapter XIII for a detailed analysis of the role of the press in the last Presidential campaign.

fore that, given the demands of journalistic writing, the face-to-face relationship of the press conferences, and the personality types who are attracted to newspaper work, there is every reason to believe it will happen again. Adulation—guilt—debunking. Newspapermen greet the new statesman with a deep hope that here, at last, is the great man incarnate. There is evidence to support this in the traditional honeymoon psychology of the first months. The great man's talents are sung, over-sung in the struggle for journalistic existence. Then "incidents" occur, a political compromise of not admirable hue, a political setback, attacks from the opposition. The newspapermen begin to see the pedal clay. They have been "taken in." Their faith has been outraged. How did they ever "fall for the stuff"? The demon on the desk in the home office sends them sarcastic reminders of their first euphoria. Other newspapermen, columnists, editors, publishers cry that the press corps was hamstrung by phrases. The correspondents are hurt; they are irritated; and they feel guilty. The breaking of the myth begins, by the men who erected it.

This writer inclines to the view that had Governor Landon been elected to the Presidency in 1936 he would have been hailed by many correspondents as the Fox from Kansas ("the greatest President since Calvin Coolidge") in 1937, that articles called "Is Landon Slipping?" (written for the Sunday pages) would appear in 1938, that public recantations by newspapermen would mount in 1939, and that—assuming no spectacular boom—the majority of the correspondents would be dreaming of "a *real* leader" in 1940.

XII. "News" and the Washington Correspondents

NO newspaper prints *all* the news. A newspaper is neither a chronology, an almanac, nor a history. It is a business enterprise selling a commodity, and it must interest its customers in that commodity. The commodity is news.

The entire process of journalism, from the "leg-man" on the street to the make-up editor at the desk, rests upon *selection*. This selective process is exercised according to "news judgment." The first test to which any constellation of events is subjected is the test of its news-value: "Is it news?" Or, in the parlance of the trade, "Is it a good story?" It is important to notice that the appraisal is not, "Is it significant?" or, "Is it important?"—but, "Is it news?" It is obvious that events which have a high degree of social or historical importance are generally charged with news-value. A Presidential announcement, a change in policy of the Federal Reserve Board, a statement from the State Department—these are, beyond a doubt, news of the first order. But it is doubtful whether an injury to the limbs of Marlene Dietrich is more consequential, by any sober estimation of human affairs, than the progress of a South American war. In the lexicon of journalism even the President's dog and the way he scratches himself may be front-page matter: the New York

Herald Tribune thought so, in its issue of June 21, 1932.* The concept of news varies with different newspapers, different editors, and different publishers. What is news for Denver is not news for Norfolk; what is news for the New York *American* is not news for the New York *World-Telegram.* By trial-and-error the reporter learns what values his particular paper places on different items.

Newspapers differ among themselves as to what constitutes news because they appeal to different publics, because their editors have different perspectives, because their publishers have different preferences as persons and different motivations as publishers.

Newspapers are published by business men whose chief concern, in most cases, is to make profit. Profit comes from advertising revenues. Advertising rates mount with ad-

---

* On November 22, 1935, Mme. Gertrud Wettergren, a Swedish contralto, arrived in New York for her debut at the Metropolitan Opera. She asked two reporters to oblige her with a kick—an old Swedish custom supposed to bring good luck to the kickee. This novel procedure brought more than good luck to Mme. Wettergren: it gave her fabulous newspaper publicity which she could not have purchased. The New York *Post* ran her picture on the front page. The New York *American, News,* and *Herald Tribune* ran feature stories embellished with photographs. The New York *Sun, World-Telegram,* and *Journal* reported the event carefully. The Washington *Herald,* using a lengthy Universal Service dispatch, devoted eleven precious column inches to the great event. The New York *Times* merely noted the arrival of Mme. Wettergren, quoting from a statement the Metropolitan Opera issued about the lady's vocal talent. It need hardly be argued that a polite kick administered to a Swedish contralto is an event of ephemeral interest and negligible consequence; by any standards other than those of journalism, Mme. Wettergren's arrival was hardly worthy of more than mention. But—and this is the crucial point—it was a "good story."

vances in circulation. To increase circulation means to appeal to a wider body of readers; this means lowering the level of attraction to the widest—and lowest—common denominator of interest. This presents a serious limitation to the work of the Washington correspondent.

The Washington correspondents must simplify issues for a public which has neither the background nor the time to analyze what it reads. They must emphasize personalities rather than forces. They must etch those personalities into sharp stereotypes which the reader can find analogous to the ordinary types of his own experience. They must inject into politics the elements of melodrama.

"The newspaper's function is not to instruct but to startle," said James Gordon Bennett, father of the modern conception of news and its first exponent. ". . . and to entertain," adds Silas Bent.[1] The press corps is often obliged to startle and entertain. The realization that the American newspaper, in a competitive commercial society, is an organ of information only in part, will clarify the dilemma in which many critics of the press find themselves. The modern newspaper, with its comics, beauty hints, Daily Romance stories, society pages, radio, sport and entertainment news, is an entertainment sheet, a purveyor of fiction, and a service bureau—as well as a journal of record.

The daily newspaper has become possessed of the thinking of a variety show. John T. Flynn has described it eloquently:

Being a show, it must, of course, have a cast of characters—its villains, its heroes, its funny men, its ingénues, its kind old fathers, its lovers. If these gentlemen do not exist in life and in the news, the paper will invent them. All characters are drawn with heavy, bold, broad strokes—caricatures, in fact—so that a deft sweep of the pen is all that is needed to depict any character in any way.

Now let a man or woman of importance stray into the news, no matter how: the copy desk will pounce upon him and put a label on him suggested by the introductory incident. Once this is done, the label will stand for good. . . . Nothing this side of heaven can rescue the victim of that label. Let a more or less talkative old Vermonter wander into the news columns with his lips closed tight and a limited dialogue for the day: the desk promptly labels him "the silent man." He becomes quickly "the strong, silent man." With that label on him he will run through ten thousand editions and a whole career, garrulous, erupting words at every opportunity, but he will always be "the strong, silent man." [2]

The Washington correspondents, like other journalists, place a premium on conflict, particularly conflict between well-known persons. An attack is news. It does not matter how shallow the grounds, how questionable the motivation, or how meretricious the personality of the attacker. An attack is news. This point has been exploited by politicians and publicity seekers. Congressmen have learned that they can always reach the front page by verbal assaults on the President. The Senator who achieved immortality by referring to some of his colleagues as "sons of the wild jackass" could not make page 1 with one of his best speeches in the Senate.[3] The public is regaled with the declamatory imbecilities of a Thomas L. Blanton, former representative from Texas, because his oratorical highjinks, though despised by the press corps, are "news." Ex-

Senator Henry Allen has suggested the ·problem which
legislators face:

> You get nowhere in modern statesmanship by standing by
> in honest defense. . . . I acquired . . . the habit of watch-
> ing certain Senators. . . . Whenever there was a big gallery
> I could see them responding consciously to the inspiring pres-
> ence of visitors. I could see them rise, glance at the Press Gal-
> lery to see if the press was on duty, and then turn loose the
> daily strafe of bathos, realizing that if they made it hot enough,
> they would reach the front page. . . .[4]

It is worth noting that the journalistic emphasis on
personalized conflict has created a striking coincidence between the language of journalism and the language of
pugilism. The reader has merely to recall such phrases as:
"The President struck a telling blow at—," "In a fighting
speech Secretary Ickes today hit back at—," "Harry Hopkins lashed out at his critics—"

A series of news dispatches is like a newsreel. From day
to day they have little continuity, vague rootings, daily
climaxes, and no fulfillment. It has been remarked that
political reporting in the United States portrays the country as being in deadly peril on November 2nd, but by November 5th, "after the enemies of the Republic have
throttled the goddess of Liberty and triumphed over the
righteous and terrified minority, all is well." [5]

The necessity of extracting startling "angles" from
events, for the sake of either creating or enhancing news-
values, leads newspapermen to take liberties with the material and often do injustice to the facts. In October of
1935, for example, the press corps in the capital had a

Roman holiday with the first part of a report called *Milk: A Study of the Ways of An Industry,* which was prepared by Irene Till, under the direction of Dr. Walton H. Hamilton and issued by the Consumers' Division of the National Recovery Administration. This study appeared in eighty-one mimeographed pages. It was a scholarly analysis of the relationship existing between the cow as a milk-producing instrument and the petty economy of the farm. It showed the influence of big business and the power of the distributor. The sobriety of the report was relieved by occasional lapses into academic humor. And it was precisely these sections that the newspapermen seized upon as a good story. Feature items appeared throughout the nation on "The Thwarted Love Life of the Cow," as examples of the waste and imbecility of an administration which was spending money for "crack-pot" projects.[6]

One publisher, at least, has revolted against the distortions which news-standards create in the treating of political events.

> We do not get the full, clear reports of what is going on in our legislature nor our Congress. Somebody gets up and says some silly, smart thing, and gets out some jokes that are amusing, and that is a leading article to publish in the headlines. . . . Our people are misled and not fully informed by the daily press on public affairs.[7]

In this connection, the success of *Time* magazine, which offers a weekly synthesis-outline of events, has led many newspapers to institute Sunday "Events of the Week" sections which give their readers a more intelligible view of the march of contemporary affairs.

News is highly imitative. And because news in the last analysis is what newspapers choose to print, a correspondent may be forced into writing a story for which he has no particular taste simply because his competitor has brought it into the focus of public attention. If nothing else, he may be required to write a story disproving the contents of competitive dispatches.*

The competition of newspapers leads to a curious practice: a deliberate effort to raise doubts about a story on which a competitor has had a "scoop." The New York *Times* ran a long account of the departure of Colonel Lindbergh and his family to England on Christmas Eve, 1935. It was an exclusive story, written by Lauren Lyman of the New York *Times* staff, to whom Colonel Lindbergh had given the details in advance. In the next few days competing papers and the press associations indulged in what appears to have been a deliberate effort to break down the validity of the story in the *Times*.

The value of a news-item at any given time depends upon the quantity of news available. A story which is featured on page 1 during a dull spell may not be included

* On November 8, 1935, the tabloid New York *News* ran a story on its front page. under a headline which almost covered the whole page:

STALIN

reported

SHOT

The story dealt with the fact that a Norwegian surgeon had left Oslo by plane for Moscow. This dispatch, sent from the Oslo United Press bureau, was available to many papers. The New York *Times* and *Herald Tribune* questioned its validity and did not use it, but on the next day both papers printed special dispatches showing that the rumor was unfounded.

on page 28 when news is rich and plentiful. "Crime waves," those invaluable aids to circulation, occur with a remarkable regard for the paucity of alternative news.* In the same way, news in Washington changes in value. When events are moving at a swift, dramatic pace, news must be of salient importance to win place in the papers. But in the political doldrums of the summer months the antics of third-rate officials and the petty squabbles of minor politicians may be heralded throughout the land.

There is an excellent phrase heard in Washington newspaper circles which suggests how news is "manufactured" when the season or the day is dull: "I'll write a think-piece," or, "I'll suck my thumb." A correspondent with no news of major consequence will sit down, "suck his thumb" and write a "think-piece" or "a flub-dub"—i.e., an article in which cerebration takes precedence over fact, interpretation over content, speculation over news.

One may wonder why, in a news-center as prolific as Washington, it should be necessary for correspondents to create news: "So much happens in Washington. . . ." But not all that happens in Washington is "hot news." Many occurrences do not possess what reporters call the "emotional wallop." Besides, most routine affairs are covered by the press associations. The special correspondent, to

---

* The Cleveland Foundation made a study of crime in Cleveland in January, 1919: in the first half of the month there were 345 felonies, to which the press devoted 925 column inches (including news pertaining to the administration of justice). During the second half of the month, when the newspapers were engaged in furious publicizing of a "crime wave," analysis showed 363 felonies (an increase of 5 per cent) to which the civic-minded press devoted no less than 6,642 inches—an increase of 600 per cent.[8]

justify his existence, must develop stories which are more than a recitation of facts. Under the harassing compulsion of sending at least one story a day the ingenuity of the correspondent is often taxed. He feels the temptation to inflate mediocre news into "puffed up" items, to read subtle and diabolic meaning into innocent facts, to distill surprising possibilities from pedestrian press releases. At so presumably newsworthy an event as the 1936 convention of the Democratic Party in Philadelphia there was a deplorable lack of real news after the first day of the meetings. Correspondents emphasized all sorts of "strategies" and behind-the-scene maneuvers; they discussed political moves which they knew had little chance of being realized; they wrote feature stories about the extraordinary inebriation which held sway in the Quaker city. Paul Y. Anderson wired the St. Louis *Post-Dispatch* that there was very little worth writing about.[9]

During the sterile summer months the National Press Club in Washington resounds with the plea: "Have you got a good story?" It is at this season that "think-pieces" abound. Correspondents devote columns to writing about *possible* action, rumored political moves, realignments and policies which *may* eventuate. In the words of one correspondent, "I go through the handouts with a fine comb." Blacksheeting is widespread. Lunches at the Press Club drag out, as men pool information and work up "angles." And Washington dispatches become compact of "masterminding" and innuendoes which suggest that something profound lurks under the guarded phrases of an empty dispatch.

On a very dull day it is not uncommon for a correspondent to go through his scrap-book and re-write dispatches sent a week or a month earlier, adding a few details which have come out in the meantime, or ordering old facts in a new manner. The former head of one Washington bureau had perfected this technique: he would rummage through old press releases and, taking material which was weeks old, presented the illusion of novelty—since no other correspondent had gone back quite that far. Once he dug up a treaty which had been announced six months earlier, re-wrote it with a fresh "twist" and sent it off boldly under an "exclusive" label. On another occasion, he went through the file of handouts on the President's speeches and noticed some comments which the President had made on social security legislation, to be presented to Congress "at the earliest opportunity"; the correspondent wrote a dispatch predicting that soon after the opening of Congress the President would present a social security program. It was a "scoop" because his guess was justified by later events. Had it not been, that would not have been any disaster: the memory of the public is notoriously short, and the incessant pouring out of new facts and new stories crowds old facts and mistaken predictions out of mind. Nothing, someone has said, is as old as yesterday's newspaper.

News from Washington is particularly susceptible to journalistic manipulation. For political news is not news of observable fact, as is a fire, a flood, or an accident. It permits elaboration, interpretation, inference, prophecy. Of no other news is Tiffany Blake's definition more apropos: "News is not fact. It is gossip about facts." [10]

But a revolution has taken place in the character of Washington news in the last four years. News from the capital has changed because the function and the jurisdiction of the American government has changed. Whether for better or for worse, the Roosevelt administration has assumed new powers, invaded new fields, challenged ancient jurisdictions. The federal government has become positivistic and aggressive. And in describing the conduct and philosophy of the Roosevelt régime, the Washington correspondents were forced to use new perspectives and re-cast old conceptions.

Within a few weeks after Mr. Roosevelt took office the Washington correspondents found themselves immersed in stories which were no longer "political," in the old sense. They discovered that they were expected to write about the gold standard and the devaluation of the dollar, the reconstruction of industrial relations under NRA, a farm program, collective bargaining, public works, relief measures, national resources, and national planning. At no time had news swerved so violently from traditional paths, and at no time had it been so prolific. The New Deal became a national crusade. Publicized shrewdly by the press agents of the New Deal, vivified by the tempo at which events moved and the glamor of the visions which were unloosed, the activities of the federal government became charged with a dramatic content which was, indeed, something new under the Washington sun. The American public began to devour a *kind* of news with which most newspapermen had not been trained to cope.

Labor news, for example, shot into public attention. News-values are such that the experiences of labor are traditionally publicized to its disadvantage. Thus, when wages were cut, hours lengthened, and the "speed-up" instituted, in 1931 and 1932, papers did not consider these matters to possess news-interest. But when, in 1937, improved business conditions, rising profits, and a sharp increase in the costs of living impelled labor groups to demand a recovery of the ground which they had lost—and led them to act upon their demands by sit-down strikes, that was news and merited columns of front-page space. These variations in news-standards create a picture of labor's belligerence which is only one-half of the whole story. Labor problems have long received a wholly disproportionate presentation in the American press, becoming "news" only when events reach the stage of violence. In the words of Louis Adamic: "The papers print the riots." [11]

Labor news has been at a disadvantage for another reason: reporters did not have access to the conveniences of press agents and publicity services of the type which business had instituted. Labor leaders were crude, aggressive and, often, unreliable as news-sources. But labor groups profited by experience. Competent press officers, reliable press releases, press conferences, statements from labor leaders whose names are big news—all these have improved the quality and raised the quantity of dispatches on the subject of labor. Most important, the New Deal legitimized news of labor's claims and rights. In October, 1933, seven months after the Roosevelt administration took office, Louis Stark of the New York *Times*, one of the ablest labor correspondents in the country, declared: "Normally the news in Washington is 10 per cent economic and 90 per cent political. Today it is about 90 per cent economic and 10 per cent political." [12]

The Washington correspondents were caught quite unprepared for this radical transformation in the subject-matter with which they were preoccupied. Some correspondents discovered, late in their careers, that they did not understand the full meaning of the news which they were dispatching and about which they were forced, *pari passu*, to pose as amateur experts. Some correspondents made an earnest effort to become versed in the intricacies of applied economics. Most correspondents adopted the attitude expressed in the words: "If I can't understand the stuff I'm sure my readers won't either. So I give it to them just as I see it—even if it is naïve—and that's about as much as I can expect them to absorb."

Many newspapermen, adept in filtering all news through old stereotypes, merely continued to interpret events according to the stylized pattern of persons and fights. It was not an antagonism of purposes and ends in the NRA, for example: it was a fight between Donald Richberg and Hugh S. Johnson. It was not a disagreement on the efficacy of money spent for permanent public works and hasty "made-relief" labor; it was a squabble between Harry Hopkins and Harold Ickes. This is not meant to give the impression that friction between personalities did not exercise an important influence in the politics and administration of the New Deal; but personal bouts were given prominence disproportionate to the role they played in the deeper conflicts between philosophies of action. The former were "news," the latter "theories."

The individual correspondent maintains that where the nature of news is concerned he is helpless. His editors print dispatches which they consider news, and he develops an evaluating mechanism which reflects their preferences. The editors in turn claim that they too are helpless; that they are subject to "the daily referendum of pennies," that the public does not care to read about tariff debates but does exhibit a ravenous appetite for political vaudeville. They claim that they merely give the public "what it wants." Since "giving the public what it wants" is, more properly, "giving the public what we have taught it to want" or "what we *say* the public wants," this defense may be open to skepticism. Professor Frank H. Knight has committed himself to the view that "giving the public what it wants" usually means corrupting the public taste.[13]

One Washington correspondent gave the writer an illuminating example of the restrictions which he felt his reading public imposed upon him. This newspaperman had labeled Dr. Rexford Guy Tugwell a radical with Communistic leanings. "I know that Tugwell is no Communist," he said. "I am well aware that he is probably a Social Democrat in the European sense. But how can you convey that impression to your readers? They are ignorant of what a Social Democrat is. They have got to have labels which they understand. They do know what 'radical' means and what 'Communist' means." An old Washington correspondent has said that "the Brain Trust" was really a newspaperman's fabrication. J. Fred Essary of the Baltimore *Sun* confessed that the professors in government positions who have been subjected to a merciless attack by the press were intelligent and decent citizens and that he was "really a little ashamed at some of the derisive matter written about them." [14]

The Washington correspondent brings to his work at the capital a long and thorough training in the arts of the police reporter. He brings to it the skills and perspective of one who has written for editors concerned exclusively with the spectacular value of stories. His dispatches from Washington compete for newspaper space and placing with stories from all corners of the world. He must describe the events of his artificial city so that they may compete with the robust news of industrial warfare and Balkan conspiracies. [15]

Newspapermen do not have the time to pursue careful research. They do not have the space to present more than a swift, colorful account of the happenings of the day. In a larger sense it is improper to blame the Washington newspapermen for interpreting events in personalized, melodramatic stereotypes. They operate with a system of values which is natural and inherent in a competitive society. Capitalism, with its strident emphasis upon individual achievement and pecuniary estimations, has created normative images which reporters, no less than other citizens, accept uncritically. It has created a cult of the Big Man, the business and financial Hero. It has applauded opportunism. It has nourished a materialistic scale of appraisal which De Tocqueville long ago recognized as confusing individual successes with social welfare. These brittle norms are part of the world in which Americans are raised and in which they have learned to interpret their universe. They are incorporated into the whole weird structure of tastes which is encompassed by the word "news." The Washington correspondents are children of their society and they interpret it in the grammar which that society has offered them with an iron hand.

XIII. The Corps, the Press, and Democracy

THERE is ample evidence to support the belief that some newspapers are more interested in furthering the interests of their publishers than in enlightening the public. Other newspapers possess great journalistic integrity, permit their reporters freedom to operate as honest newspapermen, and draw a meticulous line between the editorial and the news columns. This point of view was expressed several years ago by Paul Y. Anderson:

It required no particular courage to write the truth for the *Baltimore Sun,* the *St. Louis Post-Dispatch* or the Scripps-Howard papers. Such newspapers as these expect it. But what would happen to the correspondent who tried to write the truth about "Coolidge economy" for the *Boston Transcript,* or about the Mellon tax refunds for the *Philadelphia Public Ledger,* or about the social lobby for the *Washington Star?* What would happen to any man who insisted on dishing up the bald truth about any Republican administration for such papers as the *New York Herald Tribune,* the *Detroit Free Press,* the *St. Louis Globe-Democrat,* the *Chicago Tribune,* or the *Los Angeles Times?* The Washington corps of correspondents has its inevitable percentage of sycophants, climbers, politicians and lads with an eye on the main chance, and it has, sad to relate, a solemn bevy of "gallery statesmen" who have been duped into a bogus sense of being "part" of the government, and hence bound to conceal its blunders and knaveries. But on the whole they are ten times better men than the owners of their papers.[1]

How much journalistic integrity is to be expected from the reporter who testified, in an interview with Professor H. Gilpatrick of Columbia University:

Hearst decided he wanted the McLeod Bill to go through. We were instructed that we were in favor of the bill and were to go out and make everyone else in favor of it. We were instructed to get one hundred telegrams from various people sent to Congress saying they favored the bill. I don't think I found a single person who knew what the bill was or cared, but we got the telegrams because of the obligations they felt to the paper.[2]

Or from the reporter who said:

We do just what the Old Man orders. One week he orders a campaign against rats. The next week he orders a campaign against dope peddlers. Pretty soon he is going to campaign against college professors. It's all the bunk, but orders are orders.[3]

Newspaper "policy" is sharpened during political controversies in which the interests of publishers are involved, or during the heat of national elections. In the Presidential campaign of 1936 the newspapers of the nation were characterized by singularly undisguised preferences; the issue was not merely that of a choice between Roosevelt and Landon but between a program and philosophy of government which directly threatened the estates of the wealthy —including newspaper proprietors—and one which proposed to free them from the legislative and economic attacks of the four years in which the New Deal had operated. A swift examination of the emphases of the press during this campaign will place the meaning of newspaper policy in bolder relief.

The Baltimore *Sun,* the St. Louis *Post-Dispatch,* and the Kansas City *Star* conducted energetic criticisms of Mr. Roosevelt and the New Deal in their editorial columns. (Roy Roberts of the Kansas City *Star* acted as Governor Landon's campaign manager.) But these papers did not carry their political disposition into the news columns. News about Roosevelt and Landon was treated with a regard for the equities of both space and emphasis. Similarly, although the New York *Times* supported Mr. Roosevelt in its editorials, Mr. Landon received scrupulously fair treatment in its news columns. This is one type of journalism.

A less laudable record was left by other newspapers. The honest reporting of their Washington correspondents was negated by misleading headlines, inconspicuous placing, and the sundry devices of what is most euphemistically called "unethical journalism." Correspondents found that the impartiality of their dispatches from the capital was lost in the total effect of their papers' make-up. In some cases members of the press corps were subjected to such psychological pressure that they took the safe path of least resistance. One Washington correspondent told this writer: "I'm sick of fighting my home office. I'm sick of being criticized, accused of being 'sold' on the New Deal simply because I don't attack Roosevelt and because I honestly think he will make a better President than Landon. From now on I'm giving my paper what it wants. That's what

I'm being paid to do, I suppose. If I don't swing into line they can fire me in a second and get some trained seal who will write to please the Boss."

The Chicago *Tribune,* for example, was transformed into what was virtually a personal organ, disseminating the biases of its publisher in its news columns. For over a week, during the height of the Presidential campaign, the President of the United States, a candidate for re-election, was mentioned on the front page of "The World's Greatest Newspaper" only once. On one day he was left out of the paper entirely. On another he was given a few perfunctory lines on page 13.[4] It is difficult to cite a more unabashed manipulation of news in the service of policy. When an investigation divulged immoral practices in two Wisconsin cities, the Chicago *Tribune* captioned its dispatch:

ROOSEVELT AREA IN WISCONSIN IS
HOTBED OF VICE.[5]

In reporting the meeting of the American Labor Party, which endorsed President Roosevelt, the *Tribune* dispatch of October 29, 1936, used this language: "More than 90 per cent of the audience . . . were persons of foreign birth. . . . The leaders of the new party who addressed the meeting one after another spoke with a foreign accent."

On September 1, 1937, the *Tribune,* in an editorial, spoke of a forthcoming La Follette senatorial investigation on labor spies and the violation of civil liberties as "a form of self-advertisement," "another New Deal importation of European methods employed by dictatorships both communist and fascist." The *Tribune* placed this editorial on its front page. There is historic irony in the spectacle of a newspaper in a democratic society labeling an investigation of civil liberties as a "Fascist-Communist" tactic.

The practices of the Hearst newspapers in 1936 are still vivid enough to make extended analysis unnecessary. During the last weeks of the campaign, reporters for the Hearst papers were estopped from writing anything that suggested the *possibility* of Mr. Roosevelt's re-election. References to the President's future plans were not welcomed. The phrase "if re-elected" disappeared from the news columns. Only near the end of October, 1936, did Mr. Hearst, in a confidential "rush" cable to all his editors, order his newspapers to give news of Roosevelt equal space and prominence with news of Landon. This policy was to go into effect on October 26, 1936—exactly eight days before the country went to the polls.[6]

The Hearst policy may be indicated more sharply by comparing the form in which the syndicated column of Robert S. Allen and Drew Pearson, "The Daily Washington Merry-Go-Round," was printed in the Hearst and other papers on several occasions. In November, 1935, Allen and Pearson conducted a poll on the question: "Should President Roosevelt Be Re-elected?" This was an effort to check upon the validity of the *Literary Digest* poll, which had asked the question: "Do you now approve of the acts and policies of the New Deal to date?" The *Literary Digest* had found 55.6 per cent of the voters against "the acts and policies of the New Deal." The Allen-Pearson poll showed that 69.7 per cent of their radio listeners favored President Roosevelt's re-election—a more pertinent issue. The comparison was striking and significant. In "The Daily Washington Merry-Go-Round" for December 9, 1935, these facts were analyzed. The Washington *Herald,* a Hearst property, simply deleted this part of the column: the rest was intact, exactly similar to the column as printed that day in the Philadelphia *Record,* for example. The space which had been occupied by the paragraphs discussing the 69.7 per cent majority for Roosevelt was filled in, instead, by "filler" material which Messrs. Allen and Pearson supply to their clients: comments on processing taxes, farm contracts, "The Mail Bag," etc.

At the end of 1935, Messrs. Allen and Pearson reviewed what they called "The End of the Pedestal Era," pointing out that President Roosevelt's popularity had declined in the early part of 1935 but had risen strongly since the adjournment of Congress. A comparison of the column as printed in the Philadelphia *Record* and the Washington *Herald* on December 31, 1935, shows that the Hearst paper printed that part of the column which analyzed the *decline* in Mr. Roosevelt's popularity, but cut out the part which discussed his rise back to public favor. This time the space was filled in with miscellaneous tid-bits about the Department of Agriculture's ice-cream reports.

Random items from the news columns of several other newspapers are illuminating examples of policy-governed "news." For several months before the election, the New York *Herald Tribune* printed the daily Jeremiads of Mrs. Preston Davie, famous for the slogan, "Twelve days left before election. Twelve days left to save the American way of life." Mrs. Davie, an amateur journalist, ended her daily attack on the President with these words:

> Will you join us?
> Call, write or telephone,
> Forty-one East Forty-second Street,
> Twelfth floor, Vanderbilt 3-5600.

This can hardly be called news. It was not marked advertising. It was propaganda—on the news pages. Mrs. Davie urged voters "to save our country, our homes, and our children from Communism, from the Dubinskys, the Hillmans, the Zaritskys." [7] That this type of tub-thumping was permitted in the columns of the *Herald Tribune* is no tribute to its record.

Colonel Frank Knox's Chicago *Daily News* is part-owner of Westbrook Pegler's daily column, "Fair Enough." In several instances, when Pegler's speculations were pointedly unfavorable to the Republican cause, the column was omitted from the Chicago *Daily News*.[8]

The coloring, slanting, or suppression of political news in the 1936 campaign was not confined to Republican or anti-Roosevelt papers.* Many papers in the South did not welcome news favorable to the cause of Governor Landon. The Washington correspondent for one of the most powerful Southern newspapers told this writer that he "wouldn't dream" of sending a story which did not support President Roosevelt and the Democratic party, or

* Professor Barlow of the University of Illinois analyzed the news columns of several dozen papers and concluded that of twenty-nine large dailies examined, nineteen consistently printed more pro-Landon than pro-Roosevelt news.[9]

The Washington Correspondents

which did not seem to injure the chances of Mr. Landon and "the other party." The New York *Post* (and the Philadelphia *Record*) set about an uncompromising pro-Roosevelt campaign which resulted in such misrepresentation as this:

PRO-HITLER STAFF AT HEADQUARTERS OF REPUBLICANS.[10]

Robert S. Lynd has shown that in Middletown both daily newspapers are committed to the same political party; the assumption of the founding fathers that each community will develop an "opposition" newspaper has thus been negated.

The fact that the heavy majority of American newspapers sided with big business interests in actively backing the campaign of Governor Landon in 1936 suggests that this clash between symbol and reality, between the newspaper as a public agency for the dissemination of necessary information and the newspaper as a privately owned business venture is in no sense peculiar to Middletown.[11]

Underlying the behavior of publishers there is a structure of interests which makes their journalistic strategies intelligible.

1. Newspapers are properties. As properties they are dedicated to the making of profit. And as men of property, publishers find their interests coinciding with the interests of other property-holding groups. Their sincere editorial policies may, *without* deliberate intent, mirror the preferences of the economic stratum with which they are identified. Hence the precision with which newspapers reflected

the anti-Roosevelt line which characterized those whose property and estate were threatened by the New Deal.

Newspapers are not necessarily guardians of the public welfare or organs of political enlightenment. Given the private ownership and freedom from social responsibility of the American press, it is gratuitous to expect publishers, with acknowledged exceptions, to adhere to a different ethic or a more detached consideration of the public good than bankers, business magnates, or manufacturers of patent medicines. The *Wall Street Journal,* in an editorial on January 20, 1925, printed a refreshingly candid statement of this point:

A newspaper is a private enterprise, owing nothing whatever to the public, which grants it no franchise. It is therefore "affected" with no public interest. It is emphatically the property of its owner who is selling a manufactured product at his own risk. . . . Editors, except where they own their own newspapers, take their policy from their employers. . . . But for ridiculously obvious reasons, there are many newspaper owners willing enough to encourage the public in the delusion that it is the editor of a newspaper who dictates the selection of news and expression of opinion. He only does so subject to correction and suggestion of the proprietor of the paper who, most properly, considers his newspaper as a plain business proposition. It is just that, no more and certainly no less.

R. G. Bauer of the University of Wisconsin investigated the editorial policies of leading American newspapers from 1895 to 1923, using outstanding decisions of the Supreme Court as points of analysis. Wherever clear-cut issues were involved (States rights versus federal centralization, for example, or individualism versus collectivism) newspapers which had traditionally championed one side promptly deserted it when their own economic interests were involved. The study concluded that editorial policies tend to reflect not a philosophical point of view or a set of political principles but "sympathy for an economic class." [12]

2. Publishers are employers. The publisher's relation to his employees is precisely that of any other employer to his employees: he can hire, fire, promote, penalize. He faces the same industrial problems that other employing groups do: the challenge of unionization, the problem of wages, the threat of strikes.

Many newspaper publishers make no pretense at maintaining "objectivity" during industrial crises. During the San Francisco General Strike of 1934, the publishers of that city and Oakland formed a council which, according to *Editor and Publisher*, was responsible for breaking the strike. Despite the protestations of Secretary of Labor Perkins ("You have no right to say there is radicalism or communism in this situation.") newspaper owners adopted a red-baiting, red-herring strategy. They treated the suggestions of General Hugh S. Johnson in such a manner that, upon leaving San Francisco, he remarked: "This is the first time I have ever been up against a newspaper oligarchy." [13]

In the field of social legislation the attitude of newspaper proprietors springs, once again, from their employer status. The Committee on Social Security of the American Newspaper Publishers' Association urged publishers to join with "other employer groups . . . (to) watch closely every rule, instruction or interpretation issued by your respective state administration" with reference to the social security laws. The committee urged "co-operation wherever possible with representatives of other industries" and said rather flatly:

Newspaper publishers as employers have interests that are identical and in common with all other employers in their respective areas. . . . It has been the belief of your Committee that newspaper publishers, as employers, are charged with an especial responsibility to co-operate with other employer groups in studying this whole problem and its effects upon industry, developing, as a result, a constructive attitude in presenting the employers' side of the problem. It is our feeling that newspaper publishers as employers fail to . . . appreciate the extent to which business generally looks to them for guidance and leadership, especially with respect to problems that are as broad in their effect and definite in their form as the ones contained in this social security program. Wherever possible, in an informal manner, the members of your Committeee have endeavored to meet this situation and render constructive service.[14]

The Wagner Bill, before it was upheld by the Supreme Court, was attacked by newspapers on every ground from "un-Americanism" to "bureaucracy." Most publishers fought the Child Labor clause of the NRA code proposals bitterly. They protested on every ground from the sacrosanct "Freedom of the Press" to the claim that the government was trying to "regiment" American youth.*

---

* The Louisville *Courier-Journal* had its carriers deliver letters to all subscribers asking them to write General Hugh S. Johnson "in my behalf" because "reformers are attempting to prohibit . . . boys under eighteen years from being gainfully employed." The newsboys provided the writing paper and picked up the letters the next day; they were mailed from the *Courier-Journal* office at that newspaper's expense.[15]

In a confidential bulletin issued November 20, 1935, the A.N.P.A. warned its members against the progress of the Child Labor Amendment, referred to as the "federal control of youth [*sic*] amendment." [16] In the news columns of the New York *Herald Tribune*, the Child Labor Amendment was referred to as "youth control," a term which scarcely suggests objective news treatment.

The fight of most publishers against the American Newspaper Guild is another illustration of primary business behavior. Unionization will unquestionably result in higher salaries, shorter hours, greater security of tenure, and improved working conditions. It will also raise publishing costs and cut into publishing profits. Publishers contend that membership in a union will rob the reporter of his detachment and will result in his "slanting" the news with a pro-union or pro-labor bias. They insist that reporters should avoid extra-journalistic ties. Such logic is a two-edged weapon, for reporters may legitimately reply that, to safeguard the objectivity of the press, the American Newspaper Publishers' Association should promptly disband, publishers should give up their business connections and club memberships, publishers should withdraw their investments in stocks, bonds, and factories, etc. In England, Sweden and Australia, reporters' unions have bettered working conditions and raised the quality and the dignity of journalism without interfering with editorial policy.[17]

When the directors of the Associated Press were considering a more expensive wire-photo service, Roy Howard of the Scripps-Howard papers said tartly: "We shortly will be met with the task of meeting the arguments of the newspaper guilds, and they can't be laughed off. When they say we have money for everything but editorial brains, they've got to be answered." [18]

Mr. William Randolph Hearst's argument against a guild is worthy of preservation for future historians. Mr. Hearst said: "Frankly, I do not believe in a newspaper guild. . . . I like to feel that a newspaperman is like a soldier in war. . . . The guild would tend to deprive the reporter of the character which makes the newspaperman a romantic figure." [19]

4. Publishers have vested interests in non-journalistic enterprises. A newspaper owner may also be a mine owner, a real estate operator, a large investor in utilities, a stockholder in a manufacturing plant, a director of a bank. Elizabeth Maier studied the biographies of 162 living editors and publishers and discovered that 30 per cent of them were directors of business corporations.[20] Elmer O. Fehlhaber examined the "Purely Personal" columns of *Editor and Publisher* and concluded that editors and publishers were identified, personally or financially, "with practically every non-journalistic enterprise in their respective communities." Editors and publishers were on committees pushing the sale of refunding bonds; one was president of the local telephone company; one was president of the Chamber of Commerce; one was district governor of Rotary International; one was head of the American Legion; one was running for State Senator.[21]

A publisher's temptation to use his newspaper to buttress his extra-journalistic stakes is difficult to resist. Newspaper proprietors do not publish newspapers in one insulated compartment of their identity, and own stocks, direct banks, or vote on corporation policies in another.

Mr. Moses (New York Commissioner of Parks) came out with the statement that he didn't like the approach to the Tri-Borough Bridge. The next morning we all got instructions that we were to kill that idea—stir up people, get telegrams, etc., to the effect that people didn't want the approach changed. Well, we all knew *Hearst had been buying up property around there.* [22]

5. Publishers possess human preferences and inhibitions which are projected, often unconsciously, into the organization which they control. According to *Time* magazine, the publisher of the Kansas City *Star* has "snake phobia." The *Star* avoids snake stories, and where that is impossible refers to snakes as "moving objects." When a Moon Mullins cartoon strip had a picture of a circus character charming snakes, the sequence was cut out and a strip from 1927 was substituted.[23] Now the injection of a publisher's snake phobia into news-treatment is of trivial consequence. But what if a publisher has a political "red," "yellow," or "pink" phobia and incorporates this into his newspaper policy? The consequences to the community are too serious to be ignored.

6. As men of property, wealth, and power, publishers rotate in certain sets. They marry into certain families; they move in rarefied social circles; their children study, play, and travel together. Publishers cannot help absorbing the psychology of their associates and approximating a

* The italics are the writer's.

social philosophy which is common to their circle. William Allen White has said:

> I know of no editor so high that his mind is not affected by his industrial environment. The fact that he lives in daily contact with the rich people of his community, whether the community be large or small, that he gangs with them at the country clubs, eats with them at leading hotels, and, indeed, prays with what might be called a plutocratic congregation, colors his mind and he sees things as his friends and associates see them.[24]

The testimony of the late Arthur Brisbane, intellectual doyen of the Hearst properties, is equally pertinent:

> Newspaper success today means great wealth, and the rich man . . . 99 times out of 100, lets his money think for him. There are men owning newspapers in this country who could not be bribed by any amount of money outside of their own pockets. But the money in their pockets edits their editorial columns every day. . . . A man's newspaper, like his God, is likely to reflect his own peculiarities.[25]

7. Newspapers derive the largest part of their income from advertising, not circulation.* (Increased circulation is valued primarily because it raises advertising rates.) But direct advertising control over the news columns is far less common than is generally assumed, and thrives, for

* A survey of a dozen representative newspapers in 1935 concluded that the average revenue from circulation was 20.6 per cent of the total income. Evening and Sunday papers got only 13.3 per cent of their receipts from circulation. Six morning metropolitan newspapers reached the highest circulation percentage, which was only 28.9 per cent.[26] Advertising superseded sales-to-readers as a major source of revenue in the period from 1830 to 1840.[27]

the most part, in smaller towns and with less successful newspapers.[28] The well-known feud which exists between the city room and the business office of a newspaper generally revolves around the desire of a large advertiser to get free publicity in the news columns for a sales campaign, the annual employees' dance, or some anniversary. Such items may be marked "B.O.M." ("Business Office Must") but they are about as harmful as the free publicity given to church picnics or club outings. Department stores generally succeed in keeping the names of their institutions out of stories of accidents, and often a prominent advertiser's wayward son is spared publicity on some unfortunate *amour* or arrest for speeding. Paul Bellamy of the Cleveland *Plain Dealer* told the 1928 convention of the American Society of Newspaper Editors:

> Better be frank and admit that we have one rule for the strong and another for the weak. . . . Who of us will deny that the paper he serves (excepting only the *Christian Science Monitor*) has published scores, if not hundreds of . . . misadventures . . . when the actors were humble persons? Why, such stories are the warp and woof of the newspaper. . . . But here, forsooth, stands the great John Goodman, pillar in society and an advertiser to boot. At once that kind of editorial sixth sense, the trouble detector, flashes red, and we hesitate. . . .[29]

In larger matters the power of the advertiser has again and again been checked by metropolitan newspapers.* For

* John B. Sheridan, publicity man for certain Missouri utilities, offered the bait of million-dollar advertising contracts for favorable utilities stories, but he could get nowhere with such journals as the St. Louis *Post-Dispatch* and the Kansas City *Star*.[30] The examples can be multiplied at length.

advertisers need newspapers no less than newspapers need them. Rising rates have driven business concerns to try many substitutes for newspaper advertising: "Shopper's dailies," leaflets, neighborhood papers, "fliers" delivered to homes, etc. In no case have these been satisfactory. Advertisers generally find it difficult to suppress news of significance for several reasons. Such suppression cannot be kept secret: too many men participate in the mechanism of publishing. Furthermore, *all* newspapers cannot be bribed; an item suppressed in one sheet may be given prominence in another precisely because of the pressure brought to bear.

The solicitude of newspapers for the interests of their advertisers takes a less overt but a more important form. The Tugwell Bill, a significant move in government service and an effort to check the false advertising of commodities which affect the health and even the lives of consumers, threatened some $350,000,000 worth of publishers' revenue. The bill was fought tooth-and-nail by newspapers and advertisers. So aroused were newspaper publishers by this threat to their income that many of them would not print such unmistakable news as Mrs. Franklin D. Roosevelt's endorsement of the bill.[31]

Where consumers' problems are concerned, the affinity which exists between newspaper owners and their advertisers has resulted in offenses against the public welfare. Perhaps the most consistent violations of accepted journalistic ethics occur with reference to rulings of the Federal Trade Commission, the Food and Drug Administration, or the reports of the Departments of Labor and Agriculture. When a nationally advertised cosmetic is found to contain dangerous ingredients that fact is ignored by the press. When a standard brand of peaches or soap or gasoline is condemned by an official government bureau the public is given no wide recognition of it. Washington correspondents have learned that it is pointless to "waste telegraph tolls" on such stories. Within one week in 1935 the Federal Trade Commission called the following organizations to account for misleading advertising claims: the Jergen-Woodbury Sales Corporation, the Musterole Company, Pine Brothers, and the distributors of Feen-a-mint, and Pro Ker (a treatment for baldness). Few, if any, newspapers opened an inch of their news-space for any account of these events.[32] Apologists may retort that the "news" element was missing in these items; but it is clear that *had* the newspapers printed the stories they would have been news. If news is that which interests or affects a great number of readers then events which affect the consumers' health or purse * are news of unquestionable legitimacy.

In the larger view, the press is most vitally affected not by advertisers but by *advertising*. Because the welfare of newspapers rests upon the profitability of their advertising, publishers tend to emphasize a psychological setting which fosters buying—and therefore more advertising. One of the most marked characteristics of the American press is its continuous, self-conscious, and spurious optimism. Newspapers are singularly sensitive, in both their editorial and news columns, to the general business conditions from which their major source of income flows. Thus, a paper

* Taxation stories are always considered good news.

as intelligent as the Baltimore *Sun* used "idle" instead of
"unemployed" during the early part of the depression,
and preferred "the business situation" to "the depression."
Similarly, several newspapers in the Middle West cut out
the gloomy notes of their Washington correspondents in
describing the Supreme Court's decision on the AAA and
suggested a preference for "optimistic angles."

It may be argued that in a time of economic uncertainty
enormous damage may result if newspapers act the dour
Cassandra: banks may be wrecked by depositors' runs, pur-
chasing habits upset, the vicious spiral of depression set
into motion. But it is proper to examine the harm done by
the efforts of the press to disseminate a misleading optimism in a day when reality contradicts it. Newspapers may
deepen the severity of cyclical unemployment, for instance,
by accentuating the general outlines of the business cycle.
The American press played a significant role from 1926 to
1929 in building up a speculative psychology and a boom—
with a correspondingly sharp deflation as its aftermath.
The false hopes for business recovery aroused by optimistic
treatments of the depression led to "unhealthy speculative
situations and greater maladjustment." [33] Marlan Pew,
then editor of *Editor and Publisher*, said that in the years
preceding 1929 financial pages were loaded with " 'inspired' news, press-agent written" and that this "consti-
tuted as wicked an exploitation of the reading public as
our press has ever been guilty of." [34] In *Mobilizing for
Chaos*, Professor O. W. Riegel has commented upon the
tendency of the American press to defend the *status quo*,
and to indulge in "only those forms of sensationalism that
will not shake the political and economic set-up of the

country and thus endanger the financial security of the big newspaper properties or the great business interests which support them." [35]

8. Newspapers are Big Businesses. The character of American journalism has been radically transformed from what the founding fathers visualized. In the eighteenth and early nineteenth century, publishing was a profession. Newspapers were published by men to whom journalism was a career. It took relatively little capital for a journalistically minded man to become a publisher. Today the press is an industry and a business, subject to the laws, the problems, and the aspirations of economic enterprise. Newspaper publishing involves enormous investments and expenditures. The Chicago *Daily News* was placed on the market at a price of $13,000,000. The value of the Kansas City *Star* was set at $11,000,000. The Dallas *News*, in a city which had a population of less than 160,000 at the time, was appraised at over $2,000,000.[36]

Publishing has become an enterprise *which is no longer accessible* except to the wealthy. This means that, as in other realms of our economy, power has gravitated to few hands, power has tended to multiply itself, economic power has been translated into political power of a magnitude incongruous with the assumptions of a democratic society. Competition, from which the general good of a free competitive society is assumed to grow, has been limited, restrained, and strangulated. Competition has given way to imperfect competition or to near-monopoly. The consequences are far-reaching—perhaps more so in the realm of public opinion, where men have become lords over facts, than in the sphere of finance. For control over the dissemination of the information upon which a democratic society acts and according to which democratic citizens make political choices, is exercised by men who often recognize no social responsibility, and who may manipulate what is almost a public agency for the sake of private ends.

This does not ignore the fact that the radio has entered the scene and may publicize facts, or interpretations of fact, which newspapers suppress, mutilate, or de-emphasize. For the radio does not possess the curious authority of print; nor does the spoken word contain the *permanence* of the printed word. More important, the radio listener is conscious of the human agent, whereas the newspaper reader tends to accept printed dispatches as impersonal events. The newspaper is still "the bible of democracy, the only serious book most people read. It is the only book they read every day." [37] Nor can one dismiss the influence of the press with the blithe statement that people *know* that newspapers are not to be trusted. Charles E. Merriam has made the seminal suggestion that even where readers are skeptical of the reliability of newspapers the repetition of news has a somewhat hypnotic effect. "Journalistic repetition is in some ways reminiscent of the beat, beat, beat, of the drum in the primitive tribe." [38]

Ten years ago the Lynds said that it was safe to predict that in any given controversy the two leading papers in Middletown could be expected "to support . . . the business class rather than the working class, the Republican party against any other, but especially against any 'radical' party." [39] Today, "Middletown's press, like its pulpit, has largely surrendered its traditional role of leader; both have bartered their peculiar rights to proclaim sharply dissident truths for the right to be well supported by the reigning economy." [40] If these conditions exist in a town which at least has formally competing newspapers, how much more dire is the situation in cities in which the inhabitants have access to only one morning or evening newspaper? Even in such important centers as the following, there is only one morning newspaper: Pittsburgh, Buffalo, Cleveland, Cincinnati, Detroit, Milwaukee, Baltimore, Indianapolis, Kansas City, St. Louis, Des Moines, Louisville, Memphis, Seattle, Denver, Atlanta, Minneapolis, Syracuse, Portland (Ore.), Houston, Dallas.[41] The historical movement of journalism, reflecting the movement of the larger economy of which it is a part, is suggested by the fact that in 1890, when Chicago was one-half its present size, it had no less than eleven newspapers; today it has but five.*

Book publishing does not demand the investments or

---

* The semi-monopolistic character of journalism is strikingly indicated by the following: one newspaper (or publishing company) has an exclusive monopoly in 93 per cent of the cities in the United States with populations under 10,000; in 87 per cent of the cities between 10,000 and 25,000; in 78 per cent of the cities between 25,000 and 50,000; in 66 per cent of the cities between 60,000 and 75,000; in 46 per cent of the cities between 75,000 and 100,000. Of all the dailies in the United States 82 per cent had a complete monopoly in their communities in 1934. And of the 1,305 cities in the United States with populations under 100,000 only 163 have more than one newspaper, or one newspaper publishing company. The extraordinary growth of "chain ownership" has accentuated this movement towards monopolization. In 1933, sixty-four chains owned over 315 daily newspapers in the United States.[42]

the advertising foundation of newspaper publishing. And the American reader of books has access to political concepts and interpretations of fact which range from the most reactionary to the most radical; he has a similar choice in weekly or monthly magazines. But what choice does the vast majority of American readers have in the political emphases of the editorial columns of daily newspapers, or the political color of their news columns? Of Middletown, the Lynds have written:

> Here, then, is a community of nearly 40,000 individuals, founded upon the two principles that one adult's judgment is as good as another's and that ignorance is no excuse for incompetency, and increasingly dependent upon information furnished by its daily press. But despite the assumption of the adequacy of the information of each citizen, it is left to the whim and economic status of the individual whether he shall see a paper at all, obstructions, political, economic and personal, are thrown at many points in the way of our newspapers . . . (publishing) . . . the facts needed by the citizens to carry on a democratic form of government.[43]

In a democratic society one cannot challenge the right of Mr. William Randolph Hearst to utter the most arrant nonsense in his editorial columns, nor the privilege of Colonel Robert R. McCormick to project his personal phobias into the Chicago *Tribune's* editorials, nor the license of the respective publishers and editors of the Los Angeles *Times*, the Philadelphia *Record*, or the *Daily Worker* to stride through their editorial columns breathing hell-fire of their own particular type. Editorials are the soap-boxes of journalism. They are approached by readers as recognizable efforts to influence opinion. Their influence may be discounted accordingly. But when editorial opinions are stamped into the news columns, when facts are colored, twisted, suppressed, or mutilated, then a crime is being committed against the society which sanctions journalistic freedom. For the news columns are common carriers. As Walter Lippmann pointed out some twenty years ago:

> When those who control them (the news columns) arrogate to themselves the right to determine by their own consciences what shall be reported and for what purpose, democracy is unworkable. Public opinion is blockaded. For when a people can no longer confidently repair "to the best fountains" for their information, then anyone's guess and anyone's rumor, each man's hope and each man's whim becomes the basis of government. All that the sharpest critics of democracy have alleged is true, if there is no steady supply of trustworthy and relevant news.[44]

In the larger view, the ills with which contemporary journalism is afflicted are an integral aspect of our society rather than a disease with an etiology of its own. One may question whether newspapers are any more derelict in their duty to democratic society than the schools, the church, or the bar. The character of American journalism is, in a sense, an indictment of our educational system, for insofar as readers have not learned to be critical of evidence, or to effect better journalism by protesting against that which is offered to them, our schools have neglected an important task. "We must advance, if we are to advance at all, along the entire front at once. Our journalism can never be truly free until our society is free."[45] But long-range perspectives may tend to obscure immediate problems. Mature political orientation consists partly in subordinating utopian preferences to the recognition of available alternatives. This is not the place to suggest panaceas for our society, but we may properly devote some attention to the newspapers which are so influential an aspect of it.

A free press can exist only in a free society. It would appear, therefore, that publishers would defend the greater, inclusive freedom of the order in which they thrive. They would recognize and seek to help in the solution of the contradictions into which the growth of our economy has plunged our polity: the disparity between political and economic freedom; the precipitation of federal centralization, unionization, collective bargaining, etc., partly *as a consequence* of monopolies, the corporate structure, and imperfect competition; the violations of basic civil liberties by men more determined to defend their power than the political rights upon which the system from which they derived their power is founded; the new role of the United States in the international scene. The Washington correspondents probably recognize these manifestations of historical change more sharply than do their employers. In the scramble for immediate profit, and in the fight to keep immediate gains, men of property lose sight of the consequences of their behavior. The steel baron who defies his union is more concerned over the threat of collective bargaining than the implications of his defiance of what is now national law. The publisher who corrupts his news-columns or ignores his duties under the Wagner Labor Relations Act is, in no less measure, blind to the attack on orderly democratic government which his intransigence entails. One of the leading economists in the country has written:

> In an individualistic-utilitarian view of life, freedom means freedom to use power, and economic freedom means freedom to use economic power, without political interference or restraint. Such freedom may in effect become slavery for the person who has little power at his disposal, since life itself requires practically continuous control of a certain minimum of economic power.[46]

The historical line along which the United States seems to be traveling cannot leave the proprietary foundations of the press unaffected. The movement towards centralization of political authority is commensurate with the scale and the problems of the American economy and—perhaps more critical—with the position of the United States in the world "balancing of power" process. The rise to political self-consciousness of workers, and their identification in terms other than "Republican" or "Democrat," is a revolution which, for better or for worse, has begun. This, too, the Washington correspondents seem to recognize with more precision than do their employers. Insofar as publishers are indifferent to, or overly apologetic for, the excesses of contemporary society, and insofar as they fail to expose its weakness and its problems simply by the untrammeled publication of facts, they function to undermine the very political structure with which their own welfare is inextricably identified. It is not gratuitous to remind newspaper proprietors that the result of the 1936 Presidential campaign was a severe blow to their methods and philosophy. The press was discredited, in effect, by the size of the vote for the candidate they had so vehemently opposed.

There is a disturbing side to the publishers' conduct in the 1936 campaign which has not been commented upon. By the manner in which they presented the issues and the candidates, the newspapers increased the importance of an area of political combat which it would be better for democratic citizens to treat with skepticism: the competition of personalities and of oratory. In proportion as the newspapers did not grant a just hearing to Mr. Roosevelt they increased the public's receptivity to his voice, his phrases, and his oratorical virtuosity. They forced the public, as it were, to turn to the radio. They forced the public to give greater credence to the very things which they warned against: dramatic phrases. Those who rejoice over Mr. Roosevelt's victory may well ask themselves whether they would have welcomed a vote influenced by vocal brilliance had Mr. Landon been the better speaker and showman. Suppose, for example, that in the 1940's the Presidency becomes a contest between an honest democratic leader and a demagogue with dictatorial aspirations. Suppose the press once again enters the campaign with such undisguised animus that citizens discount even its legitimate points and turn, in disgust, to the radio as a guide? Suppose this time it is the democratic candidate, the "American" candidate, who is no master of the golden voice, but, rather, the demagogue. . . . By branding Mr. Roosevelt as a "dictator," a "radical," or a "Communist," the newspapers have robbed the words of their meaning and have built an indifference to them as negative concepts in political controversy.* The thoughtless reiteration of "red scare" phrases calculated to stampede the public had the paradoxical effect of accustoming people to the words and, by identifying a man as popular as Mr. Roosevelt with them, tended to *legitimize* their sound. Similarly, by using "freedom of the press" as a moral smokescreen behind which to defend child labor and low salaries, publishers dissipate the moral authority of the slogan; in doing so they negate its potency for some day when freedom of the press may actually be endangered. One might without flippancy recommend a reading of the "Wolf! Wolf!" fable to the next convention of the A.N.P.A.

The norms of contemporary journalism are anachronistic. The individualism of an earlier and more healthy competitive system still dominates the substance of newspaper

* In an article entitled "AWAKE, AMERICAN PATRIOTS!" published in the Los Angeles *Examiner*, November 24, 1935, Robert H. Hemphill, "financial authority" of the Hearst press, declared: "I do not know what catastrophe will be required to shock this nation into a realization of the enormous consequences which are planned and ARE BEING EXECUTED by the Federal Administration and its little band of fanatic adventurers. . . .

"This band of revolutionary radicals PROPOSE TO OVERTHROW THIS GOVERNMENT.

"AND THEY ARE DOING IT!" [47]

In the New York *American* Mr. Hearst addressed the President and his associates as "you and your fellow Communists." On October 8, 1936, the *American* printed a poem, under an inflammatory cartoon, of which the first stanza read:

> A Red New Deal with a Soviet seal
> Endorsed by a Moscow hand,
> The strange result of an alien cult
> In a liberty-loving land. [48]

dispatches. Personal ingenuity, personal success, and personal responsibility are over-emphasized and extolled at a time when widespread recognition is being given to the social foundations of individual success and the social responsibilities of individual power. The dislocations of industrial conflict are interpreted in terms of over-simplified personal equations. The wider and more important aspects of social change and political growth are lost sight of in the emphasis upon romantic personalities. "Reds" or "agitators" are blamed for protest formations which transcend the influence of persons. "John L. Lewis" becomes a too-simple rhetorical substitute for "the labor movement." Newspaper dispatches operate to concentrate attention on the individual at the expense of the societal.

The focus of attention is thus absorbed by personal problems. . . . The particular incident is not written about as representative of a context of relationships. Not desperation through unemployment, not insecurity through crop failure, not diminished administrative efficiency because of greater burdens of prohibitory regulation, but personal motives and struggles are the subject matter of the secondary means of communication in the bourgeois world.

When such an ideology impregnates life from start to finish, the thesis of collective responsibility runs against a wall of non-comprehension.[49]

The premium which journalism places upon an attack, and the spurious daily "crises" which clutter the pages of the newspapers, tend to (1) over-emphasize the errors and inefficiencies of representative government at a time when democratic agencies should concern themselves with buttressing its prestige; (2) deaden the perception of the public in advance to genuine crises which may arise; (3) heighten tensions and foster an impatience with democratic government which demagogues may use to their advantage. The campaign of the newspapers against "professors," "theories," and "theorists" has exalted the pragmatic at the expense of the analytic; it has, in effect, disparaged the value of the expert and discouraged the contribution to government of knowledge derived from systematic study. It is ironic that in a country which values education so highly that it has made it compulsory (a democracy must deny the freedom to be ignorant), the men who help make opinion have discouraged the application of knowledge to social problems.

It is worth noticing that American journalism does not possess any agency, public, private, or professional, to guard its standards and supervise its practitioners. We have an American Medical Association, bar associations, societies of engineers, architects, etc.; but we have no comparable organization of journalists. The American Newspaper Publishers' Association is primarily interested in publishers' problems and is dominated by a business ethic. The American Society of Newspaper Editors does not reach into the ranks of journalism and lacks both scope and authority. The American Newspaper Guild has devoted its brief life to the problems of unionization and recognition and has so far indicated no program along personnel lines.

In England two organizations guard the professional standards of their craft: the Institute of Journalism, founded in 1880 and composed of newspaper proprietors as well as workers, and the National Union of Journalists, which publishes the monthly organ *The Journalist*.[50] Efforts to license journalists in our country, to set up standards by which newspapermen are to be judged, or by which their integrity and competence may be tested, have invariably failed.* Since newspapermen are skeptical of the suggestions of laymen or scholars it is valuable, at this point, to quote the admonition of one of the most distinguished editors in the country, William Allen White:

> Until the people of this country get it well into their heads that journalism is a profession that must be licensed and controlled, as the medical and legal profession are licensed and controlled, there can be no freedom of the press that is not liable to abuses. . . . The most important thing in a democracy is the dissemination of intelligent information upon important matters. Until a man is equipped to know what are important matters and until he is trained to discuss important matters and disseminate facts intelligently, democracy is in danger. . . . Until journalism is recognized as a profession for trained men who have certain defined qualifications the newspaper business will vacillate.[51]

For over 150 years the right of American publishers to print what they please has not been challenged. They have enjoyed freedom of expression and freedom of reporting. But they have not been held responsible for the *uses* to which they put their constitutional prerogative. If a doctor falsely or incompetently prescribes strychnine and his patient dies, the doctor is subject to prosecution. If a maniac puts poison into a public-drinking system, he is incarcerated in a stronghold where his possibilities of injuring society

---

* In many cases there was an understandable fear that such measures might be an encroachment on the freedom of the press.

are minimized. But a newspaper publisher can give criminal advice, lie to the public, poison its intelligence, and conduct campaigns against civil liberties, decent morals, and the democratic system itself without being held accountable for his conduct, or without having to accept responsibility for the consequences of his action. He is granted legal sanction for behavior which may range from the incendiary to the psychopathic.

The journalist with a power comprehending all things requires no sanction. He derives his authority from no election, he receives support from no one. . . . It is hard to imagine a despotism more irresponsible than the despotism of printed words. Is it not strange and irrational that those who struggle most for the preservation of this despotism are the most impassioned champions of freedom, the ferocious enemies of legal restrictions and of all interference by established authority? . . . For conduct such as this a monarch would lose his throne, a minister would be disgraced, impeached and punished; but the journalist stands dry above the waters he has disturbed; from the ruin he has caused he rises triumphant and briskly continues his destructive work.[52]

Professor Merriam has said that in one sense newspaper proprietors have become an informal and irresponsible House of Lords.[53] This position assumes enormous significance if we remember that the newspaper becomes to the layman what the school is to the child: a dispensary of facts; a crucible in which political ideas are resolved; an opinion-making institution which disseminates the symbols of political life and, however unintentionally, assigns moral values to them.

The American press is free in the sense that there are

no legal or political interferences with its editorial and news-columns. But the freedom of the press does not mean the freedom of the *news*. It is the contention of this writer that in abusing the freedom which they possess newspaper publishers are strengthening the possibility of political interference with that freedom. The danger of distorted news-columns and of colored dispatches lies not merely in the fact that the public is misled—(the radio has removed some of the dangers in this direction)—but that aspiring demagogues and potential dictators are provided with impressive arguments for controlling the press. A public which has learned to be skeptical of the sources of its news, and which has been given evidence of the falsifications practiced by its newspapers, may be receptive to the oratory of those who ask for the power to "cleanse" the press and "remove" those who pollute the news. This is a danger which few publishers seem to recognize, but it cannot be ignored in a day in which democratic society is being threatened. The best guarantee of freedom is the intelligent use of it. In no society has license long gone uncorrected: when liberty is used to violate the privileges which liberty confers, men of force and eloquence may win public support to suppress those violations—and freedom with it. It is not academic to suggest to the proprietors of the American newspapers that one of the gravest threats to their freedom lies in the very use which they are making of it. They would do well to ponder the words of Franz Höllering, formerly editor of the Berlin *Zeitung am Mittag*, who speaks from direct experience when he says:

But I must say that Hitler had a fatal attraction for the big publishers as he did for the rest of big business. He promised to free them from labor unions and from government regulations. In economic matters he promised them absolute freedom. Many things which today are said in America against the New Deal, Hitler said against the Weimar Republic.[54]

From whatever point of departure one chooses to analyze the function and the influence of the Washington representatives of the American press, the following generalizations, suggested in earlier chapters, seem defensible: newspapers get the type of reporting which they encourage; publishers get the kind of Washington correspondents that they deserve; and the public receives Washington correspondence of a character which newspaper publishers, and ultimately they alone, make possible.

APPENDICES

APPENDIX A

A NOTE ON METHOD:
HOW THE 127 WERE CHOSEN

THIS study was begun on September 3, 1935. The *Congressional Directory* for April, 1935, the latest issued at the time, served as the first guide in selecting the correspondents to be studied. Later, the *Directory* for January, 1936, was substituted. This listed 497 persons as "members of the press entitled to admission to the press galleries" of the Senate and the House of Representatives.* The list was misleading. It included correspondents who were no longer in Washington (or who had died), secretaries, telegraph operators, cartoonists, representatives of foreign newspapers, managing editors, news editors, society columnists, editorial writers, feature writers, and specialists. The field of inquiry for this study was restricted to active political correspondents for American newspapers and press associations, specifically to (a) writers of news-dispatches or columns (b) of national political content (c) for daily United States newspapers or press associations (d) of a general, rather than trade, circulation (e) of 75,000 or over. Freelance correspondents who represented more than one American paper were included if the combined circulation of their clients was above 75,000.

According to these qualifications the following groups were ruled out as ineligible for study:

* Pp. 617-626.

1. Newspapermen who do not write news. (Managing editors of Washington papers, editorial writers, desk men, copy editors, telegraph editors or operators, secretaries.)

2. Correspondents who do not write political news or columns. (Sports writers, society columnists, feature writers, financial experts.)

3. Correspondents who do not write political news of national content. (Many regional reporters for the Associated Press, local reporters for the Washington papers, part-time free-lance writers who supply such items as "Kansans in Washington.")

4. Correspondents who do not work for daily newspapers. (Representatives of weekly or monthly magazines, news-letter writers.)

5. Correspondents whose newspapers are not of general circulation. (Business organs, trade journals, technical publications.)

6. Correspondents for foreign newspapers or press agencies.

An application of these standards to the 497 correspondents included in the *Congressional Directory* for January, 1936, eliminated the following:

Deceased	4
Foreign correspondents	24
Persons no longer in Washington, or no longer active in newspaper work	19
Office or secretarial help	11
Correspondents for trade and business journals	9
Correspondents not sending daily dispatches or sending non-political dispatches (science, radio, editorial services)	19
Correspondents for newspapers which have a circulation under 75,000, or correspondents concentrating on news only of interest to their localities	49

Appendices

Correspondents for foreign-language newspapers published in the United States ... 1
Associated Press
    Reporters on the Regional Staff ... 26
    News editors, filing editors, copy and re-write men, photo editors ... 14
    Reporters covering features, sports, science, etc. ... 8
    Correspondents covering Latin-American and Insular Affairs ... 2
United Press
    Desk men ... 5
    Correspondents covering Latin-American and Insular Affairs, and feature writers ... 4
International News Service
    Desk men and telegraph editors or operators ... 4
    Sports and feature writers ... 2
Universal Service
    Editorial columnists, feature writers ... 4
Central News Association
    Financial experts and writers (Central News is largely a financial ticker service) ... 6
Scripps-Howard Newspaper Alliance
    Editorial writers, foreign experts, feature writers, cartoonists ... 7
United States News Association
    (The entire staff; this is a weekly publication) ... 12
Wall Street Journal
    Telegraph operators, office help, non-political writers ... 8
Washington City News Service
    (A local news service for newspapers and newspapermen) ... 2
Washington Newspapers
    Washington *Herald* ... 16

Washington *Times*   10
Washington *Daily News*   11
    (These papers list their reportorial staffs in the
       Congressional Directory; but the majority of
       these men cover local District of Columbia news,
       or features, human-interest stories, society, etc.
       The Washington *Herald* relies on Universal
       Service dispatches for items of national political
       importance; the Washington *Times,* on the
       INS; the Washington *Daily News* uses the
       Scripps-Howard Newspaper Alliance.)
Washington Evening *Star*
    Desk men, local reporters, editorial writers   5
Washington *Post*
    Desk men, local reporters, editorial writers   7
            Total   289

Thus, 289 out of the 497 newspapermen and women listed
in the *Congressional Directory* were considered ineligible for
the purposes of the study. That left 208 correspondents. I
began to interview the most important of these * covering as
wide and representative a field as possible. Efforts to contact
certain newspapermen failed: telephone calls and letters received no response from nineteen of the lesser correspondents,
many of whom had no offices listed in the *Congressional Directory.* This reduced the number to 189.

    By June of 1936, I had interviewed 154 correspondents.
Of this number, 127 filled out the first questionnaire. They
became the control group; and the second questionnaire was

    * Obviously a reporter for the Chicago *Tribune* is more important
than a reporter for a small morning newspaper in Evanston, Illinois,
which the *Tribune* invades. Similarly, a correspondent for an inconspicuous Iowa paper was passed up for the correspondent for the Des
Moines *Register* and *Tribune.*

sent to them. 107 filled out the second questionnaire. It is obvious that, by statistical law, the "sample" is more than adequate to permit generalization about the press corps—especially since it is a selected sample of correspondents for the most influential papers in the country.

After analyzing the questionnaire materials, three months were spent in the Library of Congress examining literature and monographs which impinged upon special aspects of the study. The Press Intelligence Bureau of the government, in the Department of Commerce Building, was valuable in supplying "clips" of dispatches from over 400 newspapers distributed throughout the country. This made it possible to analyze the regional and policy differences in newspaper treatments of the same political events.

Editor and Publisher and the *American Press* (trade journals), the *Guild Reporter* (bi-weekly publication of the American Newspaper Guild), the *Journalism Quarterly* (published by the University of Minnesota), and the weekly Press section of *Time* magazine were essential sources of information. Editorial comments and articles in the *Nation* and the *New Republic* were followed for criticisms of news-treatment. The annotated bibliography on *Propaganda and Promotional Activities*, by Lasswell, Casey, and Smith, was used as a guide to published materials in the field of public opinion to which the facts, interpretations and impressions rising from the research might be compared.

APPENDIX B

NEWSPAPERS REPRESENTED IN THIS STUDY (186)

NEWSPAPER	WASHINGTON CORRESPONDENT
Akron (Ohio) *Beacon-Journal*	Radford Mobley, Jr.
Akron (Ohio) *Times-Press*	Ned Brooks
	Robert S. Brown
Albuquerque (N. M.) *Tribune*	Max Stern
Anderson (S. C.) *Independent &* *Tribune*	Jesse S. Cottrell
Anderson (S. C.) *Mail*	Jesse S. Cottrell
Ann Arbor (Mich.) *News*	Mark Foote
Appleton (Wis.) *Post-Crescent*	Ruby A. Black
Arizona *Daily Star* (Tucson)	Jesse S. Cottrell
Arkansas *Democrat* (Little Rock)	Bascom N. Timmons
Atlanta (Ga.) *Constitution*	Gladstone Williams
Baltimore *Evening Sun*	Frederick Barkley
	Henry M. Hyde
Baltimore *Sun*	J. Fred Essary
	Dewey Fleming
	Charles P. Trussell
	Paul W. Ward
Bay City (Mich.) *Times*	Mark Foote
Beacon (N. Y.) *News*	George H. Manning, Jr.
	James J. Butler
Birmingham (Ala.) *Age-Herald*	Russell Kent
Birmingham *News*	Russell Kent
Birmingham *Post*	Robert W. Horton

NEWSPAPER	WASHINGTON CORRESPONDENT
Boston *Evening Transcript*	Oliver McKee, Jr.
Boston *Herald*	William Kennedy
Boston *Traveler*	William Kennedy
Brockton (Mass.) *Enterprise &*	
Times	Bulkley S. Griffin
Brooklyn (N. Y.) *Daily Eagle*	Clinton W. Mosher
Buffalo (N. Y.) *Evening News*	James L. Wright
	Arthur W. Weil
	Merwin H. Browne
Buffalo *Times*	Herbert Little
Camden (N. J.) *Courier*	George H. Manning, Jr.
Camden *Post*	George H. Manning, Jr.
Charleston (S. C.) *News &*	
Courier	K. Foster Murray
Charlotte (N. C.) *Observer*	Jesse S. Cottrell
Chattanooga (Tenn.) *Times*	Russell Kent
Chicago *Daily News*	Paul R. Leach
	Fred A. Reed
Chicago *Tribune*	Arthur S. Henning
	Walter Trohan
Christian Science Monitor	Erwin D. Canham
(Boston)	Richard L. Strout
	Mary Hornaday
Cincinnati *Enquirer*	Edwin W. Gableman
Cincinnati *Post*	Ned Brooks
	Robert S. Brown
Cincinnati *Times-Star*	Morris D. Ervin
Cleveland *News*	Bascom N. Timmons
Cleveland *Plain Dealer*	Paul Hodges
Cleveland *Press*	Ned Brooks
	Robert S. Brown
Columbia (S. C.) *Record*	Ralph C. Mulligan

NEWSPAPER	WASHINGTON CORRESPONDENT
Columbus (Ohio) *Citizen*	Ned Brooks
	Robert S. Brown
Daily Northwestern (Oshkosh, Wis.)	Ruby A. Black
Dallas (Tex.) *Evening Journal*	Parke F. Engle
Dallas *News*	Parke F. Engle
Dallas *Times-Herald*	Bascom N. Timmons
Denver (Colo.) *Post*	Charles O. Gridley
Des Moines (Iowa) *Register*	Richard L. Wilson
Des Moines *Tribune*	Richard L. Wilson
Detroit *Free Press*	Clifford A. Prevost
Detroit *News*	Jay G. Hayden
Detroit *Times*	Felix Cotten
Eau Claire (Wis.) *Telegram*	Ruby A. Black
Elmira (N. Y.) *State Gazette*	George H. Manning, Jr.
El Paso (Tex.) *Herald-Post*	Max Stern
Evansville (Ind.) *Courier*	Mark Thistlewaite
Evansville *Journal*	Mark Thistlewaite
Flint (Mich.) *Journal*	Mark Foote
	Lawrence E. Stafford
Fort Wayne (Ind.) *Journal Gazette*	Lawrence E. Stafford
	Mark Thistlewaite
Fresno (Calif.) *Bee & Republican*	Gladstone Williams
Grand Rapids (Mich.) *Press*	Mark Foote
	Lawrence Stafford
Green Bay (Wis.) *Press-Gazette*	Ruby A. Black
Harrisburg (Pa.) *News-Patriot*	George H. Manning, Jr.
	James J. Butler
Hartford (Conn.) *Courant*	Arthur C. Wimer
Hartford (Conn.) *Times*	Bulkley S. Griffin
Haverhill (Mass.) *Gazette*	Bulkley S. Griffin
Houston (Tex.) *Chronicle*	Bascom N. Timmons

NEWSPAPER	WASHINGTON CORRESPONDENT
Houston *Post*	George W. Stimpson
Indianapolis (Ind.) *News*	Mark Thistlewaite
	Frederick Morhart, Jr.
Indianapolis *Star*	Everett C. Watkins
Jackson (Mich.) *Citizen Patriot*	Mark Foote
	Lawrence Stafford
Jamestown (N. Y.) *Evening Journal*	Ruby A. Black
Jamestown (N. Y.) *Post*	George H. Manning, Jr.
	James J. Butler
Jamaica (N. Y.) Long Island *Daily Press*	George H. Manning, Jr.
	James J. Butler
Jersey City (N. J.) *Journal*	George H. Manning, Jr.
	James J. Butler
Joliet (Ill.) *Herald-News*	Frederic W. Wile
Kalamazoo (Mich.) *Gazette*	Marke Foote
	Lawrence E. Stafford
Kansas City (Mo.) *Journal-Post*	William P. Helm
Kentucky *Post* (Covington) *	Ned Brooks
	Robert S. Brown
Kentucky *Times Star* †	Morris D. Ervin
Knoxville (Tenn.) *Journal*	John D. Erwin
Knoxville *News-Sentinel*	Robert W. Horton
LaCrosse (Wis.) *Tribune & Leader-Press*	Ruby A. Black
Lancaster (Pa.) *New Era*	George H. Manning, Jr.
	James J. Butler
Los Angeles *Times*	Warren B. Francis
Lynn (Mass.) *Item*	Bulkley S. Griffin
Madison (Wis.) *Capital Times*	Radford Mobley, Jr.

* An edition of the Cincinnati *Post*.
† An edition of the Cincinnati *Times-Star*.

NEWSPAPER	WASHINGTON CORRESPONDENT
Madison (Wis.) *State Journal*	Ruby A. Black
Manchester (N. H.) *Union Leader*	Bulkley S. Griffin
Memphis (Tenn.) *Commercial-Appeal*	John D. Erwin
Memphis (Tenn.) *Press-Scimitar*	Robert W. Horton
Miami (Fla.) *Herald*	Gladstone Williams
Middletown (N. Y.) *Times-Herald*	Edwin E. Hartrich
Milwaukee *Sentinel*	Raymond Z. Henle
Minneapolis *Journal*	George A. Benson
Minneapolis *Star*	Richard L. Wilson
Mobile (Ala.) *Press Register*	Radford Mobley, Jr.
Modesto (Calif.) *Bee*	Gladstone Williams
Moline (Ill.) *Dispatch*	Charles O. Gridley
Mount Vernon (N. Y.) *Daily Argus*	George H. Manning, Jr.
	James J. Butler
Muskegon (Mich.) *Chronicle*	Mark Foote
Nashville (Tenn.) *Tennesseean*	John D. Erwin
Newark (N. J.) *Evening News*	Walter Karig
Newark (N. J.) *Ledger*	George H. Manning, Jr.
	James J. Butler
New Britain (Conn.) *Herald*	James J. Butler
Newburgh (N. Y.) *Beacon-News*	Edwin E. Hartrich
New Castle (Pa.) *News*	Arthur C. Wimer
New Haven (Conn.) *Register*	Bulkley S. Griffin
New Mexico *State Tribune* (Albuquerque)	Max Stern
New Orleans *Item*	J. Fred Essary
New Orleans *States*	Bascom N. Timmons
New Orleans *Times-Picayune*	Paul Wooton

NEWSPAPER	WASHINGTON CORRESPONDENT
New Orleans *Tribune*	J. Fred Essary
New Rochelle (N. Y.) *Standard Star*	George H. Manning, Jr.
	James J. Butler
New York *Daily News*	John O'Donnell
New York *Daily Worker*	Marguerite Young
New York *Evening Post*	Robert S. Allen
	Kenneth Crawford
	Charles Malcolmson
New York *Herald Tribune*	Albert L. Warner
	Ernest K. Lindley
	Joseph W. Alsop, Jr.
New York *Sun*	Phelps J. Adams
New York *Times*	Arthur Krock
	Felix Belair, Jr.
	Delbert Clark
	W. Turner Catledge
	Frank Kluckhohn
	Charles R. Michael
	Louis Stark
New York *World-Telegram*	Thomas L. Stokes
Niagara Falls (N. Y.) *Gazette*	James J. Butler
Norfolk *Virginian-Pilot*	K. Foster Murray
Omaha (Neb.) *World-Herald*	Radford Mobley, Jr.
Ossining (N. Y.) *City Register*	George H. Manning, Jr.
	James J. Butler
Pawtucket (R. I.) *Times*	Bulkley S. Griffin
Peoria (Ill.) *Evening Star*	Charles O. Gridley
Philadelphia *Inquirer*	Paul J. McGahan
Philadelphia *Public Ledger*	Harold Brayman
	Frank H. Weir

NEWSPAPER	WASHINGTON CORRESPONDENT
Philadelphia *Record*	Robert S. Allen
	Kenneth Crawford
	Charles Malcolmson
Pittsburgh *Post-Gazette*	Raymond Z. Henle
Pittsburgh (Pa.) *Press*	Fred W. Perkins
Pittsfield (Mass.) *Eagle*	Bulkley S. Griffin
Port Chester (N. Y.) *Daily Times*	George H. Manning, Jr.
	James J. Butler
Portland (Me.) *Evening News*	Ruby A. Black
Portland (Ore.) *Oregonian*	John W. Kelly
Providence (R. I.) *Bulletin*	Ashmun Brown
	Stanley Chipman
Providence (R. I.) *Journal*	Ashmun Brown
	Stanley Chipman
Reading (Pa.) *Eagle*	George H. Manning, Jr.
	James J. Butler
Reno (Nevada) *Gazette*	Radford Mobley, Jr.
Richmond (Va.) *Times-Dispatch*	Radford Mobley, Jr.
Rochester (N. Y.) *Chronicle and Democrat*	Jesse S. Cottrell
Rochester *Times-Union*	Jesse S. Cottrell
Rock Island (Ill.) *Argus*	Radford Mobley, Jr.
Sacramento (Cal.) *Bee*	Gladstone Williams
Saginaw (Mich.) *News*	Mark Foote
	Lawrence E. Stafford
St. Louis *Globe-Democrat*	Charles P. Keyser
St. Louis *Post-Dispatch*	Raymond P. Brandt
	Paul Y. Anderson
	Marquis W. Childs
St. Paul *Dispatch*	J. R. Wiggins
St. Paul *Pioneer Press*	J. R. Wiggins
Salem (Mass.) *Evening News*	William P. Kennedy

NEWSPAPER	WASHINGTON CORRESPONDENT
San Antonio (Tex.) *Express*	Bascom N. Timmons
San Diego (Calif.) *Sun*	Max Stern
San Francisco *Daily News*	Max Stern
San Francisco *Examiner*	Arthur W. Hachten
Savannah (Ga.) *Morning News*	K. Foster Murray
Scranton *Republican*	George H. Manning, Jr.
Schenectady (N. Y.) *Gazette*	James J. Butler
Shreveport (La.) *Times*	Bascom N. Timmons
Springfield (Mass.) *Daily News*	William P. Kennedy
Springfield (Mass.) *Republican*	William P. Kennedy
Springfield (Mass.) *Union*	Bulkley S. Griffin
Staten Island *Advance*	George H. Manning, Jr.
	James J. Butler
Superior (N. H.) *Telegram*	Bascom N. Timmons
Syracuse (N. Y.) *Herald*	William P. Helm
Terre Haute (Ind.) *Star*	Everett C. Watkins
	Mark Thistlewaite
Terre Haute *Tribune*	Mark Thistlewaite
Toledo *News-Bee*	Ned Brooks
	Robert S. Brown
Troy (N. Y.) *Times-Record*	George H. Manning, Jr.
	Jesse S. Cottrell
Tulsa (Okla.) *World*	Bascom N. Timmons
Utica (N. Y.) *Observer-Dispatch*	James J. Butler
Wall Street *Journal*	Bernard Kilgore
	Eugene S. Duffield
Washington (D. C.) *Daily News*	(listed under Scripps-Howard Alliance, Appendix C.)
Washington (D. C.) *Evening Star*	Frederic William Wile
	G. Gould Lincoln
	William P. Kennedy

NEWSPAPER	WASHINGTON CORRESPONDENT
Washington (D. C.) *Herald*	John T. Lambert
	Arthur Hachten
Washington (D. C.) *Post*	Felix Bruner
	Franklyn Waltman, Jr.
Washington (D. C.) *Star*	William P. Kennedy
	G. Gould Lincoln
Washington (D. C.) *Times*	(listed under International News Service, Appendix C.)
Waterbury (Conn.) *American*	Bulkley S. Griffin
Watertown (N. Y.) *Daily Times*	Jesse S. Cottrell
Williamsport (Pa.) *Times & Gazette Bulletin*	George H. Manning, Jr.
	James J. Butler
Worcester (Mass.) *Gazette*	Ruby A. Black
Worcester (Mass.) *Post*	Bulkley S. Griffin
Worcester (Mass.) *Telegram*	Ralph C. Mulligan
Yonkers (N. Y.) *Statesman*	George H. Manning, Jr.
	James J. Butler
York (Pa.) *Dispatch*	George H. Manning, Jr.
	James J. Butler
Youngstown (O.) *Telegram*	Ned Brooks
	Robert S. Brown
Youngstown *Vindicator*	Bascom N. Timmons

DISTRIBUTION BY STATES OF THE 186 NEWSPAPERS WHOSE
SPECIAL CORRESPONDENTS ARE INCLUDED

STATE	NUMBER	STATE	NUMBER
Alabama	4	Colorado	1
Arizona	1	Connecticut	5
Arkansas	1	Delaware	0
California	7	D. of C.	6

STATE	NUMBER	STATE	NUMBER
Florida	1	New Mexico	2
Georgia	2	New York	32
Idaho	0	North Carolina	1
Illinois	6	North Dakota	0
Indiana	7	Ohio	12
Iowa	2	Oklahoma	1
Kansas	0	Oregon	1
Kentucky	2	Pennsylvania	12
Louisiana	5	Rhode Island	3
Maine	1	South Carolina	4
Maryland	2	South Dakota	0
Massachusetts	15	Tennessee	6
Michigan	11	Texas	7
Minnesota	4	Utah	0
Missouri	3	Vermont	0
Mississippi	0	Virginia	2
Montana	0	Washington	0
Nebraska	1	West Virginia	0
Nevada	1	Wisconsin	8
New Hampshire	2	Wyoming	0
New Jersey	5		

APPENDIX C

PRESS ASSOCIATIONS, SYNDICATES, AND INDEPENDENT COLUMNISTS REPRE-SENTED IN THIS STUDY

ASSOCIATION	WASHINGTON CORRESPONDENT
Associated Press	Byron Price
	Kirke L. Simpson
	D. Harold Oliver
	Nathan W. Robertson
	Joseph L. Miller
	J. R. Brackett
	Douglas Cornell
	Lloyd L. Lehrbas
	Thomas J. Hamilton, Jr.
	Preston L. Grover
Central News of America	Felix Cotten
Federated Press	Henry Zon
Independent Columnists	Carlisle Bargeron
	David Lawrence
International News Service	George R. Holmes
	William K. Hutchinson
	William S. Neal
	George Durno
	Kingsbury Smith
Newspaper Enterprise Association	Rodney Dutcher
North American Newspaper Alliance	Paul Mallon
	Genevieve F. Herrick

ASSOCIATION	WASHINGTON CORRESPONDENT
Scripps-Howard Newspaper Alliance	Ruth Finney
	Thomas L. Stokes
	Robert W. Horton
	Max Stern
	Fred W. Perkins
	Robert S. Brown
	Ned Brooks
	Raymond Clapper
United Features Syndicate	Robert S. Allen
	Drew Pearson
United Press Association	Lyle C. Wilson
	Harry W. Frantz
	H. O. Thompson
	Arthur F. DeGreve
	Edward W. Lewis
	John R. Beal
	Carlton Skinner
Universal Service *	John T. Lambert
	Arthur W. Hachten

* Consolidated with International News Service on August 14, 1937.

APPENDIX D

TABLES: THE COMPOSITION OF THE PRESS CORPS

LIST OF TABLES *

In Appendix D

I. AGE DISTRIBUTION OF 127 WASHINGTON CORRE-SPONDENTS.

II. DISTRIBUTION OF PLACES OF BIRTH ACCORDING TO POPULATION IN 1900.

III. PLACE OF BIRTH: 127 CORRESPONDENTS.

IV. TEN LEADING STATES OF BIRTH.

V. EDUCATIONAL BACKGROUND.

VI. FIELD OF SPECIALIZATION IN COLLEGE.

VII. RELIGIOUS TRAINING OF THE CORRESPONDENTS.

VIII. OCCUPATIONS OF THE FATHERS OF 123 CORRESPOND-ENTS.

IX. PROFESSIONS OF THE FATHERS OF THE CORRESPOND-ENTS.

X. FATHERS' ANNUAL INCOME LEVEL.

XI. FATHERS' POLITICAL IDENTIFICATION.

XII. REASONS GIVEN BY CORRESPONDENTS FOR ENTERING JOURNALISM.

* All tables are as of 1936.

324

Appendices 325

I. AGE DISTRIBUTION OF 127 WASHINGTON CORRESPONDENTS *

AGE	NUMBER	AGE	NUMBER	AGE	NUMBER
23	1	39	4	55	3
24	2	40	6	56	1
25	. .	41	2	57	1
26	1	42	2	58	2
27	2	43	3	59	. .
28	4	44	3	60	3
29	5	45	2	61	1
30	5	46	4	62	. .
31	3	47	1	63	1
32	4	48	4	64	1
33	9	49	1	65	. .
34	4	50	3	66	. .
35	4	51	4	67	1
36	11	52	1	68	. .
37	8	53	1	69	. .
38	7	54	1	70	1

II. DISTRIBUTION OF PLACES OF BIRTH ACCORDING TO POPULATION IN 1900 †

POPULATION	NUMBER	PER CENT	POPULATION	NUMBER	PER CENT
Under 2,500	50	38.5	75-100,000	6	4.7
2,500-5,000	5	3.9	100-250,000	7	5.5
5-10,000	8	6.2	250-500,000	10	7.8
10-25,000	16	12.5	500-750,000	3	2.3
25-50,000	8	6.2	750-1,000,000	. .	. . .
50-75,000	4	3.1	1-2,000,000	2	1.5

* As of 1936.

† Population figures were taken from *Fourteenth Census of the United States*, vol. I, pp. 178-331. For the reasons for which 1900 was chosen as a date of reference, see reference note 7, Chapter VI.

III. PLACE OF BIRTH: 127 CORRESPONDENTS

STATE	NUMBER	STATE	NUMBER
Alabama	2	New Jersey	2
California	2	New York	7
Colorado	1	Ohio	5
Connecticut	2	Oregon	1
D. of C.	8	Pennsylvania	8
Georgia	4	South Dakota	1
Idaho	1	Tennessee	3
Illinois	12	Texas	2
Indiana	13	Utah	1
Iowa	5	Vermont	1
Kansas	3	Virginia	1
Kentucky	4	Washington	1
Louisiana	1	West Virginia	2
Maine	1	Wisconsin	1
Maryland	3		
Massachusetts	8	*Foreign*	
Michigan	5	Canada	1
Minnesota	5	Hungary	1
Mississippi	2	India	1
Missouri	3	Russia	1
Nebraska	1	Total	127
New Hampshire	1		

IV. TEN LEADING STATES OF BIRTH

STATE	NUMBER	PER CENT
1. Indiana	13	10.2
2. Illinois	12	9.4
3. District of Columbia *	9	7.0

* The position of the District of Columbia must be discounted since correspondents born in the capital have been in a singularly fortunate position for work on either a Washington newspaper or in a Wash-

STATE	NUMBER	PER CENT
4. Pennsylvania	8	6.2
5. Massachusetts	8	6.2
6. New York	7	5.5
7. Iowa	5	4.0
8. Michigan	5	4.0
9. Minnesota	5	4.0
10. Ohio	5	4.0

V. EDUCATIONAL BACKGROUND

TYPE	NUMBER	PER CENT
Higher Degrees	8	6.2
A.M. (Oxon)	3	2.3
A.B. (Oxon)	1	..
A.M.	4	3.1
Graduate work (no higher degree)	8	6.2
2 years	1	..
1 year	7	5.5
Degrees *	66	51.9
Four-year (A.B., Ph.B., J.B., Litt.B.)	65	51.1
Two-year (A.A.)	1	..
Years in College (no degree)	36	28.3
5 years	1	..
4 years	5	3.9
3 years	8	6.2
2 years	12	9.4
1 year	10	7.8

ington press bureau. They differ from the rest of the corps in that they were not promoted to the capital.

* Figures for college degrees of course include those men who received higher degrees as well.

TYPE	NUMBER	PER CENT
Years in High School (no college education)	23	18.1
4 years	15	11.8
3 years	4	3.1
2 years	4	3.1
Years in Grammar School (no high school education)	2	1.5
8 years	1	..
4 years	1	..

VI. FIELD OF SPECIALIZATION IN COLLEGE

FIELD	NUMBER	PER CENT	FIELD	NUMBER	PER CENT
Liberal Arts	25	19.6			
Journalism *	13	10.2	Economics	3	2.3
Law (or pre-legal)	7	5.5	Education	1	..
English	5	3.9	Engineering	1	..
Political Science (Government)	4	3.1	Agriculture	1	..

VII. RELIGIOUS TRAINING OF THE CORRESPONDENTS

CHURCH	NUMBER	PER CENT	CHURCH	NUMBER	PER CENT
Methodist	18	14.1	Baptist	8	6.2
Presbyterian	17	13.3	Jewish	4	3.1
Episcopalian	16	12.5	Church of Christ		
Roman Catholic	13	10.2	(Scientist)	3	2.3
Congregationalist	11	8.6	United Presby-		
Methodist-Episc.	11	8.6	terian	2	1.5

* Since the first school of journalism was not founded until 1908, the older correspondents show little specialization in this field. Correspondents who specialized in journalism are thirty-seven years of age or under.

CHURCH	NUMBER	PER CENT	CHURCH	NUMBER	PER CENT
Junker Congre-			Lutheran Baptist	1	..
gation	1	..	Unitarian	1	..
Free Methodist	1	..	United Baptist	1	..
Ind. Congrega-			United Brethren	1	..
tion	1	..	Mormon	1	..

CHURCH ATTENDANCE OF CORRESPONDENTS TODAY

ATTENDANCE	NUMBER	PER CENT
Never	65	51.1
Occasionally	30	23.6
Rarely	17	13.3
Regularly	12	9.4

VIII. OCCUPATIONS OF THE FATHERS OF 123 CORRESPONDENTS *

OCCUPATIONS	NUMBER	PER CENT
Professional (editors, lawyers, doctors, teachers)	55	43.3
Proprietary (merchants, executives, office managers)	31	24.4
Farmers	12	9.4
Clerical (salesmen, clerks, agents, etc.)	11	8.6
Unskilled labor (manual labor)	8	6.2
Skilled labor (printers, painters, etc.)	4	3.1
Semi-skilled labor (conductors, etc.)	2	1.5

* Six of the categories follow the occupational classification of Professor William F. Ogburn in "The Family and Its Functions," *Recent Social Trends* (p. 685). I have added "farmers." The total is 123 instead of 127 because four correspondents did not list the occupation of their fathers, who died while the newspapermen were under three years of age.

IX. PROFESSIONS OF THE FATHERS * OF THE CORRESPONDENTS

PROFESSION	NUMBER	PROFESSION	NUMBER
Newspapermen and Editors	14	Engineers	3
Lawyers	13	Advertising	2
Physicians	7	University Pres.	2
Clergymen	6	University Prof.	1
Teachers	5	Authors	1
		Accountants	1
			55

X. FATHERS' ANNUAL INCOME LEVEL †

WHILE CORRESPONDENTS WERE IN:	UNDER $2,500		$2,500- 5,000		$5,000- 10,000		OVER $10,000	
	NO.	%	NO.	%	NO.	%	NO.	%
Grammar School	44	42.3	43	41.3	11	10.5	6	5.7
High School	37	37.7	42	42.8	11	11.2	8	8.1
College (or between 16-21)	34	35.4	43	44.7	10	10.4	9	9.3

XI. FATHERS' POLITICAL IDENTIFICATION

POLITICS	NUMBER	POLITICS	NUMBER
Republican	44	Progressive	2
Democrat	41	"Radical"	2
Independent	16	"Labor"	1
Liberal	5	"No Party"	4
Socialist	2	No Answer	10
		Total	127

* For the 55 who fall into the Professional category.

† It was to be expected that a high proportion would not fill in these figures. Some correspondents wrote "don't know." Furthermore, the fathers of twenty-three correspondents died before the newspapermen were sixteen years of age.

XII. REASONS GIVEN BY CORRESPONDENTS FOR ENTERING JOURNALISM

REASON	NUMBER	PER CENT
Choice (or "desire to write")	96	75.5
Accident *	15	11.8
Personal contact	13	10.2
Fathers' "pull" †	3	2.3

XIII. JOURNALISTIC POSTS HELD PRIOR TO WASHINGTON ‡

POST	NUMBER CORRESPONDENTS	POST	NUMBER CORRESPONDENTS
Managing Editor	13	Finance Editor	1
Editor	7	Labor Editor	1
Associate Editor	1	Railroad Editor	1
Editorial Writer	10	Columnist	3
Sunday Editor	1	Special Writer	4
City Editor	19	Theater Critic	3
Asst. City Editor	4	Book Critic	2
Foreign Correspondent	12	Music Critic	1
News Editor	4	Features	9
Night Editor	2	Sports	10
State Editor	3	Re-write	19
Wire (Teleg.) Editor	15	Copy Desk	22
Political Editor	2	Make-up	1

* This includes one correspondent who began as a cartoonist, one who began working in his father's office, and four who began in the mechanical or commercial end of a newspaper organization.

† This category was written in by three newspapermen.

‡ This table represents all the positions held by all correspondents. Many individual correspondents held more than one of the posts listed.

XIV. YEARS OF EXPERIENCE IN JOURNALISM

NUMBER YEARS	NUMBER CORRESPONDENTS	NUMBER YEARS	NUMBER CORRESPONDENTS	NUMBER YEARS	NUMBER CORRESPONDENTS
3	2	17	4	29	2
4	4	18	6	30	3
6	1	19	4	31	2
8	4	20	4	32	4
9	6	21	2	33	3
10	10	22	3	34	1
11	5	23	4	37	1
12	3	24	4	38	2
13	9	25	4	40	2
14	7	26	1	44	1
15	8	27	3	46	1
16	5	28	1	49	1

XV. YEARS OF EXPERIENCE IN JOURNALISM BEFORE BECOMING WASHINGTON CORRESPONDENTS *

NUMBER YEARS	NUMBER CORRESPONDENTS	NUMBER YEARS	NUMBER CORRESPONDENTS	NUMBER YEARS	NUMBER CORRESPONDENTS
..	..	9	8	18	1
1	1	10	8	19	..
2	11	11	4	20	4
3	3	12	6	21	3
4	10	13	8	22	..
5	8	14	2	23	1
6	10	15	2	24	1
7	15	16	1	30	1
8	7	17	2	40	1

* For 118 correspondents. This table excludes the nine correspondents who were born in Washington, D. C., since their experience and

XVI. JOURNALISTIC EXPERIENCE BEFORE PROMOTION TO
WASHINGTON (BY AGE GROUPS)

PRESENT AGE	NUMBER IN GROUP	TOTAL NUMBER YEARS EXPERI- ENCE BEFORE WASHINGTON	AVERAGE NUMBER YEARS EXPERI- ENCE BEFORE WASHINGTON
23-33	29	162	5.5
33-38	30	229	7.6
38-47	30	307	10.2
48-70	29	361	12.4

XVII. NUMBER OF YEARS AS WASHINGTON CORRESPONDENT

NUMBER YEARS	NUMBER CORRE- SPONDENTS	NUMBER YEARS	NUMBER CORRE- SPONDENTS	NUMBER YEARS	NUMBER CORRE- SPONDENTS
1	4	12	4	23	. .
2	15	13	5	24	. .
3	12	14	7	25	6
4	6	15	5	26	1
5	10	16	3	27	1
6	8	17	1	28	. .
7	3	18	3	29	. .
8	8	19	. .	30	. .
9	4	20	2	31	. .
10	7	21	4	32	2
11	5	22	1		

status are distinct from those of newspapermen who were promoted to
Washington. Of the nine men, six had no previous journalistic experience. Two had two years; one had six.

XVIII. AGES OF APPOINTMENT TO THE POST OF WASHINGTON
CORRESPONDENT

AGE	NUMBER	AGE	NUMBER	AGE	NUMBER
18	1	33	4	48	1
19	1	34	5	49	. .
20	2	35	6	50	. .
21	4	36	3	51	. .
22	5	37	4	52	. .
23	6	38	1	53	. .
24	7	39	. .	54	. .
25	10	40	. .	55	1
26	10	41	3	56	. .
27	3	42	1	57	. .
28	12	43	1	58	. .
29	6	44	1	59	. .
30	10	45	3	60	1
31	10	46	. .	Unknown	1
32	5	47	. .		

XIX. NUMBER OF PAPERS FOR WHICH CORRESPONDENTS
HAVE WORKED, INCLUDING THEIR PRESENT ONE*

NUMBER PAPERS	NUMBER SPECIAL CORRESPOND-ENTS	NUMBER REPORTERS FOR PRESS ASSOCIATIONS	NUMBER COLUMNISTS AND SYND. WRITERS	TOTAL
0	. .	4	. .	4
1	14	9	1	24
2	15	3	1	19
3	21	5	2	28
4	20	4	1	25
5	8	1	1	10

* For 124 correspondents. Three did not answer this question.

NUMBER PAPERS	NUMBER SPECIAL CORRESPOND-ENTS	NUMBER REPORTERS FOR PRESS ASSOCIATIONS	NUMBER COLUMNISTS AND SYND. WRITERS	TOTAL
6	8	..	1	9
7	..	1	..	1
8	1	..	..	1
9	1	..	..	1
10	2	..	..	2
				124

XX. AGES AT WHICH CORRESPONDENTS BEGAN SUPPORTING THEMSELVES WHOLLY *

AGE	NUMBER	PER CENT	AGE	NUMBER	PER CENT
13	2	1.5	20	19	14.9
14	0	..	21	21	15.7
15	4	3.1	22	18	14.1
16	4	3.1	23	9	7.08
17	9	7.08	24	5	3.9
18	15	11.8	25	2	1.5
19	14	11.0	28	1	..

* For 123. Four did not answer.

XXI. SIBLING PATTERN: 126 CORRESPONDENTS *

NUMBER CORRE-SPONDENTS	YOUNGER BROTHERS	YOUNGER SISTERS	OLDER BROTHERS	OLDER SISTERS	NUMBER CORRE-SPONDENTS	YOUNGER BROTHERS	YOUNGER SISTERS	OLDER BROTHERS	OLDER SISTERS
20	..	..	..	..	1	1	1	2	..
12	1	..	..	..	1	..	1	..	2
11	1	1	..	..	1	..	1	2	1
11	..	1	..	..	1	1	..	1	1
7	..	..	..	1	1	..	..	2	1
4	..	2	.	..	1	2	1	2	..
4	1	1	1	1	1	1	..	..	3
4	1	..	1	..	1	..	..	2	..
4	..	..	1	1	1	..	..	1	2
3	..	1	1	1	1	..	..	2	3
2	2	1	..	..	1	3	..	..	..
2	..	1	1	..	1	..	..	5	1
2	..	1	..	1	1	..	4	..	..
2	1	2	..	..	1	..	..	2	4
2	2	..	..	..	1	1	1	5	3
2	..	..	1	..	1	..	1	4	3
2	..	..	3	..	1	..	..	2	2
2	1	3	..	..	1	..	..	..	3
2	..	1	5	2	1	..	1	4	1
1	1	1	1	..	1	1	..	4	1

* Psychologists may be interested in analyzing this material: the high number of Washington correspondents who are either only children or oldest children (see Summary, above) may warrant more detailed statistical inquiry.

Important research in sibling relationships and individual success, "genius," "problem children," neuropathic tendencies, insanity, etc., has been conducted by L. L. Thurstone and R. L. Jenkins in *Order of Birth, Parent-Age, and Intelligence* (University of Chicago Press: 1931).

NUMBER CORRE-SPONDENTS	YOUNGER BROTHERS	YOUNGER SISTERS	OLDER BROTHERS	OLDER SISTERS	NUMBER CORRE-SPONDENTS	YOUNGER BROTHERS	YOUNGER SISTERS	OLDER BROTHERS	OLDER SISTERS
1	1	1	4	1	1	..	..	3	1
1	..	..	4	3	1	..	..	2*	2†
1	2	..	..	1	1	2	3	..	..
1	1	..	2	..					

Summary

Only child	20
No older siblings	68
	—
Only child or oldest child	88

One sibling	32	Six siblings	4
Two siblings	30	Seven "	2
Three "	18	Eight "	3
Four "	13	Nine "	..
Five "	3	Ten "	1

XXII. MARITAL STATUS OF CORRESPONDENTS

STATUS	NUMBER	PER CENT
Married	111	87.4
Divorced	12	9.4
Divorced and re-married	11	8.6
Single (never married)	16	12.5

* Half-brothers.
† Half-sisters.

XXIII. NUMBER OF CORRESPONDENTS WHO WRITE COLUMNS

Daily (six times a week) *	18
Five times a week	2
Three times a week	5
Twice a week	4
Once a week	9
"Occasionally"	5
Twice a month	1

* This includes columnists who do not send spot news dispatches (e.g., Raymond Clapper, David Lawrence, Paul Mallon), and correspondents who both cover spot news and write a column daily (e.g., Robert S. Allen). Some correspondents are primarily columnists but write news dispatches on important events from time to time (e.g., Arthur Krock).

APPENDIX E

SUMMARY OF ANONYMOUS QUESTIONNAIRE: ATTITUDES AND PREFERENCES

FORM LETTER SENT WITH SECOND QUESTIONNAIRE

February 15, 1936

Dear Mr. Jones:

I wish to thank you for your co-operation on my study of "The Washington Newspaper Correspondents." The receipt of your biographical questionnaire was greatly appreciated. It will interest you to know that 126 correspondents have made similar returns. This makes available, for the first time, an important and objective body of information about a significant group of journalists.

I have spent six months in interviewing newspapermen. I have heard many different points of view expressed about a correspondent's function, problems, freedom and limitations. Now it would be unfair to generalize from individual opinions. You, for example, would certainly disagree with many of the attitudes expressed. The only way to get a scientific, factual basis for generalization is to discover *what percentage* of the correspondents support or deny these separate attitudes. I have therefore mimeographed a list of opinions, taken literally from interviews, and am asking the correspondents to check in their reactions—*anonymously*.

The list is *short*. It is *simple*. It is *ANONYMOUS*. It can be checked in 7 minutes according to tests. (There is practically no writing.) Your name is nowhere to be affixed.

340

I think you will agree that the attitudes solicited through this form are highly important, and that it is necessary to get the widest number of men to express their agreement or disagreement. For this reason I am asking you to spare 6 or 7 minutes and check it in. A stamped, addressed return envelope is enclosed.

You will be making a valued contribution to what I hope will be a significant study conducted in a dispassionate manner.

Sincerely yours,

Leo C. Rosten

P.S. Many men have asked about the Social Science Research Council, whose fellowship to me has made this research possible. The Council is composed of representatives of the American Political Science, Economics, Sociology, Statistical and History Associations. It aids scientific research in these fields by grants and fellowships. It has no political connections. It has no control over the research itself or the conclusions reached.

THE ATTITUDES AND PREFERENCES OF 107 WASHINGTON
CORRESPONDENTS

127 correspondents filled in the questionnaire pertaining to biographical material and experience which is reproduced on page 151. To this group, which served as the subject-matter of this research, a second questionnaire was sent: questions designed to elicit attitudes, preferences, choices and similar information. Because of the confidential nature of these questions this second questionnaire was necessarily anonymous. Each correspondent was asked to designate his reaction in one of

three manners: a check for "Yes"; a zero for "No"; a question mark for "Uncertain."

Of the 127 forms mailed, 107 returns were received. They are summarized below.

"I believe that 'rugged individualism' is the best economic philosophy today."

	NUMBER	PER CENT
Yes	22	21.7
No	67	66.3
Uncertain	12	11.8
Total answers	101	99.8
No answer	6	

"I favor government operation of mines, public utilities and railroads."

	NUMBER	PER CENT
Yes	40	38.4
No	56	53.9
Uncertain	8	7.6
Total answers	104	99.9
No answer	3	

"If European nations can afford to arm they can pay us the War Debts."

	NUMBER	PER CENT
Yes	46	43.8
No	43	40.9
Uncertain	16	15.2
Total answers	105	99.9
No answer	2	

"The United States should co-operate more energetically with the League of Nations."

	NUMBER	PER CENT
Yes	32	30.4
No	58	55.2
Uncertain	15	14.2
Total answers	105	99.8
No answer	2	

"The United States should enter the World Court, with reservations as to its jurisdiction."

	NUMBER	PER CENT
Yes	47	44.8
No	46	43.8
Uncertain	12	10.4
Total answers	105	99.0
No answer	2	

"I favor higher taxes on the upper income brackets, on huge profits, etc."

	NUMBER	PER CENT
Yes	70	67.3
No	24	23.0
Uncertain	10	9.6
Total answers	104	99.9
No answer	3	

Appendices

"Some form of government regulation over big business has become imperative."

	NUMBER	PER CENT
Yes	84	80.0
No	18	17.1
Uncertain	3	2.8
Total answers	105	99.9
No answer	2	

"I prefer the stories of (check one):

	NUMBER	PER CENT
* Associated Press	44	45.3
* United Press	48	49.4
International News Service	4	.41
Universal Service	1	1.0
Total answers	97	99.8
No answer	10	

". . . because they are: †

	AP	UP	INS	US
better written	5	42	3	1
more reliable	43	19	4	0
more liberal	0	27	0	0

"The *three* newspapers (U. S.) which give the most fair and reliable news are:"

(See Table XXIV.)

* Several correspondents checked two associations; their votes were considered as ½ each and are included in the totals.
† Some correspondents checked more than one category.

Appendices 345

"The three papers which are *least* fair and reliable (Don't give more than *one* from any one chain):"

(See Table XXV.)

"The press devotes too much space to trivialities: scandals, sensations, divorces, etc."

	NUMBER	PER CENT
Yes	63	60.5
No	31	29.8
Uncertain	10	9.6
Total answers	104	99.9
No answer	3	

"In general, news columns are equally fair to big business and labor."

	NUMBER	PER CENT
Yes	46	43.8
No	51	48.5
Uncertain	8	7.6
Total answers	105	99.9
No answer	2	

"Comparatively few papers give significant accounts of our basic economic conflicts."

	NUMBER	PER CENT
Yes	91	86.6
No	12	11.4
Uncertain	2	1.9
Total answers	105	99.9
No answer	2	

"The publishers' cry of 'Freedom of the Press' in fighting the NRA code was a ruse."

	NUMBER	PER CENT
Yes	67	63.8
No	26	24.7
Uncertain	12	11.4
Total answers	105	99.9
No answer	2	

"Most papers printed unfair or distorted stories about the Tugwell Pure Foods Bill."

	NUMBER	PER CENT
Yes	49	46.2
No	23	21.6
Uncertain	34	32.0
Total answers	106	99.8
No answer	1	

"If salary and security were no consideration, for which three U. S. papers would you most prefer to be a Washington correspondent?" (In order of preference.)

(See Table XXVI.)

"Which *one* of the following posts would you most prefer to fill (ignoring salary)?" (The following categories were given.)

Washington Correspondent	52
Roving Reporter	16
Daily Columnist	13
Foreign Correspondent	10
Managing Editor	6

Editor-in-Chief	3
Business Department	2
Editorial Writer	1
Total answers	103
No answer	4

"If you had your choice over, would you choose journalism as a profession?"

	NUMBER	PER CENT
Yes	87	82.0
No	15	14.1
Uncertain	4	3.7
Total answers	106	99.8
No answer	1	

"Which field, *other than journalism*, would you choose today?" *

Law	17
Medicine	5
Writing ("more serious"; "magazine")	4
Diplomatic service	3
Radio or stage	3
Teaching	3
Economics	2
Politics	2
Publishing	2

One for each of the following: Bio-chemist, Business office of newspaper, Commercial attaché, Farming, Gambling, Painting, Political

* Many of those who answered "yes" to the question "If you had your choice over, would you choose journalism as a profession?" did not answer this question.

Science, Public Service, Science, Social research, Social worker.

"Of the current candidates for President, who is your choice?" *

Roosevelt	54	*Summary*	
Landon	8		
Vandenberg	8		PER CENT
Borah	4	Roosevelt	63.5
Thomas	4	Republican candidate	30.5
Hoover	2	Socialist	4.7
Knox	1	Third party	
Taft	1	(Browder)	1.1
Wadsworth	1		
"The Republican"	1	Total percentage	99.8
Browder	1		
Total answers	85		
No answer	22		

"Whose daily column do you consider most significant, fair and reliable?" †

Raymond Clapper	25
Paul Mallon	13
Walter Lippmann	9
Arthur Krock	7

* These questionnaires were being filled in from February, 1936, through April, 1936, before the Republican candidate was chosen. The combined vote for Republican candidates is 26, less than half of the vote for Mr. Roosevelt.

† Some correspondents informed me later that they had assumed that only columns issuing from Washington were involved and that they might otherwise have listed New York columnists. These figures should be discounted accordingly.

Robert S. Allen and Drew Pearson 5
Heywood Broun 5
"What's the News" (Wall St. *Journal*) 3
John T. Flynn 2

One for each of the following: Rodney Dutcher, Frank Kent, Clinton Mosher, O'Donnell and Fleeson,. Eleanor Roosevelt, Mark Sullivan, Ray Tucker, Franklyn Waltman.

Total answers 77
No answer 30

"Ignoring salary, what is the worst part of the Washington correspondent's job?" *

COMPLAINTS OF 94 CORRESPONDENTS

NUMBER
MEN

Hours ("long," "uncertain," "no home life," "few vacations," "on call 24 hours a day," etc.) 21

Home Office Queries ("ignorance of editors," "covering unimportant local news," "poor co-operation from home office," etc.) 18

Routine ("daily grind," "checking facts," "covering third-rate events for protection," "getting trivial details," etc.) 13

Politicians, Congressmen ("covering petty and ignorant men," "enforced association with Congressmen," "reporting hypocrites," "treating insincere, self-minded men seriously," etc.) 12

* No categories were suggested; replies have been summarized according to groups. Many correspondents listed more than one complaint: each complaint has been recorded separately.

NUMBER
MEN

Publishers' Interference ("running publisher's chores," "lobbying for the boss," "requests to use influence," "pleasing the publisher," "writing what is wanted, not what is important," etc.)   11

Subject Matter ("range of stories," "complexity of news," "difficulty of interpreting events," "covering too many stories in limited time," etc.)   6

Government Routine and Officials ("red tape," "government agencies' handling of news," "bureaucracy," "dumb press relations men," etc.)   5

Tension ("inability to relax," "tension of work all the time")   5

Propagandists ("Spotting propagandists," "handling too many government handouts," "fighting off special pleaders")   5

A Daily Story ("Having to produce one story a day, whether important or not," "pressure to produce daily")   5

Boredom ("keeping from being bored in the capital," "ennui")   2

Personal ("doing someone else's proselytizing instead of my own")   1

Social Life ("artificial circles to mix in")   1

Total answers   94
No answer   13

Note: The next seven questions were omitted from the form which was sent to press association reporters and columnists, since the questions are concerned with the "policy" of one newspaper or publisher. Eighty answers were received.

"I often feel the need of knowing more economics for my job."

	NUMBER	PER CENT
Yes	65	86.6
No	8	10.6
Uncertain	2	2.6
Total answers	75	99.8
No answer	5	

"It is almost impossible to be objective. You read your paper, notice its editorials, get praised for some stories and criticized for others. You 'sense policy' and are psychologically driven to slant your stories accordingly."

	NUMBER	PER CENT
Yes	42	60.0
No	24	34.2
Uncertain	4	5.6
Total answers	70	99.8
No answer	10	

"I am not aware of any definite fixed 'policy' on my paper."

	NUMBER	PER CENT
Yes	23	32.8
No	42	60.0
Uncertain	5	7.1
Total answers	70	99.9
No answer	10	

"My orders are to be objective, but I *know* how my paper wants stories played."

	NUMBER	PER CENT
Yes	40	60.6
No	23	34.8
Uncertain	3	4.5
Total answers	66	99.9
No answer	14	

"Correspondents try too hard to please their editors. If they had more independence they would discover that they really have more freedom than they assume."

	NUMBER	PER CENT
Yes	45	60.8
No	21	28.3
Uncertain	8	10.8
Total answers	74	99.9
No answer	16	

"In my experience I've had stories played down, cut or killed for 'policy' reasons."

	NUMBER	PER CENT
Yes	40	55.5
No	30	41.6
Uncertain	2	2.7
Total answers	72	99.8
No answer	8	

"In general, I agree with my paper's political point of view."

	NUMBER	PER CENT
Yes	49	65.3
No	19	25.3
Uncertain	7	9.3
Total answers	75	99.9
No answer	5	

Note: The next questions were on all the questionnaires sent.

"I favor *a* Newspaper Guild to improve salaries, contract and bargain collectively."

	NUMBER	PER CENT
Yes	58	56.3
No	38	36.8
Uncertain	7	6.7
Total answers	103	99.8
No answer	4	

"Apropos a Newspaper Guild, I feel:
"—newspapermen are individualists and craftsmen, not in a class with labor."

	NUMBER	PER CENT
Yes	57	60.0
No	35	36.8
Uncertain	3	3.1
Total answers	95	99.9
No answer	12	

"—it is unethical for newspapermen to form into unions."

	NUMBER	PER CENT
Yes	15	16.1
No	69	74.1
Uncertain	9	9.6
Total answers	93	99.8
No answer	14	

"—I have nothing to gain by joining a Guild."

	NUMBER	PER CENT
Yes	53	56.9
No	31	33.3
Uncertain	9	9.6
Total answers	93	99.8
No answer	14	

"—a Guild would make reporters partisan in treating labor and union news."

	NUMBER	PER CENT
Yes	35	37.2
No	44	46.8
Uncertain	15	16.0
Total answers	94	100.0
No answer	13	

"—newspapermen should not strike, nor use the threat of strike."

	NUMBER	PER CENT
Yes	27	29.0
No	50	53.6
Uncertain	16	17.2
Total answers	93	99.8
No answer	14	

"—a good newspaperman doesn't need a Guild: it is organized for the lazy, the incompetent or the mediocre."

	NUMBER	PER CENT
Yes	28	29.4
No	58	61.0
Uncertain	9	9.4
Total answers	95	99.8
No answer	12	

"—it would become too radical."

	NUMBER	PER CENT
Yes	21	22.8
No	47	51.0
Uncertain	24	26.0
Total answers	92	99.8
No answer	15	

(*Finally:* Many correspondents have urged me to discover the average salary of the corps. They have offered to state theirs in this *anonymous* form. It will be a great help to this research if you would give your annual salary below. If you handle several papers please state your total *net* salary.)

Salary (per annum): $
(See Table XXVII.)

XXIV. THE NEWSPAPERS CONSIDERED "MOST FAIR AND RELIABLE" BY 99 WASHINGTON CORRESPONDENTS

PAPER	1ST CHOICE	POINTS	2ND	POINTS	3RD	POINTS	NUMBER MENTIONS	TOTAL POINTS
N. Y. *Times*	64	640	16	80	9	27	89	747
Baltimore *Sun*	14	140	21	105	13	39	48	284
Christian Science *Monitor*	3	30	9	45	5	15	17	90
Scripps-Howard Papers *	4	40	6	30	5	15	15	85
St. Louis *Post-Dispatch*	2	20	8	40	8	24	18	84
Washington *Star*	2	20	8	40	4	12	14	72
N. Y. *Herald Tribune*	..	..	8	40	9	27	17	67
Washington *Post*	3	30	2	10	..	..	5	40
Phila. *Record*	2	20	3	15	..	..	5	35
Kans. City *Star*	..	..	1	5	6	18	7	23
Newark *Evening News*	..	..	2	10	1	3	3	13
Des Moines *Register & Tribune*	..	..	..	..	2	6	2	6
Chicago *Daily News*	..	..	..	..	2	6	2	6

One vote for *first* choice was cast for each of the following papers: Brooklyn *Daily Eagle*, Chicago *Tribune*, Cincinnati *Enquirer*, *Daily Worker*, Providence *Journal*.

* Some correspondents wrote "Scripps-Howard," others named a Scripps-Howard paper. It was thought advisable to combine the votes in one group.

One vote for *second* place was cast for each of the following papers: Boston *Globe,* New York *Daily News,* Providence *Evening Bulletin,* San Francisco *Chronicle.*

One vote for *third* place was cast for each of the following papers: Akron *Beacon-Journal,* Dallas *Evening News,* Detroit *News,* Cleveland *Plain-Dealer,* Boston *Transcript,* New York *American,* New York *Sun,* New York *Journal of Commerce,* Philadelphia *Bulletin,* Springfield *Republican,* Salt Lake City *Tribune,* Washington *Herald.*

Total answers	99
No answer	8

XXV. THE NEWSPAPERS CONSIDERED "LEAST FAIR AND RELIABLE" BY 93 WASHINGTON CORRESPONDENTS

PAPER	1ST CHOICE	POINTS	2ND	POINTS	3RD	POINTS	NUMBER MENTIONS	TOTAL POINTS
Hearst newspapers *	59	590	20	100	8	24	87	714
Chicago *Tribune*	24	240	37	185	10	30	71	455
Los Angeles *Times*	2	20	7	35	16	48	25	103
Scripps-Howard papers †	4	40	5	25	4	12	13	77
Denver *Post*	..	..	4	20	6	18	10	38
N. Y. *Herald Tribune*	..	..	4	20	4	12	8	32
Washington *Post*	2	20	1	5	2	6	5	31

* Many correspondents merely stated "Hearst," "Hearst papers" or "any Hearst paper." They have been combined, in the total figures, with Hearst papers which were named.

† Footnote above applies to returns which listed "Scripps-Howard papers."

PAPER	1ST CHOICE	POINTS	2ND	POINTS	3RD	POINTS	NUMBER MENTIONS	TOTAL POINTS
Phila. *Record*			3	15	5	15	8	30
Daily Worker	1	10	1	5	2	6	4	21
Phila. *Inquirer*	1	10	1	5	2	6	4	21
N. Y. *Daily News*			1	5	1	3	2	8
Detroit *Free Press*					2	6	2	6

One vote for *second* place was cast for the New York *Post* and the Kansas City *Star*.

One vote for *third* place was cast for each of the following papers: Baltimore *Sun*, Boston *Transcript*, Des Moines *Register & Tribune*, "Paul Block papers."

Total answers   93
No answer   14

XXVI. NEWSPAPERS FOR WHICH 87 CORRESPONDENTS WOULD
PREFER TO WORK "IF SALARY AND SECURITY WERE
NO CONSIDERATION"

PAPER	1ST CHOICE	POINTS	2ND	POINTS	3RD	POINTS	NUMBER MENTIONS	TOTAL POINTS
New York *Times*	31	310	16	80	21	63	68	453
Baltimore *Sun* *	11	110	19	95	32	96	62	291
St. Louis *Post-Dispatch*	6	60	8	40	17	51	32	151
N. Y. *Herald Tribune*	4	40	12	60	8	24	24	124

* Two of the second choices were for the Baltimore *Evening Sun*, but are included here since the papers are under the same management.

PAPER	1ST CHOICE	POINTS	2ND	POINTS	3RD	POINTS	NUMBER MENTIONS	TOTAL POINTS
Scripps-Howard	9	90	3	15	6	18	18	123
Phila. *Record* or N. Y. *Post* *	5	50	6	30	1	3	12	81
Christian Science Monitor	4	40	0	0	3	9	7	49
Hearst papers	2	20	1	5	1	3	4	28
Kans. City *Star*	1	10	0	0	5	15	6	25
Chicago *Daily News*	1	10	1	5	1	3	3	18
Cleveland *Plain Dealer*	1	10	1	5	1	3	3	18
Chicago *Tribune*	1	10	1	5	0	0	2	15
N. Y. *Daily News*	0	0	2	10	1	3	3	13
Washington *Post*	1	10	0	0	1	3	2	13
Detroit *News*	0	0	2	10	0	0	2	10

One vote for first place was cast for each of the following: Brooklyn *Daily Eagle*, Buffalo *Evening News*, *Daily Worker*, Des Moines *Register & Tribune*, *People's Press*, Providence *Journal*, Washington *Star*.

One vote for second place was cast for each of the following: Booth Papers (Mich.), Boston *Herald*, Chicago *Times*, Providence *Evening Bulletin*.

One vote for third place was cast for each of the following: Indianapolis *News*, Memphis *Commercial-Appeal*, Milwaukee *Journal*, *Wall Street Journal*, Kansas City *Star*, Indianapolis *Star*, New York *Sun*, San Francisco *Chronicle*.

Twenty correspondents made no return for first place, thirty-two for second place, forty-one for third place.

Four correspondents gave "my own paper" or "present paper" as first choice.

* Both owned by J. David Stern.

XXVII. ANNUAL SALARIES OF 87 CORRESPONDENTS *

SALARY IN DOLLARS	NO.	SALARY IN DOLLARS	NO.	SALARY IN DOLLARS	NO.	SALARY IN DOLLARS	NO.
1,500	2	3,450	1	5,500	2	8,000	2
1,560	1	3,500	1	5,720	1	8,250	1
1,800	2	3,900	2	5,980	1	8,500	1
1,820	1	4,000	3	6,000	5	8,620	1
2,200	1	4,100	1	6,200	1	9,000	2
2,400	1	4,160	1	6,240	1	9,360	1
2,570	1	4,200	2	6,500	7	9,900	1
2,600	1	4,500	1	6,780	1	10,400	1
2,640	1	4,800	1	7,000	1	10,560	1
2,650	1	5,000	4	7,020	1	12,000	1
3,000	2	5,040	1	7,120	1	13,000	1
3,200	1	5,100	1	7,300	1	15,000	2
3,300	1	5,200	6	7,500	2	16,000	1
3,380	2	5,300	1	7,800	1	18,000	1

* Newspaper salaries only. Income from magazine writing, radio services, etc., is not included. The list includes the salaries of syndicated correspondents, columnists, etc. For correspondents who serve several papers, their total income is stated.

APPENDIX F

RULES GOVERNING ADMISSION TO THE PRESS GALLERIES OF CONGRESS *

1. Persons desiring admission to the press galleries of Congress shall make application to the Speaker, as required by Rule XXXV of the House of Representatives, and to the Committee on Rules of the Senate, as required by Rule VI for the regulation of the Senate Wing of the Capitol; and shall state in writing the names of all newspapers or publications or news associations by which they are employed, and what other occupation or employment they may have, if any; and they shall further declare that they are not engaged in the prosecution of claims pending before Congress or the departments, and will not become so engaged while allowed admission to the galleries; that they are not employed in any legislative or executive department of the Government, or by any foreign Government or any representative thereof; and that they are not employed, directly or indirectly, by any stock exchange, board of trade, or other organization, or member thereof, or brokerage house, or broker, engaged in the buying and selling of any security or commodity or by any person or corporation having legislation before Congress, and will not become so engaged while retaining membership in the galleries. Holders of visitor's cards who may be allowed temporary admission to the galleries must conform to the restrictions of this rule.

2. The applications required by the above rule shall be authenticated in a manner that shall be satisfactory to the standing committee of correspondents who shall see that the occu-

* Copied from *Congressional Directory*, January, 1936, p. 611.

pation of the galleries is confined to bona fide correspondents of reputable standing in their business, who represent daily newspapers or newspaper associations requiring telegraphic service; and it shall be the duty of the standing committee at their discretion, to report violation of the privileges of the galleries to the Speaker, or to the Senate Committee on Rules, and pending action thereon the offending correspondent may be suspended.

3. Persons engaged in other occupations whose chief attention is not given to newspaper correspondence or to newspaper associations requiring telegraphic service shall not be entitled to admission to the press galleries; and the Press List in the CONGRESSIONAL DIRECTORY shall be a list only of persons whose chief attention is given to telegraphic correspondence for daily newspapers or newspaper associations requiring telegraphic service.

4. Members of the families of correspondents are not entitled to the privileges of the galleries.

5. The press galleries shall be under the control of the standing committee of correspondents, subject to the approval and supervision of the Speaker of the House of Representatives and the Senate Committee on Rules.

Approved.

JOSEPH W. BYRNS,
Speaker of the House of Representatives
Approved by the Committee on Rules of the Senate.

THOMAS L. STOKES,
Chairman,
HARRY B. GAUSS,
WILLIAM K. HUTCHINSON,
WILLIAM P. KENNEDY,
PAUL J. McGAHAN,
Secretary,
Standing Committee of Correspondents.

APPENDIX G

HISTORICAL NOTE ON THE PRESS CORPS

SILAS BENT says that in 1813-14 there were four Washington correspondents, and that the press gallery was set aside in 1823, with twelve correspondents in attendance.* According to Professor Willard Grosvenor Bleyer, special correspondence began in Washington around 1825, supplementing the reports of Congressional Proceedings taken from Gale and Seaton's *National Intelligencer*.†

I have gone through the *Congressional Directory* since 1868, and counted the number of members of the official press corps representing newspapers, press associations and syndicates *in the United States*. At approximate ten-year intervals the lists show: ‡

1868	58
1878	153
1888	127
1900	171
1910	166
1920	209
1930	251

* *Ballyhoo*, p. 76.

† *Main Currents in the History of American Journalism*, pp. 152-53.

‡ The following page references for these figures refer to the *Congressional Directory* for the year cited: 1868, p. 55; 1878, pp. 92-93; 1888, pp. 158-60; 1900, pp. 322-24; 1910, pp. 392-94; 1920, pp. 447-50; January, 1930, pp. 555-62.

In 1892 T. C. Crawford, a Washington correspondent, stated that there were 100 or more occasional correspondents with clerkships in the government departments, or attached to the private service of Senators or Representatives. Private Secretaries of Congressmen often corresponded with the leading journal of the Congressman's district. Clerkships of leading Congressional committees used to be given to the representatives of prominent papers.*

Malcolm Willey and Stuart A. Rice point out that from 1902 to 1929 press representation in Washington was being extended in cities of medium size and in smaller cities above 25,000 population; papers in the larger cities, already well represented in the capital, were expanding their Washington staffs, becoming more independent of the press associations, expressing greater individuality. Although smaller papers began to make more frequent use of the "specials," they still depended largely upon press association coverage. During this period the greatest increase was in New England papers represented in Washington; next, the papers in the West, South and Central states. Representation of the Rocky Mountain section showed a loss.†

In 1899 only three press associations and syndicates were represented, with fourteen men; in 1929, nineteen were represented, with 113 men and women.‡

In 1899, sixty-two cities in the United States had newspapers with special correspondents in the capital; in 1929, 183 cities fell in this category. The maximum tendency toward individual representation occurred "in cities of middle size." §

* "The Special Correspondent at Washington," *Cosmopolitan*, January, 1892, p. 356.

† *Communication Agencies and Social Life* (New York and London: McGraw-Hill, 1933), p. 170.

‡ *Ibid.*, pp. 168-69.

§ *Ibid.*, p. 169.

APPENDIX H

MISCELLANEOUS EXHIBITS

I.

THE following correspondents were contacted but did not fill out questionnaires.

Alford, Theodore C.	Kansas *City Star*
Bates, Edwin	Los Angeles Illustrated *Dail News*
Bell, Ulric	Louisville *Courier-Journal*
Brown, Constantine A.	Washington *Star*
Buel, Walker S.	Cleveland *Plain Dealer*
Doyle, James F.	Buffalo *Courier-Express*
Fleeson, Doris	New York *Daily News*
Fulton, William	Chicago *Tribune*
Gilroy, Harry	Newark *Evening News*
Goodwin, Mark L.	Dallas *News,* Dallas *Evening Journal*
Gridley, R. L.	United Press Association
Groves, Charles S.	Boston *Globe*
* Hornaday, James P.	Indianapolis *News*
Kelley, Ralph J.	Atlanta *Constitution,* Miami (Fla.) *Herald,* Sacramento (Calif.) *Bee,* Fresno (Calif.) *Bee*
Kintner, Robert E.	New York *Herald Tribune*
Knorr, Ernest A.	Central News of America
Martin, Lorenzo W.	Louisville *Times*
Pearl, Philip	Universal Service

* Deceased.

Plummer, H. C.	Associated Press
Raymond, William T.	Wall Street *Journal*
Saunders, Richard E.	Omaha *Bee-News*
Scott, David R.	Sandusky *Star-Journal*, Louisville *Herald-Post*
Stephenson, Francis M.	Associated Press
Storm, Frederick A.	United Press Service
Sullivan, Mark	New York *Herald Tribune* Syndicate
Turner, Richard L.	Associated Press
Waldman, Seymour	New York *Daily Worker*

2.

The publicity-seeking of the present administration cannot compete with the twenty-three-page mimeographed letter which was sent out regularly by the Treasury Department under Secretary Andrew W. Mellon, from 1927 to 1929, to teachers, high school, and college students who wrote in for information. It read in part:

I think you will agree with me that the task of the Secretary of the Treasury is a colossal one, especially at this time when the Nation is striving to get its finances into normal condition.

We are indeed fortunate that the President of the United States has been able to prevail upon a man of such high attainments, financial experience and outstanding ability as Mr. Andrew W. Mellon, of Pittsburgh, to take upon his shoulders this great responsibility.

He is not the sort of man who talks about what he is doing, but the Nation knows that at the head of the Treasury there is a clear-headed, capable man who is giving his entire energy and time to the solution of the problems which he has assumed as his own, and who has already demonstrated that he ranks with the ablest financiers of our time.*

3.

It is to be expected that newspapers will differ in their editorial interpretations and emphases. But it is hardly to be expected that two newspapers in the same city will present directly contradictory versions of fact. On December 17, 1936, ex-President Hoover delivered an address in St. Louis, in the course of which he accused President Roosevelt of bringing about the crash of the Detroit banks through a panic precipitated by his conduct between November, 1932 (when he was elected) and March, 1933, when he took office. The sensation this statement created needs no comment. In Detroit the newspapers and the public were, obviously, whipped to a high point of interest in the charges. The following editorials of December 18, 1936, one from the Detroit *Free Press,* the other from the Detroit *News,* proved both that every fact cited by Mr. Hoover was historically accurate, and that every fact was historically false. They form a strange document for students of public opinion.

MR. HOOVER'S MEMORY	MR. HOOVER AT ST. LOUIS
Our memory of the Detroit crisis is different from that of Mr. Hoover.	Mr. Hoover's discussion of Mr. Roosevelt and his New Deal administration . . . is a smashing arraignment.
We recall no panic in Detroit previous to the closing of the banks. We remember no run on them. We do re-	The assertions of fact contained in it are all well supported by the record. Mr.

* See the Washington *Post,* December 28, 1935, p. 7.

call . . . the blank surprise of Detroiters when they learned the banks would not reopen their doors on February 14, 1933, and the almost general impression that if they needed aid, they would be granted it by the Reconstruction Finance Corporation.

. . . . .

It is our recollection that the closing of the Detroit banks by Federal bank examiners under the Hoover administration, which Mr. Hoover now finds inexcusable, did create a panic all over the country; that the Hoover administration was at its wits ends to find some way of dealing with it successfully, and finally did nothing; and that a day or two after President Roosevelt's inauguration a bank holiday was declared to give opportunity for an examination and strengthening of the banks and let the people cool off. Thereafter, the sound banks were permitted to reopen, and the unsound ones were kept closed.

Further, we do not recall that Detroit bank depositors in both the closed Banks were

Hoover says nothing he is unable to back up with evidence.

What the former Chief Executive asserts about the responsibility of President Roosevelt for the bank collapse during the transition period after the November, 1932, election, and in the first days of his incumbency is well established. . . .

And Mr. Hoover speaks with the authority of intimate, first-hand knowledge when he asserts flatly that the bank structure of the Nation was not insolvent at the time, citing the rape of the Detroit banks in proof of his assertion, and declares that the smash was the "most political and most unnecessary bank panic in all our history."

. . . . .

A general consideration of Mr. Hoover's words calls up a picture of what might have been if the Nation had understood in 1932 that it had in the White House a man specially fitted for the emergency facing it, had been patient and had retained him in his place.

—Detroit *Free Press*, Dec. 18, 1936.

paid 100 per cent. Nor has
any bank in Detroit paid 100
per cent without collecting
from the stockholders.

But we do recall that
shortly after Roosevelt's inauguration, business bounded
upward until in July its volume was equal to the 1923-5
average. Was that due to dis-
trust and panic, or was it
merely the country's unfavorable reaction to the bills
passed by Congress?

—Detroit *News*, Dec. 18,
1935.

4.

On November 11, 1935, Walter P. Chrysler, noted American automobile manufacturer, was denounced by Justice Cyril
Atkinson (in King's Bench Court, London), in delivering
judgment on a conspiracy case which lasted sixty-two days
and entailed legal costs of $200,000.* Among other things
Justice Atkinson said:

Mr. Chrysler is said to be one of the foremost industrialists in
America. Some of his answers in this case show that his standard of business morality is lamentably low.

I doubt very much whether Mr. Chrysler is proud of these
methods. In this case he and other defendants have not hesitated through their counsel to charge the plaintiff with willful

* The suit was brought by Arnold de la Poer, formerly a Chrysler
official in London, who charged that in 1928 he was forced by threats
and misrepresentations to sell the shares he held in Chrysler Motors,
Ltd., at less than half their value.

perjury, with conspiring to give false evidence, with trickery, deception and blackmail, although, as they must know, there is not the slightest justification for saying it.

I think that the less that is said about honor in this case the better.

The New York *Times* for November 12, 1935, from which the quotation is taken, gave a long and detailed account of this event (page 9), as did other New York papers.

Now surely Mr. Chrysler is news, and bigger news in Detroit than in New York. How did the Detroit papers treat this story? A careful search failed to find any reference in the Detroit *Free Press* to the sensational remarks of Justice Atkinson on Mr. Chrysler. Neither did the Detroit *News* mention the event. But the next day, on November 13, 1935, the Detroit *Free Press* ran a three-inch Associated Press story under the caption:

London Expects Chrysler Appeal

The dispatch gave a bare recitation of the formal facts. The Detroit *News*, on November 14, 1935, devoted four and a half inches, on page 21 (!), to the announcement:

Judgment Stayed in Chrysler Case

Detroit readers of these two journals had no inkling of an episode which was a news item of great interest, involving one of the most famous of Detroit personalities, and revolving around the one subject of paramount interest to Detroit —automobiles.

REFERENCE NOTES

PART ONE

CHAPTER I. THE CAPITAL

1. *The World Almanac for 1937* (New York: New York *World-Telegram*, 1937), p. 541.
2. Paul W. Ward, "Washington Weekly," *Nation*, December 5, 1936, p. 651.
3. Oswald Garrison Villard, *Some Newspapers and Newspapermen* (New York: Knopf, 1928), p. 187.
4. *World Almanac, op. cit.*, p. 54.
5. Raymond G. Carroll, "Reform vs. the Washington Correspondents," *Editor and Publisher*, July 21, 1928, p. 14.
6. *High-Low Washington* (Philadelphia: Lippincott, 1932), p. 25.

CHAPTER II. PRESS CONFERENCES

1. Villard, "The Press and the President," *Century*, December, 1925, pp. 198 ff. Compare this to J. Frederick Essary, *Covering Washington* (Boston and New York: Houghton Mifflin, 1927), p. 87. Essary suggests that McKinley was fairly approachable.
2. "First White House Reporter Dies," *Editor and Publisher*, October 31, 1931, p. 38.
3. Henry Suydam says that regular press conferences began with Theodore Roosevelt. See *Conference on the Press*,

under the auspices of the School of Public and International Affairs, Princeton University, April 23-25, 1931 (Washington, D. C.: Printing Corporation of America, 1931), pp. 66-85. This point of view, however, is not held by other commentators. See Essary, *op. cit.*, p. 88, and David Lawrence, "The President and the Press," *Saturday Evening Post*, August 27, 1927, p. 27.

4. Villard, "The Press and the President," *op. cit.*, p. 198; Essary, *op. cit.*, pp. 93-94. Robert W. Desmond, *The Press and World Affairs*, (New York and London: D. Appleton-Century, 1937), p. 309.

5. Villard, "The Press and the President," *op. cit.*, p. 198.

6. Essary, *op. cit.*, p. 98. See also Silas Bent, *Ballyhoo: the Voice of the Press* (New York: Boni and Liveright, 1927), p. 77.

7. Villard, "The Press and the President," *op. cit.*, pp. 199 ff.

8. Essary, *op. cit.*, p. 88; Bent, *op. cit.*, p. 78.

9. Quoted in Desmond, *op. cit.*, pp. 310-11. For details of Wilson's relations with the press see Essary, *op. cit.*, pp. 99 ff., Villard, "The Press and the President," *op. cit.*, p. 197, Bent, *op. cit.*, p. 78, and George Creel, "Woodrow Wilson, the Man Behind the President," *Saturday Evening Post*, March 28, 1931, pp. 37-44.

10 David Lawrence, *op. cit.*, p. 277. Villard suggests that Wilson stopped holding press conferences because of his hypersensitivity and his refusal to submit to cross-examination. See "The Press and the President," *op. cit.*, p. 197.

11. Essary, *op. cit.*, pp. 89-90.

12. Villard, "The Press and the President," *op. cit.*, p. 199.

13. Villard, *ibid.*, p. 200. See also George H. Manning, "Capital Corps Hopes for 'New Deal,' " *Editor and Publisher*, March 4, 1933, p. 5.

14. Lawrence, *op. cit.*, pp. 27, 118.
15. Villard, "The Press and the President," *op. cit.*, p. 199.
16. Paul Hanna, "The State Department and the News," *Nation*, October 13, 1920, p. 399.
17. Essary, *op. cit.*, p. 91.
18. Manning, *op. cit.*, p. 5.
19. See Lawrence, *op. cit.*, p. 118.
20. Villard, "The Press and the President," *op. cit.*, p. 194. Also "Brooklyn *Eagle's* Writer Firmly Contests White House Interview Denial," *Editor and Publisher*, January 3, 1925, pp. 3-4.
21. *Ibid.*, p. 195.
22. Bent, *op. cit.*, p. 80.
23. Ray Tucker, "Part-Time Statesmen," *Collier's*, October 28, 1933, p. 38.
24. Suydam, in *Conference on the Press*, *op. cit.*, p. 67.
25. *Ibid.*
26. "Mr. Hoover's Refusal to be 'Humanized,'" *Literary Digest*, July 25, 1931, p. 8.
27. Raymond Clapper, "Why Reporters Like Roosevelt," *Review of Reviews*, June, 1934, p. 14.
28. Suydam, *op. cit.*, p. 67.
29. Quoted in Charles and Mary Beard, *The Rise of American Civilization* (New York: Macmillan, 1927), Vol. II, p. 669.
30. *Ibid.*
31. See Essary, "Democracy and the Press," *Annals of the American Academy of Political and Social Science*, September, 1933, pp. 111-12.
32. The entire affair of the Hoover censorship on the "Goodwill Trip" is discussed by Paul Y. Anderson in "A Reporter at Large," *News, Its Scope and Limitations*, edited by T. C. Morelock, University of Missouri Jour-

nalism Series, Bulletin No. 57 (Columbia, Missouri: University of Missouri, 1929), pp. 11 ff.

33. Anderson, "Cross-Section of Washington," *Nation,* April 9, 1930, p. 420; *Time,* March 20, 1933, pp. 20-23; Robert S. Allen and Drew Pearson, *Washington Merry-Go-Round* (New York, Liveright, 1931), pp. 56-60.

34. See the following: J. Hayden, quoted in "Mr. Hoover's Refusal to be Humanized," *op. cit.;* Allen and Pearson, *op. cit.,* p. 58; Anderson, "Hoover and the Press," *Nation,* October 14, 1931, pp. 382-84.

35. Manning, "Strained Air Pervades Press Circles as White House 'Leak' Is Sought," *Editor and Publisher,* July 18, 1931, p. 10.

36. See John S. Gregory, "All Quiet on the Rapidan," *Outlook and Independent,* August 5, 1931, p. 427.

37. "Mr. Hoover's Refusal to be 'Humanized,' " *op. cit.* Cf. Manning, "Strained Air Pervades Press Circles," *op. cit.* For Hoover's objection to human-interest stories see "Hoover Seeks Source of 'Talkie' Story," *Editor and Publisher,* November 14, 1931, p. 8; cf. Will Irwin, *Propaganda and the News* (New York and London: McGraw-Hill, 1936), pp. 295-96, who defends Hoover in regard to the curtain episode. Hoover, according to Irwin, feared that a servant who would reveal such a fact might reveal others of more importance. The patched curtains were in a private room to which none of the press had access. Hence Mr. Hoover knew that a servant or a Secret Service man had been the "leak."

38. Allen and Pearson, *op. cit.,* p. 60.

39. Manning, "Subtle Censorship on Government News is Arising Steadily in Washington," *Editor and Publisher,* September 5, 1931, p. 5.

40. Allen and Pearson, *op. cit.*, pp. 75-76; Manning, "Joslin Suggests News 'Consultations,'" *Editor and Publisher*, September 19, 1931, p. 7.

41. *Ibid.*

42. Warren B. Francis, "Secrecy Policy of Shipping Board Attacked," *Editor and Publisher*, September 19, 1931, p. 16.

43. Anderson, "Hoover and the Press," *op. cit.*, pp. 383-84.

44. Manning, "White House News Ban on Bank Parley Upset by Correspondents," *Editor and Publisher*, October 10, 1931, p. 5.

45. The Department of Justice episode is mentioned by Suydam, *op. cit.*, p. 70; the Federal Farm Board incident is in Manning, "Subtle Censorship on Government News is Arising Steadily in Washington," *op. cit.*, pp. 5-6, and "Farm Board Resists News Coverage," *Editor and Publisher*, September 3, 1932, p. 15; the Shipping Board policy is in Francis, "Secrecy Policy of Shipping Board Attacked," *op. cit.*

46. Manning, "Hurley Charges Refuted by Reporters," *Editor and Publisher*, August 13, 1932, p. 7.

47. Manning, "Farm Board Resists News Coverage," *op. cit.*

48. Manning, "Joslin Suggests News 'Consultations,'" *op. cit.*, p. 7.

49. See Tucker, *op. cit.*, p. 38.

50. Manning, "President Cancels Press Conferences," *Editor and Publisher*, November 26, 1932, p. 8.

51. Ashmun Brown, "The Roosevelt Myth," *American Mercury*, April, 1936, p. 390.

52. For comments on Roosevelt's friction with the press as Governor of New York see Manning, "Capital Corps Hopes for 'New Deal,'" *op. cit.*; also "Reporters Protest Roosevelt Favors," *Editor and Publisher*, June 25, 1932, p. 18. Several correspondents informed this

writer of a mild boycott of Roosevelt's press conferences in Albany.

53. Ernest K. Lindley, *The Roosevelt Revolution: First Phase* (New York: Viking, 1933), p. 280. See also Erwin D. Canham, "Democracy's Fifth Wheel," *Literary Digest*, January 5, 1935, p. 6.

54. For a detailed description of the first press conference see Manning, "New Deal for Press Begins at Once as Nation Faces Bank Crisis," *Editor and Publisher*, March 11, 1933, pp. 3-4.

55. Quoted in "Mr. Roosevelt Ungags the Press," *Literary Digest*, March 25, 1933, p. 10.

56. Tucker, *op. cit.*, p. 26.

57. Marlan E. Pew, "Shop Talk at Thirty," *Editor and Publisher*, April 8, 1933, p. 36.

58. Clapper, *op. cit.*, p. 15. See also "Correspondents Like Roosevelt," *American Press*, March, 1933, p. 3, for general comments on the press corps' attitude.

59. Clapper, *op. cit.*, p. 17.

60. Ishbel Ross, *Ladies of the Press* (New York and London: Harpers, 1936), pp. 309-22.

61. For praise of the press-relations techniques of Cabinet members see Manning, "New Deal for Press Begins at Once," *op. cit.*

62. See comments of several correspondents on the New Deal press agents and "handouts" in Bice Clemow, "Recovery on Way, Capital Corps Feels," *Editor and Publisher*, December 29, 1934, p. 8; "Washington Correspondents Praise Press Agents," *Editor and Publisher*, December 29, 1934, p. 10. Also Arthur Krock, in a speech to the National Republican Club in New York City, January 26, 1935 (copy in my possession). For a lengthy, critical analysis of press agents, see Wil-

liam E. Berchtold, "Press Agents of the New Deal," *New Outlook*, July, 1934, pp. 23-30.

63. Henning's comment is in "New Deal for Press Praised by Henning," *Editor and Publisher*, June 10, 1933, p. 54. Holmes' praise is in Clemow, *op. cit.; Krock's comments taken from the speech cited above.

64. See for example, Lawrence, "The Lost Right of Privacy," *American Mercury*, May, 1936, pp. 12-18; Eugene A. Kelly, "Distorting the News," *ibid.*, March, 1935, pp. 307-18; Robert E. Kintner, "The SEC Dictatorship," *ibid.*, June, 1936, pp. 180-87; Paul R. Leach in Chicago *Daily News*, May 20, 1935, p. 7; Brown, *op. cit.*, pp. 390-94.

65. Clemow, "F. D. R. Retains 'Open' Conferences," *Editor and Publisher*, March 2, 1935, p. 9.

66. Brown, *op. cit.*, p. 392.

67. These matters are all discussed from the point of view of a conservative correspondent in Brown, *op. cit.*, pp. 391-94. It should be noted that Mr. Roosevelt was generally held responsible for the "preacher letter" fiasco, though the fault clearly lay with the White House secretariat.

68. *Time*, December 24, 1934, p. 14; also January 21, 1935, p. 23.

69. See comment of Raymond P. Brandt, quoted by Robert S. Mann, "Capital Corps No Propaganda Victim, Writers Tell Journalism Teachers," *Editor and Publisher*, January 4, 1936, p. 3.

70. See comments of Paul Mallon, Ulric Bell, Russell Kent, and Mark Foote in Clemow, "Recovery on Way, Capital Corps Feels," *op. cit.*, p. 8. Mr. Arthur Krock criticized the "off the record" statements as stifling budding publication in his speech, cited above.

71. Krock, in speech cited above.
72. Kelly, *op. cit.*, p. 316.
73. Krock, "The Press and Government," *Annals of the American Academy of Political and Social Science*, July, 1935, pp. 164 ff.
74. Canham, *op. cit.*, p. 6.
75. *Conference on the Press, op. cit.*, p. 86.
76. *Ibid.*, pp. 89-90.
77. "Roper Establishes a Strict Censorship," *Editor and Publisher*, March 14, 1936, p. 10.
78. Quoted in "News Regulation in Washington Seen as Step to Co-ordination," *Editor and Publisher*, April 7, 1934, p. 10.
79. Villard, "Press and the President," *op. cit.*, p. 198.
80. "News Men Criticized by Premier Bennett," *Editor and Publisher*, August 6, 1932, p. 11.

CHAPTER III. THE HANDOUT

1. See, for example, George Michael (pseud.), *The Handout* (New York: Putnams, 1935). Also Elisha Hanson, "Official Propaganda and the New Deal," *Annals of the American Academy of Political and Social Science*, May, 1935, pp. 176-86.
2. In general see Essary, *Covering Washington, passim;* George Creel, *How We Advertised America* (New York and London: Harpers, 1920) *passim;* Harold D. Lasswell, *Propaganda Technique in the World War* (New York: Knopf, 1927), *passim.*
3. Frank Cobb, in a speech to the Women's City Club of Detroit, quoted in an editorial note in the *New Republic*, December 31, 1919, p. 44.
4. Essary, "The Washington Assignment," *News and the*

Newspaper, edited by Robert S. Mann, University of Missouri Journalism Series, Bulletin No. 28 (Columbia, Missouri: University of Missouri, 1923).

5. "Federal Handouts Cost Three Millions a Year," *American Press,* July, 1931, p. 18.

6. Essary, "Uncle Sam's Ballyhoo Men," *American Mercury,* August, 1931, pp. 419-20.

7. Harper Leech and John C. Carroll, *What's the News?* (Chicago: Covici, 1926), p. 160.

8. Mr. Elisha Hanson seems to overlook this. See his article, quoted above.

9. Figures on NRA handouts were taken from Berchtold, *op. cit.,* p. 24; on AAA from Hanson, *op. cit.,* p. 180; the others were given to the writer by press agents of the respective agencies.

10. Michael (pseud.), *op. cit.*

11. E. Pendleton Herring, "Official Publicity Under the New Deal," *Annals of the American Academy of Political and Social Science,* May, 1935, p. 169. Dr. Herring gives a reasoned analysis of the function of the press agents and concludes that without them there would be much confusion and inconvenience.

12. Krock, speech to the National Republican Club, *op. cit.*

13. Kelly, *op. cit.,* p. 316.

14. Krock, remarks before the Chamber of Commerce of the United States, May 4, 1934 (copy in my possession).

15. Berchtold, *op. cit.,* p. 25.

16. "The Share-Croppers Fight for Life," *New Republic,* January 29, 1936, p. 336.

17. Clemow, "Recovery on Way, Capital Corps Feels," *op. cit.,* p. 7; see also "Washington Correspondents Praise Press Agents," *op. cit.,* p. 10.

CHAPTER IV. NEWS SOURCES AND RESTRAINTS

1. Leech and J. C. Carroll, *op. cit.*, pp. 164 ff.
2. Essary, *Covering Washington*, p. 51.
3. Bulkley S. Griffin, "The Public Man and the Newspapers," *Nation*, June 17, 1925, p. 690.
4. *High-Low Washington*, pp. 156-58.
5. *Ibid.*, pp. 155-56.
6. Leech and Carroll, *op. cit.*, pp. 94-101. Essary describes how an important treaty was communicated to a correspondent by an informal method which absolved a Senator from responsibility. See *Covering Washington*, pp. 44-47.
7. Paul Mallon, "Inquisition Dramas Staged by Congress," Sunday New York *Times*, December 9, 1934, Section 6, p. 7.
8. *High-Low Washington*, p. 152.
9. Hanson, *op. cit.*, p. 186.
10. Griffin, *op. cit.*, p. 689.
11. *High-Low Washington*, p. 122.
12. *Who Shall Survive? A New Approach to the Problem of Human Interrelations* (Washington, D. C.: Nervous and Mental Diseases Publishing Company, 1935).
13. Lindley, *op. cit.*, pp. 280 ff.
14. Clemow, "Recovery on Way, Capital Corps Feels," *op. cit.*, p. 7.
15. The entire episode is discussed by Professor Ellery C. Stowell in "A Memorable Press Conference," *International Law and Relations*, Vol. IV, Bulletin Nos. 18 and 19, American University Graduate School (Washington, D. C.: The Digest Press). The pamphlet includes photostatic copies of the dispatches which resulted from the press conference.

16. Griffin, *op. cit.*, p. 689.
17. *Ibid.*
18. The seven examples are taken from Griffin, *ibid.*

CHAPTER V. COVERING WASHINGTON

1. Kelly, *op. cit.*, p. 308.
2. See the first few chapters in John L. Given, *Making a Newspaper* (New York: Henry Holt, 1907), for the best description of this process. Walter Lippmann's discussion of the nature of news-coverage, in *Public Opinion* (New York: Harcourt, Brace, 1925), draws heavily on Given's exposition.
3. These estimates were obtained from officers of the respective associations in 1936. In an advertisement in *Editor and Publisher* on April 24, 1937 (p. 73), the United Press asserted that it now serves 1,424 newspapers; this includes many papers in Central and South America where the United Press is particularly strong.
4. James J. Butler, "Press Wires Jammed with Capital News," *Editor and Publisher*, January 11, 1936, p. 11. On January 6, 1936, the Associated Press dispatched 73,000 words, covering the Supreme Court decision on the AAA and the President's message.
5. Villard, "The Associated Press," *Nation*, April 16, 1930, p. 443.
6. "Cornering Washington News," *New Republic*, February 22, 1933, p. 34.
7. "United Press: Budget for a Worldwide News Service," *Fortune*, May, 1933, p. 98. It was impossible to obtain similar figures from other associations; none are given in the literature covered.

8. Villard, "The United Press," *Nation,* May 7, 1930, pp. 539-42.

9. See, for example, Washington *Daily News,* December 26, 1935, p. 5.

10. Villard, "The United Press," *op. cit.,* p. 541. The lower wage scale of the United Press is often mentioned in Washington newspaper circles.

11. This is the opinion of an overwhelming majority of the correspondents and is reflected in their vote on Press Associations in Chapter IX. An examination of Universal Service dispatches over any period of time will support the point. Compare, for example, the Universal Service's treatment of the American Liberty League's opinion on the Wagner National Labor Relations Act, as printed in the New York *American* for September 19, 1935 (p. 1), to dispatches of the other press associations, or the accounts of the New York *Times,* Baltimore *Sun* or Washington *Post,* for the same date.

12. Anderson in *Conference on the Press,* p. 73.

13. T. C. Crawford, "The Special Correspondent at Washington," *Cosmopolitan,* January, 1892, pp. 351-60.

14. Leech and J. C. Carroll, *op. cit.,* p. 155. For further details on the position of the correspondent as an extension of the city desk see Raymond G. Carroll, "Washingtonia," *Saturday Evening Post,* February 16, 1935, p. 30.

15. Leech and J. C. Carroll, *op. cit.,* pp. 155-57.

16. *Ibid.,* p. 157.

17. "Reform vs. the Washington Correspondent," *op. cit.,* p. 7.

18. *Ibid.*

19. "Fight the Tugwell Bill," *National Printer Journalist,* January, 1934, p. 40; George Seldes, *Freedom of the*

Press (Indianapolis and New York: Bobbs-Merrill, 1935), pp. 66-76.

20. R. G. Carroll, *op. cit.*, p. 7.
21. Quoted by Mann, "Capital Corps No Propaganda Victim," *op. cit.*, p. 12.
22. See, for example, Will Irwin, *Propaganda and the News,* p. 312.
23. Robert S. and Helen Merrell Lynd, *Middletown in Transition* (New York: Harcourt, Brace, 1937), pp. 375-76.
24. Clemow, "Recovery on Way, Capital Corps Feels," *op. cit.*, p. 7.
25. The citations from the "Daily Washington Merry-Go-Round" may be found in either the Washington *Herald,* or the Philadelphia *Record,* for the dates given. Since Allen and Pearson submit their columns by mail at least five days before publication date, the prognostications are even more impressive.
26. Clemow, "Recovery on Way, Capital Corps Feels," *op. cit.*, p. 7.
27. From figures supplied to me by the head of a large syndicate.
28. "Fortune Quarterly Survey: VII," ("Have you a Favorite Newspaper Columnist? (If yes) Who?"), *Fortune,* January, 1937, pp. 86, 156.

PART TWO

CHAPTER VI. THE SOCIAL COMPOSITION OF THE PRESS CORPS

1. See Lasswell, "The Person: Subject and Object of Propaganda," *Annals of the American Academy of Political and Social Science,* May, 1935, p. 190, and "Research

on the Distribution of Symbol Specialists," *Journalism Quarterly*, June, 1935, pp. 146-57.

2. "The Family and its Functions," *Recent Social Trends* (New York and London: McGraw-Hill, 1934), p. 685.

3. Robert Frank Harrel, "Factors Making for Success in Journalism," in R. F. Harrel and Walter B. Pitkin, *Vocational Studies in Journalism* (New York: Columbia University Press, 1931), pp. 101-02.

4. *Ibid.*, pp. 151-52.

5. Given in Robert S. Lynd, "The People as Consumers," *Recent Social Trends*, p. 860.

6. *The Movement of Money and Real Earnings in the United States, 1926-28*, quoted by Leo Wolman and Gustav Peck, "Labor Groups in the Social Structure," *Recent Social Trends*, p. 817.

7. As a labor-saving device population figures were used for 1900, the census year which corresponds most closely to the average age of the newspapermen studied. This is a necessary and unavoidable compromise for several reasons: (1) Population figures are not available for many towns and cities prior to 1900; (2) figures are not available for the percentage of present-day Americans who were born in communities of different sizes; (3) it would have involved elaborate and cumbersome statistical techniques to weight population figures for the year of birth of each separate correspondent, and to proportionalize these figures according to (a) the percentage relationship of towns of any given population figure to the general population of the United States at the same point in time, (b) the percentage of living persons born in localities of a given size at any given date. Obviously a population of 5,000 in 1890 has a

different meaning than the same population in 1910. The present compromise, using 1900 as a controlled date of reference, serves our purpose well enough to make a greater refinement of method unnecessary. There were obviously few metropolitan centers in 1900 from which the members of the corps could come.

8. 1930 population figures were taken from the *World Almanac for 1937*, p. 272. Percentages for 1900 were computed from gross population figures.

9. "The Person: Subject and Object of Propaganda," *op. cit.*, p. 190.

10. Computed from election figures in the *World Almanac for 1937*, pp. 909-10.

11. Harrel, *op. cit.*, p. 152.

12. See my article, "President Roosevelt and the Washington Correspondents," *Public Opinion Quarterly*, January, 1937, pp. 48-49; also Chapter XII.

13. Ogburn, *op. cit.*, p. 680. The youngest correspondent is twenty-three years old. Ogburn's percentage would obviously be higher for the proportion of the population twenty-three or above who are married. But these estimates are sufficiently suggestive for our purposes.

14. *Ibid.*, p. 685.

15. *Ibid.*, p. 688.

16. C. Luther Fry, "Changes in Religious Organization," *Recent Social Trends*, pp. 1021-22.

CHAPTER VII. WHAT DO THEY READ?

No reference notes.

CHAPTER VIII. THE PROFESSIONAL COMPOSITION
OF THE CORPS

1. T. C. Crawford, *op. cit.*, pp. 351-60.
2. Harrel, *op. cit.*, pp. 150-51.
3. New York *Times*, January 8, 1936, p. 13. Newspaper salaries are listed in greater detail in "U. S. Lists High Newspaper Salaries," *Editor and Publisher*, January 18, 1936, pp. 15, 50.
4. "Salaries and Working Conditions of Newspaper Editorial Employees," *Monthly Labor Review* (Bureau of Labor Statistics), May, 1935, pp. 3-4.

CHAPTER IX. THE ATTITUDES OF THE WASHINGTON
CORRESPONDENTS

1. George Gallup, "America Speaks," Los Angeles *Times*, February 16, 1936, Part I, p. 9.
2. *Time*, April 19, 1937, p. 51, footnote.
3. Alfred Meusel, "Middle Class," *Encyclopedia of the Social Sciences* (New York: Macmillan, 1930-33), Vol. X, pp. 407-15.

CHAPTER X. "POLICY" AND THE WASHINGTON
CORRESPONDENTS

1. In "Problems of Journalism," *Proceedings of the American Society of Newspaper Editors* (Washington, D. C.: published by the Society, 1930), p. 252.
2. New York *Times*, November 5, 1935, p. 22.
3. Ernest Sutherland Bates and Oliver Carlson, *Hearst: Lord of San Simeon* (New York: Viking, 1936), p. 254.

4. See the comments of Raymond Clapper, "Between You and Me," Washington *Post*, December 28, 1935, p. 2. Cf. *Time*, June 12, 1933, p. 47, and June 19, 1933, p. 48. Also James J. Butler, "12 News Executives Resign from Daily in Business Office Clash," *Editor and Publisher*, November 2, 1935, p. 8.
5. *The Ethics of Journalism* (New York: Knopf, 1924), pp. 83-85.

PART THREE

CHAPTER XI. THE PSYCHOLOGY OF THE CORRESPONDENT

1. Max Weber, *Politik als Beruf*. Zweite Auflage (München und Leipzig: Verlag von Duncker und Humblot), p. 29. I used an unpublished translation by Gabriel Almond of the University of Chicago.
2. "Why Men Work for Newspapers," *American Mercury*, May, 1929, p. 87.
3. Tucker, *op. cit.*, p. 38.
4. *Ibid.*
5. *Ibid.*
6. I. Ross, *op. cit.*, p. 341.
7. Tucker, *op. cit.*, p. 38.
8. Anderson, "Lame-Duck Diplomats," *Nation*, January 15, 1930, p. 66.
9. *Ibid.* Also see Anderson, "Washington Honor Roll," *Nation*, January 28, 1931, p. 94.
10. Richard V. Oulahan, "Capital Corps Praised for Diligence," *Editor and Publisher*, April 25, 1931, p. 32.
11. "Two News Men Found AAA Substitute," *Editor and Publisher*, January 25, 1936, p. III.
12. Bent, "Journalism and Morality," *Atlantic Monthly*, June, 1926, p. 761.
13. Brown, *op. cit.*, p. 391.

CHAPTER XII. "NEWS" AND THE WASHINGTON
CORRESPONDENTS

1. Bent, *Ballyhoo*, p. 27.
2. "Edward L. Bernays: The Science of Ballyhoo," *Atlantic Monthly*, May, 1932, p. 570.
3. Ex-Senator Henry Allen in *Conference on the Press*, p. 102.
4. *Ibid.*
5. Leech and J. C. Carroll, *op. cit.*, p. 134.
6. See, for example, Buffalo *Evening News*, October 22, 1935, p. 9.
7. William Summerill in *Conference on the Press*, p. 83.
8. Discussed by N. A. Crawford in *The Press and the Public* (Chapel Hill: University of North Carolina Newspaper Institute, No. 13, January 15, 1936.)
9. Villard, "Donkey Brays Again," *Nation*, July 4, 1936, p. 10.
10. Quoted by Irwin, "The American Newspaper: A Study of Journalism in its Relation to the Public," *Collier's Weekly*, April 1, 1911, p. 28.
11. Louis Adamic, "The Papers Print the Riots," *Scribners*, February, 1932, pp. 109-11. For a careful study of Labor and news see Burrus S. Dickinson, "The Influence of the Press in Labor Affairs," *Journalism Quarterly*, September, 1932, pp. 269-80.
12. Louis Stark, quoted by David Resnick in "Labor News Takes the Spotlight," *Editor and Publisher*, October 14, 1933, p. 7.
13. Frank H. Knight, *The Ethics of Competition* (New York and London: Harpers, 1935), p. 57.

Reference Notes   389

14. Bell and Essary are quoted in Mann, "Capital Corps No Propaganda Victim," *op. cit.*, p. 3.
15. See Leech and J. C. Carroll, *op. cit.*, p. 107.

CHAPTER XIII. THE CORPS, THE PRESS, AND DEMOCRACY

1. Quoted in George Seldes, *op. cit.*, p. 338.
2. Bates and Carlson, *op. cit.*, pp. 254-55.
3. Frederick L. Schuman, "Hearst's Campaign Against Professors," a letter to the editors of the *New Republic*, April 17, 1935, pp. 287-88.
4. "The Press and the Public," *New Republic*, Special Section, Prepared by the Editors, March 17, 1937, Part Two, pp. 180-81.
5. In Virginius Dabney, "The Press and the Election," *Public Opinion Quarterly*, April, 1937, p. 123. For a detailed analysis of the Chicago *Tribune's* methods in the 1936 campaign see "The Press and the Public," *New Republic*, *op. cit.*, pp. 180-82.
6. Paul W. Ward, "Washington Weekly: Farley Captures Labor," *Nation*, October 31, 1936, p. 512. Also *Time*, November 2, 1936, p. 14.
7. New York *Herald Tribune*, October 22, 1936, p. 15.
8. Heywood Broun, "Roosevelt Shows up the Press," *Nation*, October 31, 1936, p. 522.
9. In Virginius Dabney, *op. cit.*, p. 123.
10. *Ibid.*
11. Robert S. and Helen Merrell Lynd, *Middletown in Transition*, pp. 377-78.
12. In Chilton R. Bush, *Editorial Thinking and Writing* (New York and London: Appleton, 1932), p. 307, footnote.
13. Earl Burke, "Dailies Helped Break General Strike," *Edi-*

tor and Publisher, July 28, 1934, p. 5. Also see "The Press As Strike-Breakers," *New Republic,* August 8, 1934, p. 333.

14. "Report of the Committee on Social Security of the ANPA," *Editor and Publisher,* April 25, 1936, p. 14.
15. *Time,* June 25, 1934, p. 64.
16. *Editor and Publisher,* November 30, 1935, p. 43.
17. "Conditions of Work and Life of Journalists," *International Labor Office, Series and Reports,* Series L, No. 2 (London: E. S. King, 1928). See also Dexter Merriam Keezer, "Press," *Encyclopedia of the Social Sciences,* XII, pp. 325-43; and Allan Nevins, "Journalism," *ibid.,* VIII, pp. 420-24.
18. *Time,* May 7, 1934, p. 48.
19. *Ibid.*
20. C. R. Bush, *op. cit.,* p. 312, footnote.
21. "Whose Hands Need Washing?" *Guild Reporter,* June, 1934, p. 11.
22. In Bates and Carlson, *op. cit.,* p. 255.
23. *Time,* October 28, 1935, p. 48.
24. Quoted by C. R. Bush, *op. cit.,* p. 311.
25. John K. Winkler, *William Randolph Hearst: An American Phenomenon* (New York: Simon and Schuster, 1928), p. 120.
26. *Editor and Publisher,* March 14, 1936, p. 28.
27. "Conditions of Work and Life of Journalists," *op. cit.,* p. 2. See also Julius Ochs Adler, "Do Advertisers Control Newspaper Policy?" *American Press,* April, 1937, p. 1.
28. See "The Press and the Public," *New Republic, op. cit.,* pp. 188-89.
29. *Problems of Journalism: 1928,* Proceedings of the American Society of Newspaper Editors (Washington, D. C.: Published by the Society, 1928), pp. 139-40.

30. *Editor and Publisher,* June 30, 1928, p. 5.
31. James Rorty, "Call for Mr. Throttlebottom," *Nation,* January 10, 1934, p. 37. The National Editorial Association printed an appeal entitled: "Fight the Tugwell Bill," *National Printer Journalist,* January, 1934, p. 40. Also see Seldes, *op. cit.,* p. 56.
32. See the Consumers' columns of Ruth Brindze, *Nation,* December 18, 1935, p. 716, and November 20, 1935, pp. 592-94.
33. Burrus S. Dickinson, "The Influence of the Press in Labor Affairs," *op. cit.,* p. 280.
34. Quoted by Seldes, *op. cit.,* p. 155.
35. *Mobilizing for Chaos: the Story of the New Propaganda.* (New Haven: Yale University Press, 1934), pp. 138-39.
36. Bent, *Ballyhoo,* p. 252.
37. *Liberty and the News* (New York: Harcourt, Brace and Howe, 1920), p. 47.
38. *The Making of Citizens: A Comparative Study of Methods of Civic Training* (Chicago: University of Chicago Press, 1931), p. 267.
39. *Middletown,* p. 476.
40. *Middletown in Transition,* p. 381.
41. Willard Grosvenor Bleyer, "Freedom of the Press and the New Deal," *Journalism Quarterly,* March, 1934, p. 29.
42. *Ibid.*
43. *Middletown,* p. 477.
44. *Liberty and the News,* pp. 10-11.
45. Bruce Bliven, "Bliven Sees Losing Fight Against Press Repressions," *Editor and Publisher,* March 23, 1935, p. 14.
46. Frank Knight, *op. cit.,* p. 292.
47. Bates and Carlson, *op. cit.,* p. 269.

48. "The Press and the Public," *New Republic, op. cit.,* p. 182.
49. Lasswell, *Politics: Who Gets What, When, How* (New York and London: McGraw-Hill, 1936), p. 33.
50. Allan Nevins, *op. cit.,* p. 423.
51. Quoted by John E. Drewry, "The Journalist's Inferiority Complex," *Journalism Quarterly,* March, 1931, p. 69.
52. Count Constantine K. Pobyedenostseff, Minister of Education for Czar Nicholas II, *Recollections of a Russian Statesman,* quoted in A. J. Beveridge, *The Russian Advance* (New York: Harpers, 1903), p. 456.
53. *The Making of Citizens,* p. 213.
54. In "Newspapers, Dare To Be Free!" *Nation,* February 5, 1936, p. 145.

BIBLIOGRAPHY *

REFERENCE WORKS

"Conditions of Work and Life of Journalists." *International Labor Office, Series and Reports*, Series L, No. 2. London: E. S. King & Co., 1928.

Directory of Newspapers and Periodicals. Philadelphia: N. W. Ayer & Sons, 1936.

Editor and Publisher: International Year Book Number for 1935. Two Sections: Section Two. New York: Editor and Publisher Co., January 26, 1935.

Editor and Publisher: International Year Book Number for 1936. Two Sections: Section Two. New York: Editor and Publisher Co., January 25, 1936.

Encyclopedia of the Social Sciences. New York: Macmillan Co., 1930-33.

Propaganda and Promotional Activities: An Annotated Bibliography. Prepared under the Direction of the Advisory Committee on Pressure Groups and Propaganda, Social Science Research Council. Harold D. Lasswell, Ralph D. Casey, and Bruce Lannes Smith. Minneapolis: University of Minnesota Press, 1935.

Recent Social Trends in the United States. Report of the President's Research Committee on Social Trends (one volume edition). New York and London: Whittlesey House, McGraw-Hill, 1934.

The World Almanac for 1937. New York: New York World-Telegram, 1937.

* Selected.

BOOKS

Allen, Robert S., and Pearson, Drew. *More Merry-Go-Round*. New York: Liveright, 1932.

—— *Washington Merry-Go-Round*. New York: Liveright, 1931.

Angell, Norman. *The Press and the Organization of Society*. London: Labour Publishing Company, 1922.

Bates, Ernest Sutherland, and Carlson, Oliver. *Hearst: Lord of San Simeon*. New York: Viking Press, 1936.

Beard, Charles A., and Mary R. *The Rise of American Civilization*. New York: Macmillan Co., 1927.

Belloc, Hilaire. *The Free Press*. London: Allen and Unwin, 1918.

Bent, Silas. *Ballyhoo: the Voice of the Press*. New York: Boni and Liveright, 1927.

—— *Strange Bedfellows: A Review of Politics, Personalities and the Press*. New York: Liveright, 1928.

Bleyer, Willard G. *Main Currents in the History of American Journalism*. Boston and New York: Houghton Mifflin Co., 1927.

Bourdon, George, and others. *Le Journalisme d'Aujourd'hui*. Paris: Libraire Delagrave, 1931.

Britt, George. *Forty Years—Forty Millions: The Career of Frank A. Munsey*. New York: Farrar & Rinehart, 1935.

Bryce, James. *The American Commonwealth*. 2 vols. 3d ed. New York: Macmillan Co., 1895.

Bush, Chilton Rowlette. *Editorial Thinking and Writing*. New York and London: Appleton, 1932.

Carlson, Oliver, and Bates, Ernest Sutherland. *Hearst: Lord of San Simeon*. New York: Viking Press, 1936.

Carroll, John C., and Leech, Harper. *What's the News?* Chicago: Covici, 1926.

Clarke, Tom. *My Northcliffe Diary*. New York: Cosmopolitan Book Corporation, 1931.

Cochran, Negley. *E. W. Scripps*. New York: Harcourt, Brace & Co., 1933.

The Coming Newspaper. Edited by Merle Thorpe. New York: Henry Holt & Co., 1915.

Conference on the Press, under the Auspices of the School of Public and International Affairs, Princeton University, April 23-25, 1931. Washington, D. C.: Printing Corporation of America, 1931.

Coolidge, Louis Arthur, and Reynolds, James Burton. *The Show at Washington*. Washington, D. C.: Washington Publishing Co., 1894.

Corbin, Charles R. *Why News is News*. New York: Ronald Press Co., 1928.

Crawford, Nelson Antrim. *The Ethics of Journalism*. New York: Alfred A. Knopf, 1924.

Creel, George. *How We Advertised America*. New York and London: Harper & Bros., 1920.

Desmond, Robert W. *The Press and World Affairs*. New York and London: D. Appleton-Century Co., 1937.

Dickinson, Burrus Swinford. *The Newspaper and Labor:* An Inquiry into the Nature and Influence of Labor News and Comment in the Daily Press. Unpublished Ph.D. thesis. Urbana, Ill.: University of Illinois, 1930.

Doob, Leonard. *Propaganda*. New York: Henry Holt & Co., 1935.

Essary, J. Fred. *Covering Washington: Government Reflected to the Public in the Press, 1822-1926*. Boston and New York: Houghton Mifflin Co., 1927.

Farson, Negley. *The Way of a Transgressor*. New York: Harcourt, Brace & Co., 1936.

Flint, Leon Nelson. *The Conscience of the Newspaper: A Case*

Book in the Principles and Problems of Journalism. New York and London: D. Appleton & Co., 1925.

Fowler, Gene. *Timber Line.* New York: Covici, Friede, 1933.

Gardner, Gilson. *Lusty Scripps: The Life of E. W. Scripps.* New York: Vanguard Press, 1932.

Gibbons, William F. *Newspaper Ethics.* Ann Arbor: Edwards Brothers, 1926 (mimeographed).

Gilbert, Clinton. *The Mirrors of Washington.* New York: G. P. Putnam & Sons, 1921.

Given, John L. *Making a Newspaper.* New York: Henry Holt & Co., 1907.

Gosnell, Harold F., and Merriam, Charles E. *The American Party System.* New York: Macmillan Co., 1929 (revised edition).

Gruening, Ernest. *The Public Pays: A Study of Power Propaganda.* New York: Vanguard Press, 1931.

Hard, Anna. *Sirens of Washington.* New York: Scribners, 1931.

Harrel, Robert Frank, and Pitkin, Walter B. *Vocational Studies in Journalism.* New York: Columbia University Press, 1931.

Helm, William P. *Washington Swindle Sheet.* New York: Albert and Charles Boni, 1932.

High-Low Washington. Philadelphia: J. B. Lippincott Co., 1932.

Irwin, Will. *Propaganda and the News.* New York and London: Whittlesey House, McGraw-Hill, 1936.

Johnson, Gerald White. *What is News?* New York and London: Alfred A. Knopf, 1926.

Journalism as a Career. Edited by W. T. Cranfield. London: Sir Isaac Pitman & Sons, 1930.

Kent, Frank R. *The Great Game of Politics.* Garden City: Doubleday, Doran, 1930 (revised edition).

—— *Political Behavior.* New York: Morrow, 1928.

Knight, Frank H. *The Ethics of Competition.* New York and London: Harpers, 1935.

Lahey, Thomas A. *The Morals of Newspaper Making.* South Bend: Notre Dame University Press, 1924.

Lasswell, Harold D. *Politics: Who Gets What, When, How.* New York and London: McGraw-Hill, 1936.

—— *Propaganda Technique in the World War.* New York: Alfred A. Knopf, 1927.

—— *Psychopathology and Politics.* Chicago: University of Chicago Press, 1930.

—— *World Politics and Personal Insecurity: A Contribution to Political Psychiatry.* New York: McGraw-Hill, 1935.

Lee, James Melvin. *The History of American Journalism.* Boston and New York: Houghton Mifflin Co., 1923.

Leech, Harper, and Carroll, John C. *What's the News?* Chicago: Covici, 1926.

Levin, Jack. *Power Ethics.* New York: Alfred A. Knopf, 1931.

Lindley, Ernest K. *Franklin D. Roosevelt: A Career in Progressive Democracy.* Indianapolis: Bobbs-Merrill Co., 1931.

—— *The Roosevelt Revolution: First Phase.* New York: Viking Press, 1933.

Lippmann, Walter. *Liberty and the News.* New York: Harcourt, Brace, and Howe, 1920.

—— *The Phantom Public.* New York: Harcourt, Brace, and Howe, 1920.

—— *Public Opinion.* New York: Harcourt, Brace & Co., 1925.

Lumley, Frederick. *The Propaganda Menace.* New York and London: Century Co., 1933.

Lundberg, Ferdinand. *Imperial Hearst: a Social Biography.* New York: Equinox Cooperative Press, 1936.

Lynd, Robert S., and Helen Merrell. *Middletown.* Harcourt, Brace & Co., 1929.

Lynd, Robert S., and Helen Merrell. *Middletown in Transition*. New York: Harcourt, Brace & Co., 1937.

Luxton, Norman Neil, and Porter, Philip W. *The Reporter and the News*. New York and London: D. Appleton-Century Co., 1935.

McLean, Evalyn Walsh. *Father Struck it Rich*. Boston: Little, Brown Co., 1936.

Merriam, Charles E. *The Making of Citizens: A Comparative Study of Methods of Civic Training*. Chicago: University of Chicago Press, 1931.

Merriam, Charles E., and Gosnell, Harold F. *The American Party System*. New York: Macmillan Co., 1929 (revised edition).

"M. E. S.": His Book. A collection of the letters and addresses of Melville E. Stone. New York and London: Harper & Bros., 1918.

Michael, George. *Handout*. New York: G. P. Putnam's Sons, 1935.

Miller, Webb. *I Found No Peace*. New York: Simon and Schuster, 1936.

Minney, R. J. *The Journalist*. London: Geoffrey Bles, 1931.

Mirrors of 1932. New York: Brewer, Warren & Putnam, 1931.

Moreno, Jacob L. *Who Shall Survive? A New Approach to the Problem of Human Interrelations*. Washington, D. C.: Nervous and Mental Diseases Publishing Co., 1935.

Older, Mrs. Fremont. *William Randolph Hearst: American*. New York and London: D. Appleton-Century Co., 1936.

Overacker, Louise. *Money in Elections*. New York: Macmillan Co., 1932.

Pearson, Drew, and Allen, Robert S. *More Merry-Go-Round*. New York: Liveright, 1932.

—— *Washington Merry-Go-Round*. New York: Liveright, 1931.

Pitkin, Walter B., and Harrel, Robert F. *Vocational Studies in Journalism.* New York: Columbia University Press, 1931.

Porter, Philip W., and Luxon, Norval Neil. *The Reporter and the News.* New York and London: D. Appleton-Century Co., 1935.

Proceedings of the American Society of Newspaper Editors, *Problems of Journalism: 1928.* Washington, D. C.: Published by the Society, 1928.

Proceedings of the American Society of Newspaper Editors, *Problems of Journalism: 1930.* Washington, D. C.: Published by the Society, 1930.

Recent Social Changes. Edited by William F. Ogburn. Chicago: University of Chicago Press, 1930.

Reynolds, James Burton, and Coolidge, Louis Arthur. *The Show at Washington.* Washington, D. C.: Washington Publishing Co., 1894.

Rice, Stuart A., and Willey, Malcolm M. *Communication Agencies and Social Life.* New York and London: McGraw-Hill, 1933.

Richardson, Francis A. *Recollections of a Washington Newspaper Correspondent.* Records of the Columbia Historical Society, Vol. VI. Washington, D. C.: Columbia Historical Society, 1903.

Riegel, O. W. *Mobilizing for Chaos: the Story of the New Propaganda.* New Haven: Yale University Press, 1934.

Le Rôle Intellectuel de la Presse. Essays by Savin Cans, Henri de Jouvenal, Kingsley Martin, Paul Scott Mowrer, Friedrich Siebury. Paris: Société des Nations, Institut International de Cooperation Intellectuelle, 1933.

Rorty, James. *Our Master's Voice—Advertising.* New York: John Day Co., 1934.

Rosewater, Victor. *History of Co-operative Newsgathering in the United States*. New York and London: D. Appleton & Co., 1930.

Ross, Ishbel. *Ladies of the Press*. New York and London: Harper & Bros., 1936.

Salmon, Lucy Maynard. *The Newspaper and the Historian*. New York: Oxford University Press, American Branch, 1923.

Scott-James, Rolfe Arnold. *The Influence of the Press*. London: S. W. Partridge, 1913.

Seitz, Don C. *Joseph Pulitzer: His Life and Letters*. New York: Simon and Schuster, 1924.

Seldes, George. *Freedom of the Press*. Indianapolis and New York: Bobbs-Merrill Co., 1935.

Sinclair, Upton. *The Brass Check*. Pasadena: published by the author, 1919.

de Tocqueville, Alexis. *Democracy in America*. Translated by Henry Reeve. New York: Century Co., 1898.

Villard, Oswald Garrison. *Some Newspapers and Newspapermen*. New York: Alfred A. Knopf, 1928.

Warner, Edward Henry. *The Making of a Newspaper*. Baltimore: A. S. Abell Co., 1931.

Weber, Max. *Politik als Beruf*. Zweite Auflage. München und Leipzig: Verlag von Duncker und Humblot, 1926.

White, Leonard D. *Introduction to the Study of Public Administration*. New York: Macmillan Co., 1926.

Willey, Malcolm M., and Rice, Stuart A. *Communication Agencies and Social Life*. New York and London: McGraw-Hill, 1933.

Winkler, John K. *William Randolph Hearst: An American Phenomenon*. New York: Simon and Schuster, 1928.

Yost, Casper S. *The Principles of Journalism*. New York and London: Appleton, 1924.

ARTICLES

Abbott, Willis J. "Proportion in the News," *Journalism Quarterly*, March, 1931, pp. 100-07.

Adamic, Louis. "The Papers Print the Riots," *Scribner's*, February, 1932, pp. 109-11.

Adler, Julius Ochs. "Do Advertisers Control Newspaper Policy?" *American Press*, April, 1937, p. 1.

Allen, Eric W. "Economic Changes and Editorial Influence," *Journalism Quarterly*, September, 1931, pp. 342-59.

Anderson, Paul Y. "A Reporter at Large," *News, Its Scope and Limitations*. Edited by T. C. Morelock. Journalism Series, Bulletin No. 57. (Columbia, Missouri: University of Missouri, 1929.)

—— "Cross-Section of Washington," *Nation*, April 9, 1930, pp. 419-20.

—— "Hoover and the Press," *Nation*, October 14, 1931, pp. 382-84.

—— "In Defence of Congress," *Nation*, June 28, 1933, pp. 720-22.

—— "Is Press Unfair to Officialdom?" *American Press*, August, 1932, p. 3.

—— "Johnson and the Freedom of the Press," *Nation*, August 30, 1933, p. 234.

—— "Lame-Duck Diplomats," *Nation*, January 15, 1930, p. 66.

—— "Washington Honor Roll," *Nation*, January 28, 1931, pp. 93-94.

"AP.," *Fortune*, February, 1937, p. 89.

Asbury, Herbert. "Hearst Comes to Atlanta," *American Mercury*, January, 1926, pp. 87-95.

"Back Stage in Washington," *Outlook and Independent*, December 11, 1929, p. 578.

Barlow, Reuel R. "Research Man Says Heavy Volume of New Deal News Mostly Unbiased," *Editor and Publisher*, February 23, 1935, p. 29.

Bauer, Wilhelm. "Public Opinion," *Encyclopedia of the Social Sciences* (New York: Macmillan Co., 1933), XII, pp. 669-74.

Beale, Howard K. "Forces That Control the Schools," *Harper's*, October, 1934, pp. 604-13.

Beazell, William P. "The Party Flag Comes Down," *Atlantic Monthly*, March, 1931, pp. 366-72.

—— "Tomorrow's Newspaper," *Atlantic Monthly*, July, 1930, pp. 24-30.

Benét, Stephen Vincent. "The United Press," *Fortune*, May, 1933, pp. 67 ff.

Bent, Silas. "Journalism and Morality," *Atlantic Monthly*, June, 1926, pp. 761-69.

—— "Scarlet Journalism," *Scribner's*, November, 1928, pp. 563-69.

—— "Two Kinds of News," *Yale Review*, July, 1927, pp. 691-709.

—— "Watchman, Tell Us of the Press," *Independent*, November 13, 1926, pp. 548-49 ff.

Berchtold, William E. "Press Agents of the New Deal," *New Outlook*, July, 1934, pp. 23-30.

Bleyer, Willard G. "Freedom of the Press and the New Deal," *Journalism Quarterly*, March, 1934, pp. 22-35.

—— "Journalism in the United States: 1933," *Journalism Quarterly*, December, 1933, pp. 296-301.

Bliven, Bruce. "Bliven Sees Losing Fight Against Press Repressions," *Editor and Publisher*, March 23, 1935, p. 14.

—— "Newspaper Morals," *New Republic*, May 30, 1923, pp. 17-19.

Brody, Catherine. "Newspaper Girls," *American Mercury*, March, 1923, pp. 273-77.

"Brooklyn *Eagle's* Writer Firmly Contests White House Interview Denial," *Editor and Publisher*, January 3, 1925, pp. 3-4.

Broun, Heywood. "Loose Construction," *Nation*, February 5, 1936, pp. 157-58.

———— "Roosevelt Shows up the Press," *Nation*, October 3, 1936, p. 522.

———— "Walter Winchell's Tooth," *Nation*, January 8, 1936, pp. 47-48.

Brown, Ashmun. "The Roosevelt Myth," *American Mercury*, April, 1936, pp. 390-94.

"Bunking Trustful Readers," *Independent*, May 22, 1926, pp. 598-600.

Burgess, E. W. "Art of Communication," *Recent Social Changes*. Edited by William F. Ogburn. (Chicago: University of Chicago Press, 1930), pp. 137 ff.

Burke, Earl. "Dailies Helped Break General Strike," *Editor and Publisher*, July 28, 1934, p. 5.

Butler, James J. "Press Wires Jammed with Capital News," *Editor and Publisher*, January 11, 1936, p. 11.

———— "12 News Executives Resign from Daily in Business Office Clash," *Editor and Publisher*, November 2, 1935, p. 8.

Canham, Erwin D. "Democracy's Fifth Wheel," *Literary Digest*, January 5, 1935, p. 6.

Carr-Saunders, A. M., and Wilson, P. A. "Professions," *Encyclopedia of the Social Sciences* (New York: Macmillan Co., 1933), XII, pp. 476-80.

Carroll, Raymond G. "Reform vs. the Washington Correspondents," *Editor and Publisher*, July 21, 1928, pp. 7, 14.

———— "Washingtonia," *Saturday Evening Post*, February 16, 1935, pp. 30 ff.

Carter, John. "American Correspondents and British Delegates," *Independent,* August 13, 1927, pp. 150-52 ff.

Casey, Ralph D. "Party Campaign Propaganda," *Annals of the American Academy of Political and Social Science,* May, 1935, pp. 96-105.

—— "Republican Propaganda in the 1936 Campaign," *Public Opinion Quarterly,* April, 1937, pp. 27-44.

Catlin, George E. G. "The Role of Propaganda in a Democracy," *Annals of the American Academy of Political and Social Science,* May, 1935, pp. 219-226.

Clapper, Raymond. "All Eyes Are Turned on Washington." *Editor and Publisher,* January 13, 1934, p. 9.

—— "Why Reporters Like Roosevelt," *Review of Reviews,* June, 1934, pp. 14-17.

Clark, John Maurice. "Monopoly," *Encyclopedia of the Social Sciences* (New York: Macmillan Co., 1933), X, pp. 623-29.

Clemow, Bice. "F. D. R. Retains 'Open' Conferences," *Editor and Publisher,* March 2, 1935, p. 9.

—— "Militant Stand Against Abridgement of Freedom Taken at ANPA Meet," *Editor and Publisher,* April 25, 1936, pp. 1-6.

—— "Recovery on Way, Capital Corps Feels," *Editor and Publisher,* December 29, 1934, pp. 7-8.

"Color in Our Foreign News," *Outlook and Independent,* February 25, 1931, p. 300.

Corey, Herbert. "The Presidents and the Press," *Saturday Evening Post,* January 9, 1932, pp. 25, 96-104.

"Cornering Washington News," *New Republic,* February 22, 1933, p. 34.

"Correspondents Like Roosevelt," *American Press,* March, 1933, p. 3.

"Counting Room Holds no Menace to Editorial Freedom, Says White," *Editor and Publisher,* March 10, 1934, p. 18.

Crawford, Nelson A. "The American Newspaper and the People: A Psychological Examination," *Nation*, September 13, 1922, pp. 249-52.

Crawford, T. C. "The Special Correspondent at Washington," *Cosmopolitan*, January, 1892, pp. 351-60.

Creel, George. "Woodrow Wilson, the Man Behind the President," *Saturday Evening Post*, March 28, 1931, pp. 37-44.

Crossley, Archibald M. "Straw Polls in 1936," *Public Opinion Quarterly*, January, 1937, pp. 24-35.

Crowell, Chester. "What's in the Paper?" *New Republic*, November 22, 1933, p. 42.

Dabney, Virginius. "The Press and the Election," *Public Opinion Quarterly*, April, 1937, pp. 122-25.

Dickinson, Burrus S. "The Influence of the Press in Labor Affairs," *Journalism Quarterly*, September, 1932, pp. 269-80.

Dickinson, John. "Political Aspects of the New Deal," *American Political Science Review*, April, 1934, pp. 197-209.

Doob, Leonard W., and Robinson, Edward S. "Psychology and Propaganda," *Annals of the American Academy of Political and Social Science*, May, 1935, pp. 88-95.

Drewry, John E. "The Journalist's Inferiority Complex," *Journalism Quarterly*, March, 1931, pp. 12-23.

Duffus, R. L. "Printing and Publishing," *Encyclopedia of the Social Sciences* (New York: Macmillan Co., 1933), XII, pp. 406-14.

Erhardt, Leslie. "Day Book of a Washington Correspondent," *Quill*, July, 1934, pp. 3-4.

Essary, J. Frederick. "Democracy and the Press," *Annals of the American Academy of Political and Social Science*, September, 1933, pp. 110-20.

—— "How Presidents Deal with the Press," *American Press*, April, 1933, p. 2.

—— "President, Congress and the Press Correspondents,"

American Political Science Review, November, 1928, Vol. 22, pp. 902-09.

Essary, J. Frederick. "Uncle Sam's Ballyhoo Men," *American Mercury,* August, 1931, pp. 419-28.

—— "The Washington Assignment," *News and the Newspaper.* Edited by Robert S. Mann. Journalism Series, Bulletin No. 28. (Columbia, Missouri: University of Missouri, 1923.)

"Federal Handouts Cost Three Millions a Year," *American Press,* July, 1931, p. 18.

"Feeding the Press," *Collier's,* August 16, 1930, p. 34.

Fehlhaber, Elmer O. "Whose Hands Need Washing?" *Guild Reporter,* June, 1934, p. 11.

"Fewer Labor Troubles in Past Year," *Editor and Publisher,* April 25, 1936, pp. 19, 116.

"Fight the Tugwell Bill," *National Printer Journalist,* January, 1934, p. 40.

"First List of Correspondents," *Editor and Publisher,* July 21, 1934, p. 118.

"First White House Reporter Dies," *Editor and Publisher,* October 31, 1931, p. 38.

Flynn, John T. "Edward L. Bernays: The Science of Ballyhoo," *Atlantic Monthly,* May, 1932, pp. 562-71.

"Fortune Quarterly Survey: VII. Have you a Favorite Newspaper Columnist? (If yes) Who?" *Fortune,* January, 1937, pp. 86-87, 150 ff.

Francis, Warren B. "Secrecy Policy of Shipping Board Attacked," *Editor and Publisher,* September 19, 1931, p. 16.

"The Free Press: Court Issue Upsets 'Objective' Poise," *Guild Reporter,* March 1, 1937, p. 6.

Fry, C. Luther. "Changes in Religious Organizations," *Recent Social Trends* (New York and London: Whittlesey House, McGraw-Hill, 1934, one vol. ed.), pp. 1009-60.

Gallup, George. "A Scientific Method for Determining Reader Interest," *Journalism Quarterly*, March, 1930, pp. 1-13.

Gosnell, Harold F. "How Accurate Were the Polls?" *Public Opinion Quarterly*, January, 1937, pp. 97-105.

Gregory, Clifford V. "The American Farm Bureau Federation and the AAA," *Annals of the American Academy of Political and Social Science*, May, 1935, pp. 152-57.

Gregory, John S. "All Quiet on the Rapidan," *Outlook and Independent*, August 5, 1931, p. 427.

Griffin, Bulkley S. "The Public Man and the Newspapers," *Nation*, June 17, 1925, pp. 689-90.

Gross, Herbert. "Public Monopolies," *Encyclopedia of the Social Sciences* (New York: Macmillan Co., 1933), X, pp. 619-23.

Gruening, Ernest. "Publicity," *Encyclopedia of the Social Sciences* (New York: Macmillan Co., 1933), XII, pp. 698-701.

"Guilded Age," *Time*, April 19, 1937, p. 49.

Hamilton, William P. "The Case for the Newspapers," *Atlantic Monthly*, May, 1910, pp. 646-54.

Hanna, Paul. "The State Department and the News," *Nation*, October 13, 1920, pp. 398-99.

Hanson, Elisha. "Official Propaganda and the New Deal," *Annals of the American Academy of Political and Social Science*, May, 1935, pp. 176-86.

Harding, T. Swann. "Informational Techniques of the Department of Agriculture," *Public Opinion Quarterly*, January, 1937, pp. 83-96.

Hart, Hornell, and Kingsbury, Susan A. "Measuring the Ethics of American Newspapers," *Journalism Quarterly*, June, 1933, pp. 93-108; September, 1933, pp. 181-201; December, 1933, pp. 323-42; June, 1934, pp. 179-99.

Herring, E. Pendleton. "Official Publicity Under the New

Deal," *Annals of the American Academy of Political and Social Science*, May, 1935, pp. 167-75.

Höllering, Franz. "I Was an Editor in Germany," *Editor and Publisher*, April 25, 1936, pp. 22, 115.

Hubbell, Horace J. "Think Stuff Unwanted," *American Mercury*, March, 1927, pp. 263-67.

Hughes, Helen MacGill. "Human Interest Stories and Democracy," *Public Opinion Quarterly*, April, 1937, pp. 73-83.

Hurd, Charles W. "President and Press: A Unique Forum," New York *Times Magazine*, June 9, 1935, pp. 3, 19.

Hurlin, Ralph G., and Givens, Meredith B. "Shifting Occupational Patterns," *Recent Social Trends* (New York and London: Whittlesey House, McGraw-Hill, 1934, one vol. ed.), pp. 268-324.

Irwin, Will. "The American Newspaper: A Study of Journalism in its Relation to the Public," *Collier's Weekly*, January 21 through July 29, 1911.

Johnson, Gerald White. "Why Men Work for Newspapers," *American Mercury*, May, 1929, pp. 83-88.

Keating, Isabelle. "Reporters Come of Age," *Harper's*, April, 1935, pp. 601-12.

Keezer, Dexter Merriam. "Press," *Encyclopedia of the Social Sciences* (New York: Macmillan Co., 1933), XII, pp. 325-43.

Kelly, Eugene A. "Distorting the News," *American Mercury*, March, 1935, pp. 307-18.

Kingsbury, Susan A., and Hart, Hornell. "Measuring the Ethics of American Newspapers," *Journalism Quarterly*, June, 1933, pp. 93-108; September, 1933, pp. 181-201; December, 1933, pp. 323-42; June, 1934, pp. 179-99.

Kintner, Robert E. "The SEC Dictatorship," *American Mercury*, June, 1936, pp. 180-87.

Bibliography 409

Krock, Arthur. "The Press and Government," *Annals of the American Academy of Political and Social Science*, July, 1935, pp. 162-67.

—— "Press vs. Government—A Warning," *Public Opinion Quarterly*, April, 1937, pp. 45-49.

Landis, J. M. "Freedom of Speech and of the Press," *Encyclopedia of the Social Sciences* (New York: Macmillan Co., 1933), VI, pp. 455-58.

Laski, Harold J. "The Elite in a Democratic Society," *Harper's*, September, 1933, pp. 456-64.

Lasswell, Harold D. "Censorship," *Encyclopedia of the Social Sciences* (New York: Macmillan Co., 1933), III, pp. 290-94.

—— "The Person: Subject and Object of Propaganda," *Annals of the American Academy of Political and Social Science*, May, 1935, pp. 187-93.

—— "Propaganda," *Encyclopedia of the Social Sciences* (New York: Macmillan Co., 1933), XII, pp. 521-27.

—— "Research on the Distribution of Symbol Specialists," *Journalism Quarterly*, June, 1935, pp. 146-57.

Lawrence, David. "The Lost Right of Privacy," *American Mercury*, May, 1936, pp. 12-18.

—— "The President and the Press," *Saturday Evening Post*, August 27, 1927, p. 27.

—— "Reporting the Political News at Washington," *American Political Science Review*, November, 1928, Vol. 22, pp. 893-902.

Lippmann, Walter. "Two Revolutions in the American Press," *Yale Review*, March, 1931, pp. 433-41.

Lippmann, Walter, and Merz, Charles. "More News from the Times: Russia and Poland," *New Republic*, August 11, 1920, pp. 299-301.

Lloyd, Alfred H. "Newspaper Conscience: A Study in Half

Truths," *American Journal of Sociology,* September, 1921, pp. 197-210.

Luce, Henry R. "The Press is Peculiar," *Saturday Review of Literature,* March 7, 1931, pp. 646-47.

Lundberg, Ferdinand. "The Landon Build-up," *Nation,* June 27, 1936, p. 833.

Lundberg, George A. "The Newspaper and Public Opinion," *Journal of Social Forces,* June, 1926, pp. 709-15.

Lynd, Robert S. "The People as Consumers," *Recent Social Trends* (New York and London: Whittlesey House, Mc-Graw-Hill, 1934, one vol. ed.), pp. 857-911.

Lyon, Leverett S. "Advertising," *Encyclopedia of the Social Sciences* (New York: Macmillan Co., 1933), I, pp. 469-75.

Mallon, Paul. "Inquisition Dramas Staged by Congress," Sunday New York *Timés,* December 9, 1934, Section 6, pp. 6-7.

—— "Roosevelt Gets His Story Over," New York *Times Magazine,* November 19, 1933, pp. 1-2, 15.

Mann, Robert S. "Capital Corps No Propaganda Victim, Writers Tell Journalism Teachers," *Editor and Publisher,* January 4, 1936, pp. 3-4, 12.

Manning, George H. "Capital Corps Hopes for 'New Deal,' " *Editor and Publisher,* March 4, 1933, p. 5.

—— "Farm Board Resists News Coverage," *Editor and Publisher,* September 3, 1932, p. 15.

—— "Hoover Seeks Source of 'Talkie' Story," *Editor and Publisher,* November 14, 1931, p. 8.

—— "Hurley Charges Refuted by Reporters," *Editor and Publisher,* August 13, 1932, p. 7.

—— "Insull Propaganda Operations Told," *Editor and Publisher,* December 30, 1933, p. 5.

—— "Joslin Suggests News 'Consultations,' " *Editor and Publisher,* September 19, 1931, p. 7.

Manning, George H. "Journalism Schools File Brief Hitting Editorial Wages in Code," *Editor and Publisher*, July 28, 1934, p. 12.

—— "Liberalizing of President's Contacts with Press Hoped for from Hoover," *Editor and Publisher*, January 12, 1929, pp. 5-6.

—— " 'New Deal' for Press Begins at Once as Nation Faces Bank Crisis," *Editor and Publisher*, March 11, 1933, pp. 3-4.

—— "President Cancels Press Conferences," *Editor and Publisher*, November 26, 1932, p. 8.

—— "President Candidly Consults Reporters in Advance of Budget Announcement," *Editor and Publisher*, January 6, 1934, pp. 3-4.

—— "Reporters Protest Roosevelt Favors," *Editor and Publisher*, June 25, 1932, p. 18.

—— "Strained Air Pervades Press Circles as White House 'Leak' Is Sought," *Editor and Publisher*, July 18, 1931, p. 10.

—— "Subtle Censorship on Government News Is Arising Steadily in Washington," *Editor and Publisher*, September 5, 1931, pp. 5-6.

—— "White House News Ban on Bank Parley Upset by Correspondents," *Editor and Publisher*, October 10, 1931, p. 5.

Marquis, Don. "Men Who Make Newspapers," *Yale Review*, October, 1926, pp. 45-56.

Martin, Kingsley. "The Influence of the Press," *Political Quarterly*, April, 1930, pp. 157-78.

—— "Public Opinion: Rationalization of the Press and Democracy," *Political Quarterly*, July-September, 1930, pp. 428-35.

—— "Le Rôle Educateur de la Presse," in *Le Rôle Intellectuel de la Presse* (Paris: Société des Nations, Institut International de Cooperation Intellectuelle, 1933), pp. 81-146.

Martin, Kingsley. "The Russian Press," *Political Quarterly*, January, 1933, pp. 116-20.

Marx, Fritz Morstein. "Propaganda and Dictatorship," *Annal of the American Academy of Political and Social Science*, May, 1935, pp. 211-18.

McCabe, David A. "The American Federation of Labor and the NIRA," *Annals of the American Academy of Political and Social Science*, May, 1935, pp. 144-51.

Mencken, H. L. "Editorial," *American Mercury*, March, 1927, pp. 281-83.

—— "Footnote on Journalism," *Nation*, April 26, 1922, pp. 493-94.

Merriam, Charles E. "Government and Society," *Recent Social Trends* (New York and London: Whittlesey House, McGraw-Hill, 1934, one vol. ed.), pp. 1489-1542.

Merz, Charles. "The American Press," *Century*, November, 1926, pp. 103-10.

—— "What Makes a First Page Story," *New Republic*, December 30, 1935, pp. 156-58.

Merz, Charles, and Lippmann, Walter. "More News from the Times: Russia and Poland," *New Republic*, August 11, 1920, pp. 299-301.

Meusel, Alfred. "Middle Class," *Encyclopedia of the Social Sciences* (New York: Macmillan Co., 1933), X, pp. 407-15.

"The Morris Watson Case," *Editor and Publisher*, May 2, 1936, p. 22.

Mowrer, Paul Scott. "La Presse et le Public," in *Le Rôle Intellectuel de la Presse* (Paris: Société des Nations, Institut International de Cooperation Intellectuelle, 1933), pp. 149-80.

"Mr. Hoover's Refusal to be 'Humanized,'" *Literary Digest*, July 25, 1931, p. 8.

"Mr. Roosevelt 'Ungags' the Press," *Literary Digest*, March 25, 1933, p. 10.

Nevins, Allan. "Journalism," *Encyclopedia of the Social Sciences* (New York: Macmillan Co., 1933), VIII, pp. 420-24.

"New Deal for Press Praised by Henning," *Editor and Publisher*, June 10, 1933, p. 54.

"News Men Criticized by Premier Bennett," *Editor and Publisher*, August 6, 1932, p. 11.

"Newspapermen Play Important Rôles in Hot Presidential Campaign," *Editor and Publisher*, July 11, 1936, p. 3.

"Newspapers, Dare to be Free!," *Nation*, February 5, 1936, p. 145.

"Newsprint, Labor, Chief ANPA Topics," *Editor and Publisher*, April 24, 1937, pp. 7-8, 122.

"News Regulation in Washington Seen as Step to Coordination," *Editor and Publisher*, April 7, 1934, p. 10.

Ogburn, William F. "The Family and Its Functions," *Recent Social Trends* (New York and London: Whittlesey House, McGraw-Hill, 1934, one vol. ed.), pp. 661-708.

"$1,200,000 for Publicity; That's Uncle Sam's Annual Expenditure, Says Writer," *Editor and Publisher*, January 23, 1937, p. 40.

Oulahan, Richard V. "Capital Corps Praised for Diligence," *Editor and Publisher*, April 25, 1931, p. 32.

Owens, Dewey M. "The Associated Press," *American Mercury*, April, 1927, pp. 385-93.

Park, Robert. "Natural History of the Newspaper," *American Journal of Sociology*, November, 1923, pp. 273-89.

Peck, Gustav, and Wolman, Leo. "Labor Groups in the Social Structure," *Recent Social Trends* (New York and London: Whittlesey House, McGraw-Hill, 1934, one vol. ed.), pp. 801-56.

Perry, John W. "NRA Praises Newspaper Boy Clauses, Urges Publishers to Follow Them," *Editor and Publisher*, June 8, 1935, p. 4.

Pew, Marlan E., "Public Service Journalism," *Journalism Quarterly*, March, 1931, pp. 89-99.

—— "Shop Talk at Thirty," *Editor and Publisher*, April 8, 1933, p. 36.

Plucknett, Theodore F. T. "Libel and Slander," *Encyclopedia of the Social Sciences* (New York: Macmillan Co., 1933), IX, pp. 430-34.

"Post-Dispatch Assails ANPA for Its Business Activities," *Newsdom*, April 24, 1937, p. 9.

"The Press as Strike-Breakers," *New Republic*, August 8, 1934, p. 333.

"Press Conferences: Arthur Krock Explains Why They Are Useful," *American Press*, December, 1933, p. 3.

*"Press: Exclusive Set Gathers Capital News," *Literary Digest*, March 6, 1937, p. 28.

"Press Only Vital Critic Remaining," *Editor and Publisher*, April 25, 1936, pp. 10, 126.

"Publishers Oppose 30 Hour Week," *Editor and Publisher*, February 16, 1935, p. 11.

"Relations Between Roosevelt and Reporters Most Satisfactory in White House History," *Publishers' Auxiliary*, March 31, 1934, p. 1.

Resnick, David. "Labor News Takes the Spotlight," *Editor and Publisher*, October 14, 1933, p. 7.

Rice, Stuart A., and Willey, Malcolm M. "The Agencies of Communication," *Recent Social Trends* (New York and London: Whittlesey House, McGraw-Hill, 1934, one vol. ed.), pp. 167-217.

Riddell, Lord. "The Psychology of the Journalist," in *Journalism as a Career*. Edited by W. T. Cranfield. (London: Sir Isaac Pitman and Sons, 1930), pp. 49-63.

Riegel, O. W. "Press, Radio, and the Spanish Civil War," *Public Opinion Quarterly*, January, 1937, pp. 131-36.

—— "Propaganda and the Press," *Annals of the American Academy of Political and Social Science*, May, 1935, pp. 201-10.

"Rising Costs Concern Publishers," *Editor and Publisher*, April 24, 1937, p. 9.

Robb, Arthur. "ASNE Opposes Editorial Unionism," *Editor and Publisher*, pp. 21, 124.

Robbins, Alan Pitt. "The Parliamentary Journalist," in *Journalism as a Career*. Edited by W. T. Cranfield. (London: Sir Isaac Pitman and Sons, 1930), pp. 43-50.

Robinson, Edward S., and Doob, Leonard W. "Psychology and Propaganda," *Annals of the American Academy of Political and Social Science*, May, 1935, pp. 88-95.

"Roper Establishes a Strict Censorship," *Editor and Publisher*, March 14, 1936, p. 10.

Rorty, James. "Call for Mr. Throttlebottom," *Nation*, January 10, 1934, pp. 37-38.

—— "Who's Who in the Drug Lobby," *Nation*, February 21, 1934, pp. 213-15.

Ross, E. A. "The Suppression of Important News," *Atlantic Monthly*, March, 1910, pp. 303-11.

Rosten, Leo C. "President Roosevelt and the Washington Correspondents," *Public Opinion Quarterly*, January, 1937, pp. 36-52.

—— "The Social Composition of Washington Correspondents," *Journalism Quarterly*, June, 1937, pp. 125-32.

—— "The Professional Composition of Washington Correspondents," *Journalism Quarterly*, September, 1937, pp. 221-25.

Rowell, Chester H. "The Freedom of the Press," *Annals of the American Academy of Political and Social Science*, May, 1936, pp. 182-89.

"Salaries and Working Conditions of Newspaper Editorial Employees," *Monthly Labor Review* (Bureau of Labor Statistics, U. S. Government), May, 1935, pp. 1-23.

Saunders, Richard E. "Centralizing Press Releases of the Government," *Public Opinion Quarterly*, April, 1937, pp. 101-03.

Schuman, Frederick L. "Hearst's Campaign Against Professors" (Letter to the Editor), *New Republic*, April 17, 1935, pp. 287-88.

"The Share-Croppers Fight for Life," *New Republic*, January 29, 1936, p. 336.

Sharp, Willis. "President and the Press," *Atlantic Monthly*, August, 1927, pp. 239-45.

Shepard, W. J. "Centralization," *Encyclopedia of the Social Sciences* (New York: Macmillan Co., 1930), III, pp. 183-228.

Siebury, Friedrich. "Le Rôle Intellectuel de la Presse," in *Le Rôle Intellectuel de la Presse* (Paris: Société des Nations, Institut International de Cooperation Intellectuelle, 1933), pp. 183-228.

"Social Security Laws Need Scrutiny," *Editor and Publisher*, April 25, 1936, pp. 14, 116.

Sombart, Werner. "Capitalism," *Encyclopedia of the Social Sciences* (New York: Macmillan Co., 1930), III, pp. 195-208.

Stewart, Kenneth. "The Free Press in California," *American Mercury*, January, 1935, pp. 112-17.

Stockbridge, Frank Parker. "What Makes a Perfect Front-Page Story?" *American Press*, July, 1931, p. 1.

Sullivan, R. B. "An Unidentified Man," *Esquire*, April, 1936, pp. 63, 126 ff.

Summers, Alexander. "Future of Government News Reporting," *National Printer Journalist*, April, 1937, p. 22.

Sweet, W. E. "Public Opinion and the Chief Executive," *National Conference on Social Work, 1923*, pp. 474-77.

Swenson, Rinehart J. "The Chamber of Commerce and the New Deal," *Annals of the American Academy of Political and Social Science*, May, 1935, pp. 136-43.

"Teacher's Pet," *Nation*, April 17, 1937, p. 426.

Tucker, Ray. "The Men Who Make Our Laws," *Annals of the American Academy of Political and Social Science*, September, 1933, pp. 47-54.

—— "Part-Time Statesmen," *Collier's*, October 28, 1933, pp. 26, 38 ff.

"Two News Men Found AAA Substitute," *Editor and Publisher*, January 25, 1936, p. III.

"United Press: Budget for a Worldwide News Service," *Fortune*, May, 1933, pp. 67 ff.

"Use Freedom Vigorously, Press is Told at ANPA Golden Jubilee Meeting," *Editor and Publisher*, April 24, 1937, pp. 5-6, 125.

"U. S. Lists High Newspaper Salaries," *Editor and Publisher*, January 18, 1936, pp. 15, 50.

Villard, O. G. "The Associated Press," *Nation*, April 16, 1930, pp. 443-45; April 23, 1930, pp. 486-89.

—— "The Chain Daily," *Nation*, May 21, 1930, pp. 595-97.

—— "Donkey Brays Again," *Nation*, July 4, 1936, pp. 10-12.

—— "The Press and the President," *Century*, December, 1925, pp. 193-200.

—— "Some Weaknesses of Modern Journalism," in *University of Kansas News Bulletin*, XV, No. 6, November 2, 1914.

—— "Standardizing the Daily," *Nation*, June 4, 1930, pp. 646-47.

—— "The United Press," *Nation*, May 7, 1930, pp. 539-42.

—— "Waning Power of the Press," *Forum*, September, 1931, pp. 141-45.

"Wagner Bill Attacked by Newspaper Periodicals," *Editor and Publisher*, April 7, 1934, p. 8.

Ward, Paul W. "Roosevelt Keeps His Vow," *Nation*, September 25, 1935, pp. 347-49.

—— "Washington Weekly: Campaign Press Agents," *Nation*, July 18, 1936, pp. 63-64.

—— "Washington Weekly: Farley Captures Labor," *Nation*, October 31, 1936, p. 512.

—— "Washington Weekly: Our Ambassador to Moscow," *Nation*, December 5, 1936, pp. 651-52.

Ware, Caroline F. "Foreign Language Press," *Encyclopedia of the Social Sciences* (New York: Macmillan Co., 1933), VI, pp. 378-81.

"Washington Correspondents Demand Handouts," *American Press*, November, 1931, p. 14.

"Washington Correspondents Praise Press Agents," *Editor and Publisher*, December 29, 1934, p. 10.

Wengert, E. S. "TVA Enlists Local Cooperation," *Public Opinion Quarterly*, April, 1937, pp. 97-101.

"What Washington Thinks," *Saturday Evening Post*, July 12, 1930, p. 20.

Wheeler, Kittredge. "The Art of the Copy Reader," *American Mercury*, July, 1932, pp. 352-56.

"White House Corps Urged to 'Strike'," *Editor and Publisher*, August 18, 1928, p. 22.

White, Leonard D. "Administration, Public," *Encyclopedia of the Social Sciences* (New York: Macmillan Co., 1930), I, pp. 440-49.

—— "Public Administration," *Recent Social Trends* (New York and London: Whittlesey House, McGraw-Hill, 1934, one vol. ed.), pp. 1391-1439.

White, William Allen. "Good Newspapers and Bad," *Atlantic Monthly*, May, 1934, pp. 581-86.

Wilcox, Delos F. "The American Newspaper: A Study in Social Psychology," *Annals of the American Academy of Political and Social Science*, July, 1900, pp. 56-92.

Will, Allen Sinclair. "False Modesty of the Press," *Editor and Publisher*, May 21, 1932, p. 28.

Willey, Malcolm M. "Communication Agencies and the Volume of Propaganda," *Annals of the American Academy of Political and Social Science*, May, 1935, pp. 194-200.

Willey, Malcolm M., and Rice, Stuart A. "The Agencies of Communication," *Recent Social Trends* (New York and London: Whittlesey House, McGraw-Hill, 1934, one vol. ed.), pp. 167-217.

"William Allen White Says Big Business Status of Press Menaces Its Freedom," *Editor and Publisher*, February 14, 1931, p. 50.

Wilson, P. A., and Carr-Saunders, A. M. "Professions," *Encyclopedia of the Social Sciences* (New York: Macmillan Co., 1933), XII, pp. 476-80.

Wolman, Leo, and Peck, Gustav. "Labor Groups in the Social Structure," *Recent Social Trends* (New York and London: Whittlesey House, McGraw-Hill, 1934, one vol. ed.), pp. 801-56.

Wooddy, Carroll H. "Education and Propaganda," *Annals of the American Academy of Political and Social Science*, May, 1935, pp. 227-39.

—— "The Growth of Governmental Functions," *Recent Social Trends* (New York and London: Whittlesey House, McGraw-Hill, 1934, one vol. ed.), pp. 1274-1330.

Yarros, Victor S. "Journalism, Ethics and Common Sense," *International Journal of Ethics*, July, 1922, pp. 410-19.

—— "The Press and Public Opinion," *American Journal of Sociology*, November, 1899, p. 32.

Young, Marguerite. "Ignoble Journalism in the Nation's Capital," *American Mercury*, February, 1935, pp. 239-43.

"Your Business is Threatened," *Publishers' Auxiliary*, December 2, 1933, p. 1.

JOURNALS, PAMPHLETS, SUPPLEMENTS, ETC.

"The Constitution in the Twentieth Century," *Annals of the American Academy of Political and Social Science*, May, 1936.

Crawford, Nelson Antrim. *The Press and the Public* (Chapel Hill: University of North Carolina, Newspaper Institute, No. 13), January 15, 1926.

"The Crisis of Democracy," *Annals of the American Academy of Political and Social Science*, September, 1933.

Lippmann, Walter, and Merz, Charles. "A Test of the News," *New Republic Supplement*, August 4, 1920.

Merz, Charles, and Lippmann, Walter. "A Test of the News," *New Republic Supplement*, August 4, 1920.

News and the Newspaper. Edited by Robert S. Mann. Journalism Series, Bulletin No. 28 (Columbia, Missouri: University of Missouri, 1923).

News, Its Scope and Limitations. Edited by T. C. Morelock. Journalism Series, Bulletin No. 57 (Columbia, Missouri: University of Missouri, 1929).

News: The Story of How It Is Gathered and Printed (New York: The New York Times Co., 1935).

"The Press and the Public," *New Republic: Special Section*, March 17, 1937.

"Pressure Groups and Propaganda," *Annals of the American Academy of Political and Social Science*, May, 1935.

Sinclair, Upton. *Crimes of the "Times"* (Pasadena: published by the author, no date).

Social Frontier, February, 1935 (entire issue devoted to Hearst).

"Socialism, Fascism, and Democracy," *Annals of the American Academy of Political and Social Science*, July, 1935.

Stowell, Ellery C. "A Memorable Press Conference," *International Law and Relations*, IV, Bulletin Nos. 18 and 19. (The Digest Press: American University Graduate School, Washington, D. C.)

Index

POLITICS AND PEOPLE

The Ordeal of Self-Government in America

An Arno Press Collection

Allen, Robert S., editor. **Our Fair City.** 1947

Belmont, Perry. **Return to Secret Party Funds:** Value of Reed Committee. 1927

Berge, George W. **The Free Pass Bribery System:** Showing How the Railroads, Through the Free Pass Bribery System, Procure the Government Away from the People. 1905

Billington, Ray Allen. **The Origins of Nativism in the United States, 1800-1844.** 1933

Black, Henry Campbell. **The Relation of the Executive Power to Legislation.** 1919

Boothe, Viva Belle. **The Political Party as a Social Process.** 1923

Breen, Matthew P. **Thirty Years of New York Politics, Up-to-Date.** 1899

Brooks, Robert C. **Corruption in American Politics and Life.** 1910

Brown, George Rothwell. **The Leadership of Congress.** 1922

Bryan, William Jennings. **A Tale of Two Conventions:** Being an Account of the Republican and Democratic National Conventions of June, 1912. 1912

The Caucus System in American Politics. 1974

Childs, Harwood Lawrence. **Labor and Capital in National Politics.** 1930

Clapper, Raymond. **Racketeering in Washington.** 1933

Crawford, Kenneth G. **The Pressure Boys:** The Inside Story of Lobbying in America. 1939

Dallinger, Frederick W. **Nominations for Elective Office in the United States.** 1897

Dunn, Arthur Wallace. **Gridiron Nights:** Humorous and Satirical Views of Politics and Statesmen as Presented by the Famous Dining Club. 1915

Ervin, Spencer. **Henry Ford vs. Truman H. Newberry:** The Famous Senate Election Contest. A Study in American Politics, Legislation and Justice. 1935

Ewing, Cortez A.M. and Royden J. Dangerfield. **Documentary Source Book in American Government and Politics.** 1931

Ford, Henry Jones. **The Cost of Our National Government:** A Study in Political Pathology. 1910

Foulke, William Dudley. **Fighting the Spoilsmen:** Reminiscences of the Civil Service Reform Movement. 1919

Fuller, Hubert Bruce. **The Speakers of the House.** 1909

Griffith, Elmer C. **The Rise and Development of the Gerrymander.** 1907

Hadley, Arthur Twining. **The Relations Between Freedom and Responsibility in the Evolution of Democratic Government.** 1903

Hart, Albert Bushnell. **Practical Essays on American Government.** 1893

Holcombe, Arthur N. **The Political Parties of To-Day:** A Study in Republican and Democratic Politics. 1924

Hughes, Charles Evans. **Conditions of Progress in Democratic Government.** 1910

Kales, Albert M. **Unpopular Government in the United States.** 1914

Kent, Frank R. **The Great Game of Politics.** 1930

Lynch, Denis Tilden. **"Boss" Tweed:** The Story of a Grim Generation. 1927

McCabe, James D., Jr. (Edward Winslow Martin, pseud.) **Behind the Scenes in Washington.** 1873

Macy, Jesse. **Party Organization and Machinery.** 1912

Macy, Jesse. **Political Parties in the United States, 1846-1861.** 1900

Moley, Raymond. **Politics and Criminal Prosecution.** 1929

Munro, William Bennett. **The Invisible Government** and **Personality in Politics:** A Study of Three Types in American Public Life. 1928/1934 Two volumes in one.

Myers, Gustavus. **History of Public Franchises in New York City,** Boroughs of Manhattan and the Bronx. (Reprinted from **Municipal Affairs,** March 1900) 1900

Odegard, Peter H. and E. Allen Helms. **American Politics:** A Study in Political Dynamics. 1938

Orth, Samuel P. **Five American Politicians:** A Study in the Evolution of American Politics. 1906

Ostrogorski, M[oisei I.] **Democracy and the Party System in the United States:** A Study in Extra-Constitutional Government. 1910

Overacker, Louise. **Money in Elections.** 1932

Overacker, Louise. **The Presidential Primary.** 1926

The Party Battle. 1974

Peel, Roy V. and Thomas C. Donnelly. **The 1928 Campaign:** An Analysis. 1931

Pepper, George Wharton. **In the Senate** and **Family Quarrels:** The President, The Senate, The House. 1930/1931. Two volumes in one

Platt, Thomas Collier. **The Autobiography of Thomas Collier Platt.** Compiled and edited by Louis J. Lang. 1910

Roosevelt, Theodore. **Social Justice and Popular Rule:** Essays, Addresses, and Public Statements Relating to the Progressive Movement, 1910-1916 (*The Works of Theodore Roosevelt,* Memorial Edition, Volume XIX) 1925

Root, Elihu. **The Citizen's Part in Government** and **Experiments in Government and the Essentials of the Constitution.** 1907/1913. Two volumes in one

Rosten, Leo C. **The Washington Correspondents.** 1937

Salter, J[ohn] T[homas]. **Boss Rule:** Portraits in City Politics. 1935

Schattschneider, E[lmer] E[ric]. **Politics, Pressures and the Tariff:** A Study of Free Private Enterprise in Pressure Politics, as Shown in the 1929-1930 Revision of the Tariff. 1935

Smith, T[homas] V. and Robert A. Taft. **Foundations of Democracy:** A Series of Debates. 1939

The Spoils System in New York. 1974

Stead, W[illiam] T. **Satan's Invisible World Displayed,** Or, Despairing Democracy. A Study of Greater New York (The Review of Reviews Annual) 1898

Van Devander, Charles W. **The Big Bosses.** 1944

Wallis, J[ames] H. **The Politician:** His Habits, Outcries and Protective Coloring. 1935

Werner, M[orris] R. **Privileged Characters.** 1935

White, William Allen. **Politics:** The Citizen's Business. 1924

Wooddy, Carroll Hill. **The Case of Frank L. Smith:** A Study in Representative Government. 1931

Wooddy, Carroll Hill. **The Chicago Primary of 1926:** A Study in Election Methods. 1926